THE SAME RIVER TWICE

THE SAME RIVER TWICE

*A Season with Geno Auriemma
and the Connecticut Huskies*

BY JOHN WALTERS
FOREWORD BY REBECCA LOBO

International Standard Book Number: 0-9716999-0-9

Cover design by Kristin Helgeson

Cover and interior photographs by Maureen Grise

Text design by Brian C. Conley

Copy edited by Peter Pullman

Printed and bound in the United States of America

For Kristin

CONTENTS

Acknowledgments

Geno Auriemma welcomed me into his program and always made me feel welcome in his home, as his entire family continues to do.

Meghan Pattyson made the second-greatest sacrifice, renting me a room in her West Hartford digs.

Sarah Darras and Ann Marie Person at UConn are two huge reasons why the trains run on time in the women's basketball program. Thank you both.

To the coaching staff—Chris Dailey, Tonya Cardoza, Jamelle Elliott, and Stacy Hansmeyer—and the players—Svetlana, Marci, Shea, Rig, Schuey, Sue, Swin, Asjha, Keirsten, Tamika, KJ, Ashley, Maria, Jessica, Diana, and Morgan—I cannot repay you enough for allowing me inside the circle.

Kristin Helgeson designed the cover and through it all was my very best friend.

Maureen Grise of *Sports Illustrated* often trekked up from Manhattan to shoot the photos and as usual charmed everyone that met her.

My agent, David Black, believed in the project. Chuck Cealka at Ave Maria Press said, "Yeah, we can do this."

The Connecticut media let me join in all their reindeer games. Matt Eagan and Jeff Goldberg of *The Hartford Courant* kept me sane during the writing of this book in the summer of 2001.

To friends met along the way—Katie Post, Doris Burke, the Bortons and the Koebels, Jack and Phil Eisenmann, Danny D., Smitty, Dennis, Roy Lake, Rebecca Lobo, Paul Ghiorzi, Stacy Johnson and Chuck Klein, Amy Lundy, Nicky Kliger, Renee Carlson, Linda Genther, John the bus driver, and the master of the sentence of indeterminate length, Mel "Mr. Women's Basketball" Greenberg—thank you.

To friends who stepped up big-time—Josh Krulewitz at ESPN, Mark Beech, Marty Burns, Steve Cannella, Dick Friedman, Steve "Drawstring Nation" Rushin, and John Shostrom at *Sports Illustrated*, Sally Jenkins, Dick Patrick and Robin Roberts—thank you.

Thanks to everyone not already mentioned who made time for an interview: Carl Adamec, Bruce Arena, Ferruccio Auriemma, Nancy Bird, Doug Bruno, Joe Crawford, Charlene Curtis, Howie Dickenman, Mike DiMauro, Debbie Fiske, Jim Foster, Buddy Gardler, Marci Glenney, Theresa Grentz, Kelley Hunt, T.C. Karmel, Marsha Lake, Jody Lavin, Phil Martelli, Muffet McGraw, Pat Meiser-McKnett, Peggy Myers, Renee Najarian, Dianne Nolan, Harry Perretta, Kerry Poliquin, Rene Portland, Larry Rifkin, Cathy Rush, Joe Smith, Randy Smith, Jackie Stiles, Pat Summitt, Sheryl Swoopes, Carol Stiff, Todd Turner, the Valleys, Larry Webster, Dick "Hoops" Weiss, and George and Jo Williams

My parents, William and Phyllis, and my sister, Lorraine, lost hours of their lives providing computer assistance.

Finally, I'd like to acknowledge that I am a vehicular doofus. Thrice the car I rented, a Buick LeSabre, got a flat tire. Once I locked the keys inside it. Finally, while awaiting a jump start during a blizzard, I dropped the keys into the engine where they remained lost for the next hour. Little wonder that when I at last returned the car to Al at Rent-a-Wreck, he took me out for a drink. He was glad to be rid of me.

FOREWORD

I jumped at the chance to write the foreword to *The Same River Twice* before I had read a single word of the book. Just knowing John, his writing in *Sports Illustrated*, and his sense of humor, I was confident that he would capture the compelling, funny, behind-the-scenes world of UConn women's hoops.

Then came the actual writing of this foreword. When I asked Mr. Walters for a little direction, he told me to begin with the following:

> *"When John Walters originally phoned and told me he wanted to write a book about UConn, I nearly choked on my Skoal. Then I jumped out of the jacuzzi and said, "Hot damn, Rocket Boy, that idea's aces."*

Needless to say, I didn't choke on any Skoal, jump out of a jacuzzi (I stayed in), say "Hot damn," or call him Rocket Boy. The idea, however, was definitely aces.

Many people—especially those who live in Connecticut— come to know, love, and emotionally adopt the women who play for the Huskies. However, their relationship with these women is usually based on what the girls do on the court or an exchange during a brief meeting when soliciting an autograph.

The statewide adoration of Coach Auriemma is often based on his perfect "'do" or his witty sound bites. What most people don't see is what truly makes the UConn teams so great—the day-in and day-out work, struggles, and laughter that build the camaraderie of a true team.

I graduated from UConn in 1995 but hadn't spent much time with the subsequent Husky teams. I came to know them in the same way the rest of the fans did—by watching games on TV, checking out the news, and reading the papers.

Occasionally I would talk to the coaches to find out who was that year's Worst Post Player in America (the title Coach Auriemma bestowed upon me for four years). To avoid actually being the worst post player in America, I returned to Gampel Pavilion in November 2000 to practice with the UConn team while recovering from my second anterior cruciate ligament tear. I saw firsthand some of the crazy passes that Diana threw, the work that Shea put in, and the typical mute freshman tendencies of Morgan Valley.

I heard the friendly banter and teasing that happened off the court (I also realized how much funnier Coach Auriemma's sarcastic comments were when they weren't spouted at me.) More than anything, it hit me how my time with the team in November made me watch the games in a completely different way. Just knowing the players a little bit, watching a portion of what they went through in practice, and seeing a small display of their off-court antics made them more human and—if possible—more fun to watch.

John spent November with the 2000-01 Huskies. He also spent every other month of the season with this talented squad. He lived in the hoops-crazy state of Connecticut and traveled the country with the team. His book is an invitation to the behind-the-scenes, uncensored, blooper-filled experience that is usually reserved only for the players, coaches, and close friends of the Connecticut program. It is also an invitation to see the wonderful humor, incredible generosity and caring heart that make Geno Auriemma the best coach in the game.

If I were you, I'd RSVP, spit out my Skoal, relax in the jacuzzi, say, "Hot damn, Rocket Boy," and turn the page. If Diana doesn't hit you in the head with a pass along the way, you might even find out what *The Same River Twice* really means.

—*Rebecca Lobo*

PROLOGUE

On January 17, 1995, Geno Auriemma awoke for the first time in his life as the coach of the top-ranked women's college basketball team in the nation. He promptly pulled the covers back over his head.

A day earlier, before a sellout crowd of 8,241 and a national television audience on ESPN, his No. 2 University of Connecticut (or "UConn," pronounced like the Canadian territory) Huskies had defeated the No. 1 University of Tennessee Lady Volunteers, 77-66. Viewers nationwide who may have casually flipped to ESPN to see what was on saw a delirious on-campus gathering exhorting the Huskies to victory against Tennessee, the Goliath of women's hoops. It was a day that galvanized the sport. Certainly it did the state of Connecticut. Things would never be the same.

At 9:30 a.m. the morning after, Kathy Auriemma entered the bedroom. She found her husband, who usually rises at dawn, still buried beneath the sheets in anguished hibernation. "G!" she implored. "G! What are you doing?"

From beneath the covers she heard his hollow, muffled voice. It was the voice of a man who, having achieved his aspirations, was terrified by what he had wrought. "I want," he told her, " to be the Howard Hughes of women's college basketball."

Five years later, on the eve of the most important game in his career, Geno Auriemma was anything but reclusive. In fact, he threw a party. It was April 1, 2000. The Huskies were preparing to play Tennessee for their second national championship in six years. He had returned to Philadelphia, his hometown, an unconditional success. He had a wonderful, cool wife, Kathy, and three healthy children: Jenna, Alysa, and Michael. He had financial security—an exponentially greater salary than the $13,000 per year that had first lured him from Philly, in 1981, to an assistant's job at the University of Virginia.

Blue-eyed and blessed with an impermeable coif—a female writer once breathlessly described it as "a helmet of immaculately blow-dried, spun-gold hair"—he was still youthfully handsome. Forty-six years old and high school recruits were still heard to gush that "the UConn coach is a hottie". (Until they arrived on campus. "By the end of the first day of practice," says Kerry Bascom-Poliquin, his first blue-chip recruit, "you don't notice his looks anymore.")

As Geno's pockets got deeper, he endeavored to keep his hat size the same. Not that his friends ever let him forget from where he'd come. In 1995 Geno led the Huskies to a 35-0 season and their first national championship. The Auriemmas returned home from the women's Final Four in Minneapolis to discover 72 phone messages on their answering machine. Joe Crawford left one. Earlier that day Crawford, an NBA referee, had been voted as the league's top official in a poll conducted by *USA Today*. "You think you're number one?" Crawford, also a Philly native, had defiantly barked. "Check out the newspaper. I'm number one! *I'm* number one!"

This weekend, his homecoming, Geno was truly number one, and he intended to savor it. He was "the richest man in Bedford Falls", and there was in fact more than a little of *It's a Wonderful Life*'s George Bailey in Geno. He too had been reared in blue-collar Pennsylvania, in Norristown, some twenty miles northwest of Philly. "Norristown probably wouldn't have been my first choice," he said matter-of-factly, "but I didn't have a choice."

Geno too had become the man of the house of sorts at an early age. His parents, Donato and Marsiella, had emigrated with Luigi (his real name), his younger brother and sister, and one large suitcase from Montella, Italy, in 1961. Geno was seven. His father never learned English, and his mother only haltingly, so Geno became the family's first English speaker. The Auriemmas had no credit cards, no car. By age eight he was the family spokesman, making the rounds on foot to various creditors to pay the bills.

Unlike George Bailey, though, Geno escaped. When he was 27, he was hired as an assistant coach at the University of Virginia in Charlottesville. He and Kathy piled their belongings into their Honda Accord towing a U-Haul trailer and, like his parents before him, embarked on a journey to a new world. Before he left, Marsiella, whom everyone calls "Nona", offered two morsels of advice. "Work hard," she told her son. "Make lots of friends."

He had done both. What better validation of that than to throw a party on the eve of the biggest game of his life?

The party was tradition. The previous year Geno and Kathy had attended the Women's Final Four in San Jose, even though UConn had been eliminated two rounds earlier. On that Saturday night Geno had rented space at a bar, inviting fellow friends in coaching and former players who happened to be in attendance, such as All-Americans Rebecca Lobo, Jennifer Rizzotti and Nykesha Sales. That party had been epic. Or so the survivors said.

It had also formed bonds, Geno noticed, between the present and the past. At one point teams were divvied up for billiards, and Rizzotti, a feisty, ultra-competitive sort, had picked current Husky Svetlana Abrosimova as her teammate.

"Jen must really like you," Kathy had confided to Svetlana.

"Why is that?" Svetlana asked.

"Because you're lousy."

Shortly after 8:00 p.m. on April 1, Geno strode jauntily through the lobby of the Sheraton Society Hill in Philadelphia, playing the role of tummler. He approached the dozen or so media members who cover the Huskies. "You on the bus?" he asked them. "Get on the bus."

What was more surreal, a college basketball coach trolling for media with whom to socialize? Or that more than a dozen writers regularly cover a women's college basketball program? "You on the bus?" he repeated. "Get on the bus."

They clambered aboard the bus whose side read "Coach USA". When the group arrived at the fourth-floor landing of Finnigan's Wake, they were met by Rebecca Lobo and Jennifer Rizzotti, former National Players of the Year turned doormen for the evening.

"Adamec? Adamec?" said Jennifer, as she gazed up at Carl Adamec, a writer for *The Manchester Journal-Inquirer,* who had been chronicling the Huskies continuously longer than anyone, since 1989. "I'm sorry, I don't see that name on the list. Does Coach know you?"

He smirked. She smiled. He passed.

Midway through the bacchanal, Mike DiMauro, the ineffably good-natured beat writer for *The New London Day,* admonished Geno for having fallen short of the Final Four a year ago. If UConn does not go to the Final Four, DiMauro does not cover it for his paper. "You cost me a chance to go to this party last year!?!" he cried.

Former players, at least two dozen, attended the party. And not just UConn players. Stacy Frese, the former Iowa State University forward whose 16 points had helped eliminate UConn in the NCAA tournament's round of 16 the previous season, attended. DiMauro probably scolded her, too.

There were even party-crashers. When Geno spotted two strange-looking young men, he sauntered up to them, his blue eyes beaming, cigar in hand.

"Hey, some party, eh?" he said. "How'd you guys get in?"

"Some guy named Geno let us in," the interlopers replied.

"Guess what?" Geno smiled.

"You're Geno?"

"I'm Geno."

The revelry went late. Randy Smith, the sports editor and columnist for *The Manchester Journal-Inquirer,* approached the party's host, dubious as to how focused he was for the coming game.

"Relax," said Geno. "We're going to win."

The Huskies did win, emphatically routing their rivals, 71-52. Not only did UConn win a second national title, but the top eight players from this 36-1 team would return next fall, to be joined by a freshman class that included the most coveted high school player in the nation, Diana Taurasi.

The following weekend Geno stood on the steps of the state capitol in Hartford, addressing a crowd of thousands undaunted by the blustery, wintry weather. He sensed their excitement, their expectations. Since his Howard Hughes moment, his lot in life had been one of exceeding their expectations only to create loftier ones.

"I know what we needed to do to win the first one [in 1995, also against Tennessee] and the second one," he told the throng. "I think I know what it will take to win a third one, and I am telling you right now, in front of all these players, we are going to be back here next year with a third one. I promise you that."

OCTOBER

Saturday, October 14 . . . Shea Ralph stands alone. It is 8:00 a.m; one hour before the season's first practice. Her pigeon-toed feet line up directly behind the three-point arc as she fires three pointers, one after another. A manager rebounds for her, so that her cadence resembles someone playing an arcade Pop-a-Shot game. The first player on the court, her muscle-bound limbs already glisten with sweat.

At this moment, 25 miles west at the state capitol, the Greater Hartford Marathon is just getting underway. Here in Storrs, inside Gampel Pavilion, the Huskies' on-campus arena and practice facility, the 2000-01 women's college basketball season is about to begin.

Shea Ralph is nearing the end of her own personal marathon. She is a fifth-year senior who has endured two torn anterior cruciate ligaments (ACLs) in her right knee. She is also the reigning Women's Final Four Most Outstanding Player and a Kodak All-American.

Shea Ralph is an All-American; Shea Ralph is an action figure. "She-Ra", her mother Marsha Lake will sometimes call her, both an abbreviation of her eldest daughter's name and an allusion to the eponymous cartoon figure whose alias is "Princess of Power". On the court Shea is a grim-faced superhero. When she plays, she corrals her blonde mane in a white band, her ponytail becoming a feral whip. Her limbs, her entire bearing, are reminiscent of a princess of power.

As a freshman in 1997 Shea was so stoked for the opening day of practice, scheduled for 6:00 a.m., that she and her roommate,

Paige Sauer, did not sleep the night before. Both wore their practice uniforms to bed.

"That was Shea all freshman year," says first-year graduate assistant coach Stacy Hansmeyer, who matriculated with Shea five years earlier and has now completed her eligibility. "Shea never slept. Her diet was No-Doz and Diet Cokes."

The minutes pass, and now other players begin to filter onto the court: Junior forward Svetlana Abrosimova, the Huskies' other All-American who, only nine days earlier, had returned from a summer spent as the youngest player on the Russian Olympic Team; Sue Bird, Swin Cash, and Kelly Schumacher (aka "Schuey"), the other starters from last April's championship game; and Tamika Williams, a junior, and Diana Taurasi, a freshman, both former Naismith National High School Players of the Year.

It is a golden autumn morning in Storrs. The fall colors are ripe. *The Hartford Courant* has a photo of University of Tennessee coach Pat Summitt, or as Geno refers to her, "the coach from Knoxville", on its sports section's front page. The previous evening, Friday the 13th, Summitt was inducted into the Basketball Hall of Fame in Springfield, Massachusetts, fifty miles northwest of Storrs.

Although Summitt was behind enemy lines, Connecticut has treated her well on recent visits. In April 1999 Summitt visited a Hartford bookseller to do a signing for her recently released *Raise the Roof*, a chronicle of Tennessee's 39-0 national championship season in 1998, written with Sally Jenkins. Summitt's appearance drew 669 people, the best-attended signing in the store's four-year history and her largest outside the Volunteer State. Lori Riley of *The Hartford Courant* covered the signing and dotted the "i" on meticulous by noting that Summitt "went through four markers" during the session.

At the time Geno sent Summitt a bouquet of flowers and enclosed a note: "We hope your next visit to Connecticut is not as pleasant as this one. Congratulations on your great season."

At 9:00 a.m. Geno, looking like summer in khaki shorts and a beige golf shirt, enters the arena. He has a recruit and her parents in tow. In his left hand is a bag from Dunkin Donuts. As he enters, Nykesha Sales approaches. Now playing with the WNBA's Orlando Miracle, Sales resides near Storrs during the winter and occasionally practices with her former team. She ravenously eyes the Dunkin Donuts bag, but Geno hands it to the recruit. "You know how that goes," says Nykesha, who is only the school's all-time scoring leader. "I at least might 'a got a bagel."

At 9:10 Geno blows the whistle. The Huskies, all fifteen of them, assemble around the halfcourt circle. Associate head coach Chris Dailey hands him the *Courant* sports section. He reads blurbs from the newspaper's brief story on his team, which is buried on page six and analyzes different aspects of the team from the perspective of "Right Now" and "In a Month". He reads it chapter and verse:

> *"Right now,"* he reads, *"everyone says they have the same commitment to winning as last season.*
> *"In a month? Auriemma went philosophical this summer when he said, 'You can't stick your foot in the same river twice.' His meaning? The names may be the same, but this is a different team. It will be interesting to see if a national championship dulls their appetite for the grueling practices, which were the cornerstones to their success in March."*

"The only thing we know," Geno tells them, "is 'When's the first practice?' Today. We don't know when the last practice is. All we can worry about is today."

The team huddles, breaks with its customary mantra ("Together!"), and assembles in two lines. The first drill is a layup drill, one that Geno and Dailey, aka CD, have run since their inaugural practice in Storrs in 1985. Two lines, one at the top of the key, the other on the wing. The player with the ball at the top of the key dribbles upcourt to the opposite top of the key, jumpstops, then bounce passes to the player who has run parallel to her. The girl receiving the pass attempts a layup.

"Count 'em out," Geno says, mindful of how many players are on the court with the inclusion of Sales and Rita Williams, another ex-Husky now playing in the WNBA. "Gotta make 17 in a row."

One miss and the team starts over. The drill illustrates how far the program has come in 16 seasons. The first time it was done, it lasted 20 minutes before the team completed a flawless circuit. Today the drill is executed perfectly the first time.

He is pleased. "That was pretty good, actually," he says.

The coaches—Geno, CD, Jamelle Elliott, and Tonya Cardoza—pass each other furtive glances of approval.

Ninety minutes pass before Geno spots a galling error. Maria Conlon, a freshman guard from Derby, Connecticut, who last year was the state's top high school player, misses a layup. "Maria Conlon," Geno says, "you've already missed more layups today than some people miss in four years."

If anything, and he had expected this, the freshmen— Conlon, forwards Ashley Battle and Morgan Valley, center Jessica Moore, and Taurasi, a guard—are too reticent. To participate in a UConn practice is to constantly shout encouragement to teammates, to finish a drill, and as you run to the end of the line, to slap hands with every player you pass. In a scrimmage, when one player is substituted, she jogs to the sideline and slaps hands with every teammate there. This is standard operating procedure, every day, every drill, without exception. Introversion is not tolerated.

"Talk it up, Maria," Shea, the co-captain, encourages Conlon. "Open your mouth."

Since Geno singled her out, Maria has clammed up. Shea knows that if she doesn't admonish Maria, Geno will soon do so. Perhaps not as gently.

Shea saves Maria. She cannot save Morgan Valley. "Hey, Morgan," Geno says, "you better open your goddamn mouth, or you're not going to play. Open your mouth."

At seven minutes after noon, practice ends. Geno calls, "Five Spots" and the players line up in four corners with one player, Sue Bird, standing beneath the basket with a ball in hand. This is a variation on the old basketball camp standby, the star drill. Again, every player must make her layup or the drill starts over. Again, every player does.

Afterward they encircle Geno. "The biggest danger this team faces," he says, "is everyone just wants to catch and shoot. That's not how you win championships. The way you win championships is to play together. It is not predetermined who will shoot on this team. You know who shoots? The man who's open. You're only as good as when you play together.

"Today we played great," he says, motioning them closer in the huddle."Tomorrow we have to be better."

"Together!"

Monday, October 16 . . . "Here's what's wrong with sportswriters," Geno tells me, brandishing the latest copy of *ESPN: The Magazine.* "They make judgments on people and things they know nothing about."

In a preview story on the upcoming season, Sally Jenkins, who writes for both *The Washington Post* and *ESPN*, has provided an unflattering thumbnail of Diana Taurasi. She writes that Diana is "giggly, turnover-prone, and lacks a conscience with the ball. Even worse, her ego needs its own zip code."

"Forget that nothing we have seen in the time we have known her backs that up," says Geno, who is standing in the hallway of the women's basketball offices in the bowels of Gampel Pavilion. "How do you write that about a kid who has not even played her first college game?"

Despite the offices' subterranean locale, it is uncommon for Geno to exude a bunker mentality. He has an excellent relationship with the media, and they in turn are enchanted by him.

Geno has already written Jenkins a testy e-mail, and she has replied. That Jenkins has co-authored both of Pat Summitt's best-selling books, *Reach for the Summitt* and *Raise the Roof*, allows for Geno to harbor suspicions of unfair bias. That Diana cannot recall having met Jenkins exacerbates the issue. He replies in an e-mail that "it wasn't what you wrote, it's the way you wrote it".

I worked with Sally Jenkins at *Sports Illustrated* in the early Nineties. Her father is Dan Jenkins, a scathingly funny former *SI* senior writer. After leaving *SI* Dan Jenkins wrote *You Gotta Play Hurt*, a thinly-veiled portrait of the heroes and villains who comprise the magazine's masthead, and a must-read for anyone considering a career in sports journalism. If you still wished to pursue the field after reading *You Gotta Play Hurt*, hell, it was your own damn fault.

Jenkins inherited her dad's spunk. In much the same way that people pay tribute to Geno's teams by saying that "they don't play like girls", Sally never writes like a girl. She writes with fire. She writes the way Diana Taurasi plays. Still, her scouting report on Diana was only half-correct. Giggly, turnover-prone, and lacks a conscience with the ball? Guilty. Egotistical? No, but if you don't know her, it might appear so.

Diana Taurasi is as unself-conscious a teenager as you will ever meet. She made such a first impression on the Husky faithful last April during a high school All-America game at the Hartford Civic Center (UConn's second homecourt, which seats 16,294). When her name was called for the pre-game player introductions, Diana jogged to halfcourt and, using her arms to spell out "U-C-O-N-N", led the crowd in a cheer.

Diana Taurasi is brazen. Extroverted. Clownish.

"She's a con artist," Geno will often say.

"She's Eddie Haskell," says CD.

She's mischievous. Adventurous. She's Tom Sawyer.

"When people watch me," says Diana, whose 3,047 points at Don Lugo High School in Chino, California, ranked second in state history behind Cheryl Miller, "I want them to say, 'Boy, that kid has fun.' I watch the WNBA, and nobody ever smiles. I don't like that."

Diana put a smile on Geno's face the first time he saw her play in person. He was in Iowa, watching an Amateur Athletic Union (AAU) game in which she played. Doug Bruno, the coach at DePaul University, was seated next to him. Both men were impressed by her shooting range but were simply blown away by her passes, which caught teammates by surprise as often as they did defenses.

As yet another of Diana's no-look passes bounced off the head of an unsuspecting teammate, Bruno turned thoughtfully to Geno. "Taurasi's from southern California, right?" he asked.

"Right," said Geno.

"She was born around the time Magic Johnson was in his hey-day with the Lakers, right?" asked Bruno.

"Right," said Geno.

"I think maybe," said Bruno "she's his daughter."

Diana Taurasi's parents are in fact a quiet, Italian-born machinist named Mario and a vivacious Argentinian waitress named Lily. Mario's family moved to Argentina when he was five. There he met Lily, and the couple moved from Argentina to southern California a year before Diana was born. The primary language at *La Casa Taurasi* is Spanish.

For Geno, Diana's recruitment afforded him both unique advantages and disadvantages. He and Mario were both *paisans* from southern Italy. Geography, however, was also UConn's albatross in the matter. She is a momma's girl. Lily did not want to lose her daughter to a handsome coach from across the continent.

Diana, the younger of Mario and Lily's two daughters, had attended high school literally across the street from her home. She may have been the only kid in America whose shooting range—now there's something that needs its own zip code—covered more area than her commute. Now Geno was going to take her 3,000 miles away to Connecticut?

"When Diana and her mom made their recruiting visit," says Geno, "I remember driving them from the airport to campus. Diana's mother said, 'I don't like it here. It's very dark.'

"I said, 'Lily, it's ten o'clock at night.'"

On Geno's final recruiting visit to Chino, Diana apprised him that it was between the Huskies and UCLA, the latter being a half-hour drive from her home. "I'm just going to say this," he told her. "If you were the best men's player in the country, would you rather play at a school that gets sold-out arenas or at a school that draws five hundred people a game? Because that's what you're choosing."

Then Geno hit her right between the eyes. "You're going to do a lot of amazing things in college," he said. "It'll be a shame if no one sees you do them."

This afternoon's practice, which begins at 4:30, focuses on defense. "People talk about our offense," Geno had told the team on Saturday. "Everybody misses the point. The reason we win is it's hard to score against us."

Geno preaches defense. That's what coaches do. Ask the fans, and they will tell you that senior forward Svetlana Abrosimova, who hails from St. Petersburg, Russia, is the best player on the team. Ask the coaches, and they will tell you that she may be the worst defensive player. The offensive comparisons between Svetlana and Diana were inevitable. Will the defensive comparisons be so as well?

In one defensive drill the players line up single-file roughly three yards apart. At the whistle, they are to slide three steps out, then slide three steps back. Diana, the con artist, sees little point in sliding too far away from somewhere to which she must return. She cheats. Geno catches her.

"Hey, Diana, it don't matter if you get here first if you never left."

She has, to her chagrin, caught Geno's attention. Minutes later Diana, with the ball, is unable to find an open teammate. She takes a poorly considered shot, a chuck. "What was that?" he yells. "You shot 'cuz you didn't know what the hell else to do with it! Because when you were in high school, you shot every time you got the ball."

Lacks a conscience with the ball.

Not long afterward Diana attempts a difficult pass and turns the ball over.

Turnover-prone.

"Svet," Geno says to Svetlana, the Huskies' other returning All-American senior besides Shea Ralph. "See what it's like to play with someone like you? That was you three years ago."

Svet grins at him. *Oh God, he is picking on someone else.* English is not the only language barrier Svet has been made to overcome. "Svet understands English when I talk about offense," Geno would tell the scribes when she was a freshman, "but when it comes to defense, well, that's another story."

Geno had kicked Svet out of practice that year. He had designed a drill for a fast break and directed the players to run it over and over. Nobody was supposed to shoot. After a few repetitions of the drill, she took an open shot and drained it.

"Why'd you shoot?" he asked her.

"I was open," she replied.

"Get out!"

This game is so simple, Svetlana often thought. *Why does Coach need to make it so complicated?* Once he had admonished her for failing to set a pick on offense.

"Why set pick?" Svet had asked in her halting English. "I was already open."

"Maybe," he replied, as if he'd just thought of it himself, "to get somebody else open."

"Oh."

On the very next play after her turnover, Diana has the ball again. She is two steps behind the three-point arc. She is not closely guarded—only Nykesha shoots from that distance—and so the *chica* from Chino launches a 25-foot three-pointer. She buries it. Geno watches in grudging admiration.

"She can do that, though," he says.

After practice another e-mail from Sally Jenkins awaits. She argues that the "ego that needs its own zip code" remark is just one line in an otherwise glowing article, adding that she has tremendous respect for his program.

Geno accepts her explanation. Privately, he wonders why she was the only player criticized in the entire preview.

Wednesday, October 18 . . . Four years ago she could barely speak the language. Tonight Svetlana Abrosimova is speaking in front of 1,100 guests at a celebration dinner honoring the 2000 national championship team.

It is a rainy night. The AquaTurf, a spacious banquet facility in Plantsville that is central Connecticut's leading prom and wedding warehouse, is filled to capacity. After the players receive their national championship rings, graduate assistant coach Stacy Hansmeyer, who played on last year's team, speaks. She is a blonde, blue-eyed Oklahoma girl, a 4th of July slice of Americana. Her words are sweet and heartfelt except for a good-natured dig at Svetlana, her preternaturally gifted former teammate. "I'll remember so much about my four years," Stacy says, staring at Svet. "I'll remember stories of a girl who had four turnovers a game, and none of them were her fault."

Svetlana follows Stacy on the dais, her 6'2" frame stunningly adorned in a red cocktail dress. During her summer odyssey with the Russian Olympic team, she let her brunette pixie cut, which she had worn the last three years, grow long. Heads turn at this suddenly feminine figure.

> *"It's hard to add something else,"* Svet begins. *"What Stacy said was perfect. But CD made me do it. Actually, Coach made me do it. He knows how much I like doing these things."*

Four years ago Svetlana was living with her parents, Oleg and Ludmila, in a three-room apartment in St. Petersburg, Russia. She spoke almost no English. She was 16, the Most Valuable Player of the 1996 European Junior Championships, and an opportunity for a scholarship in the United States was presented to her. All she needed was to become proficient enough in English to pass the Scholastic Aptitude Test (SAT).

Boris Lelchitski, a United States-based Russian scout who had first suggested her to Geno, set her up with a tutor, Katya Yachnikova-Hughes. "When I learned I was to teach English to a woman basketball player, I balked," said Yachnikova-Hughes, who is British. "We had only three months."

Svetlana studied night and day. When she slept, she placed a textbook under her pillow. To take the SAT she had to take a train from Moscow, where she was practicing with the Russian Junior National Team, to St. Petersburg, a three-hour trip. She did poorly on the verbal portion of the exam but missed only one question on the math.

Meanwhile, 9,000 miles away, Chris Dailey's renowned recruiting prowess was being taxed to its limits. "Everyone in our office always knew when I was calling Russia," she recalls, "because I'd start talking really loud. As if that will help a foreigner understand you better."

In August 1997 Svetlana flew to New York with one suitcase and enough money in her pocket for a return flight home. She knew no one. She was barely 17.

> *"I tried to think of stories from last year that I would talk about tonight,"* she tells the audience. *"I watched our highlight video,* A Season to Remember. . . *and that didn't help me at all."*

From the moment the Russian immigrant player met the Italian immigrant coach, it was a unique relationship. She was Eliza Doolittle—she even spoke with a British accent gleaned from her British tutor—with a reverse layup. He was Professor Henry Higgins. All of Connecticut, which fell instantly under her spell, was Colonel Pickering.

The first official team activity that autumn, the timed mile, found Svetlana drafting behind two upperclassmen after three laps. If only she knew how many laps were in a mile. "Are two left?" she asked guard Missy Rose.

"One," Missy replied.

Svet was gone, a zephyr. She broke the tape in 5:45, a team record.

She never asked for help. On her first day of school, she missed two classes because she did not understand how to read her course schedule. Another time her economics professor informed the class that there would be a quiz the next time they met. She was terrified.

"I thought, What is 'quiz'?" Svetlana remembers. That day she went to lunch, where some creative mind had made the day's menu into a quiz. She saw the word QUIZ atop the menu and figured it out for herself.

Svetlana would write a paper in Russian then translate it to English. Paige Sauer, a center who graduated in 2000, and Shea Ralph once lent her their computer for Svet to write a paper. When they returned two hours later, she had typed two sentences in English. "Move over," said Paige, "I'll take care of this."

Her teammates rooted for her, adopted her, lent her clothes. Everyone would invite her out, but she always politely declined. She had to study. "Svet would tell me that Marci [Glenney, a former player] calls her a geek," Paige remembers. "Then she'd say, 'I do not even know what *geek* is.'"

> *"I know how my teammates came here [to UConn] dreaming of a national championship. I didn't dream that, not knowing much about college basketball."*

Svetlana's first semester grade-point average was 2.78. On the court she was on her way to establishing a freshman record for points (538). Geno was amazed by her determination. Moving to a new country. Learning a new language. Accepting burdens no one else her age could fathom and excelling nonetheless. Surely she reminded him of someone he knew.

"There's nothing for her to be afraid of," he'd say. "You're nine thousand miles from home in a strange country, with a knucklehead Italian guy yelling at you all the time, and seventeen thousand people wanting you to make every shot."

In Svetlana's first start, 14 games into her freshman season, against Providence, she had a double-double (at least 10 points and 10 rebounds) in the first half. Four games later she scored 27 points and had 11 rebounds in a mild upset of second-ranked Old Dominion. She also had a game-high seven turnovers and, with UConn leading by 20 points, fouled a player attempting a three-point shot with a minute remaining.

"I didn't know she was going to lead the league in every category," said Geno. "Points, assists, rebounds, turnovers, fouling three-point shooters when you're up by twenty."

"Coach explained that foul is not good," Svetlana replied in the clipped accent that would become so widely imitated around the state. "I think I did not foul her."

The Recalcitrant Russian. She enchanted him. She enraged him. "The Russians have got to be the most stubborn bastards in the world," he would say. "Let me tell you, Svet is so much that way."

She was turning him into a xenophobe. He was turning her into a Genophobe. This was Ricky and Lucy with a Slavic twist. The media, the fans, they lapped it up.

Against Seton Hall, Svetlana played lax defense on one possession early in the game. He sat her the next 18 minutes. The following game against Miami, she was inspired on both ends of the floor, shooting 8 for 10 from the field. Had Geno motivated her?

"I don't want to give him any credit," Svetlana said. "My goal was to play more than two minutes. I feel like I accomplished something."

She was funnier in her second language than most people are in their first. So, too, however, was he. "Oh, yeah," Geno retaliated. "Svet is the best player to play. Ever. She could probably go hardship right now to the WNBA. They could use another kid who can't dribble with her left hand."

Never did Geno let Svetlana forget how much more she had to accomplish. "You didn't come all the way over here just to be average," he would tell her. "It's time for you to be great."

> *"I remember the feeling after we lost in the Sweet Sixteen two years ago. There was a feeling that we had to change the way we played. For some players that was hard. For some foreign-born players that was exceptionally hard."*

By the end of her junior season, Svet had twice been named All-American. ("That's great," she had reacted the first time. "I am not even American and I got it.") She had learned to play within the team matrix. Still, Geno loved to rattle her cage. One time he informed the media that the Huskies as a team had gone to visit a sports psychologist. "We made the whole team go," he said, "just so Svetlana wouldn't feel self-conscious."

Back at the AquaTurf, Svetlana concludes her speech. Then Geno, as always, gets the last word.

> *"I'll be brief,"* he says. *"Svet has to return the dress she borrowed for tonight. One of the showgirls at Mohegan Sun [a casino in the southeastern corner of the state] can't go to work until Svet gets back."*

Afterward, a fan approaches Svetlana for an autograph. The fan, perhaps starstruck, garbles her first name. *It is funny*, she often muses, *I learn their entire language, and they cannot pronounce my name.*

In fact, everyone from Geno on down simply calls her "Svet." The copy editors adore the pun-ful potency of the nickname: "Svet Shop" and "No Svet" are faves. Her most ardent admirers appear at games clad in homemade "Svet Shirts".

In fact, the nickname "Svet" is improper. She never corrects anyone, unless someone asks her what she prefers. "It's Sveta," she will say. "In Russian 'Svet' has another meaning. It means light, like sunny."

Radiant.

Saturday, October 21 . . . Storrs, the home of the University of Connecticut, has no Burger King, McDonald's, Wendy's or even Starbucks. Storrs is so small that it is not profiled in UConn's media guide; the neighboring town of Mansfield is. So small that, in the words of itinerant college football coach Lou Holtz, who worked at UConn in the Sixties, "It used to be called 'Storr' but then they got another one."

Storrs is located in the northeastern corner of Connecticut, the nation's third smallest state in area. Locals call this region the Quiet Corner. It is an area of soft-hilled forests and meadows, placid lakes and gentle streams. It is a Thanksgiving postcard.

Hartford is 25 miles east, and Bradley International Airport is 12 miles further north up Interstate 91 from the state capitol. Between Hartford and Storrs, there are two routes: the direct path, which meanders along country roads, and the indirect route, which mostly follows the interstate. The latter, although eight miles longer, gives the impression of a campus that is less secluded.

"When I was an assistant coach at UConn," says Wake Forest head coach Charlene Curtis, who was on Geno's staff in 1996 and '97, "we used to drive the recruits in the long way. Less little towns to drive through."

Conversely, when Geno first picked Curtis up at the airport for her job interview in the spring of 1995, he took the shorter, *i.e.*, backwoods, route. "We've got a little way to go yet," Geno said as he drove the red Ford Explorer south on I-91. "But I'm going to show you why we're so popular."

And so he drove her through the tiny towns. Through Quarryville. Coventry. Mansfield Depot. "This," he said, "is where we get our support from."

Storrs, like Oz or Las Vegas, is a miracle and an oasis. Why build an empire here?

It is 6:30 p.m as Geno drives to Bradley to pick up high school recruit Teresa Borton, the top prep player from the state of Washington. A 6'3" brunette, she is widely considered to be one of the top post players in the nation. Accompanying her are her parents, Bill and Marla, her sister Valerie Rubright, and Valerie's husband, Jason, who is also Teresa's AAU coach.

Tonight's itinerary is a cookout with the entire team at the Auriemma home in Manchester. It is a smaller abode than you might expect the best-paid women's basketball coach in America to reside in. Not long ago a boy rode by the house and spotted Geno on the front lawn. A look of shock crossed the lad's face. "You live here?" he asked.

"Yeah," Geno replied. "I gotta live somewhere, don't I?"

The Bortons bring a few boxes of apples from the Yakima orchard on which they live. The family has been in the apple business, on the same land, for four generations. Bill Borton is 6'5" and ruggedly handsome. He could be James Brolin's older brother. His son-in-law, Jason, who played for Gonzaga University in the mid-Nineties, is 6'8". They are tall, hearty stock, these Bortons. Decent people. Apple people. Solid to the core.

Teresa appears reticent, though she could be forgiven for being in awe. These are the national champions, the most exclusive hoops sorority in the country. This, understands Teresa, who has narrowed her choices to UConn and the University of Notre Dame, is rush weekend.

"Teresa doesn't want to hurt anyone's feelings," says her mother, "and she respects both programs so much. It can be a little nerve-racking."

In September Notre Dame coach Muffet McGraw and one of her assistants, Carol Owen, visited Teresa at her school, West Valley High in Yakima. As Teresa was walking them to the parking lot, the school's security guard, Robert Morphew, spotted them. "She's gotta go to Connecticut!" he shouted.

"Robert," Teresa blushed, "they're from *Notre Dame.*"

Serendipity seems to be smiling on Geno. A still-life painting of apples has been hanging on the wall in the Auriemma kitchen for years. Marla notices and nudges her husband. "That for us?" she kids.

Recruiting visits at UConn are two-way streets. Some high school seniors visit and are immediately drawn into the coven. Shea Ralph arrived on a Thursday in September of 1996, promising to phone her mother, Marsha, that evening. Four days later Kathy Auriemma received a phone call. "Just tell me this," said Shea's mom. "Is my daughter still alive?"

Rebecca Lobo visited in 1990 and cites the easy comity between herself and Meghan Pattyson, her host, as a primary reason that she chose UConn. "We just stayed in on Saturday night," she recalls, "and made hot chocolate."

As Rebecca and fellow recruit Pam Webber sat around Pattyson's apartment, a religious debate broke out. "Meghan wondered what the 'H' in 'Jesus H. Christ' stood for," says Rebecca. "Pam claimed that it stood for Henry."

Sunday, October 22 . . . At 3 p.m. the four sets of doors at Gampel Pavilion open and 6,000 people stampede inside, seeking seats close to the court. This is Huskymania.

Today is the SuperShow, a free, open-to-the-public intrasquad scrimmage that serves as the team's annual debut. It is a beautiful day, a golden Indian summer afternoon, the likes of which are not to be seen here again for months. For many of those in attendance, it will be the only opportunity this season that they will have to see the Huskies play. Tickets to UConn women's basketball games are more cherished than beautiful days in late October.

"We're here to see the new players," says Jeanne Mullaney of Mansfield who, with her daughter Samantha, 12, waited four hours in line. "We're hoping to get front-row seats."

Six thousand people for a scrimmage. There may be 20 schools besides UConn or Tennessee in all of women's college basketball that have ever drawn that number for a game. And it's a safe bet that UConn or Tennessee was the visiting team on those occasions.

The influx of humanity creates traffic problems near Gampel. As for Geno, he has already fended with his own traffic mishap today. After a two-hour morning practice, Geno drove the Bortons around the university in his SUV. They drove past Mirror Lake on the east end of campus and as they did so Bill Borton noticed some geese. "Look at the geese," he said.

Geno looked. As he did so the vehicle in front of his stopped. He rear-ended it.

Shortly after 4:00 p.m. the players are introduced one by one to the audience. The lights have been dimmed. As their names are announced, each player poses or does a dance under a spotlight, then runs to center court. This is so "Let's Get Ready to Rumble". This is so not the Huskies' style.

There are no names on the backs of UConn jerseys. No player under Geno has ever donned a jersey with the number "1". All jerseys are tucked in at all times, even during practice, and socks, always all white, are lower-calf-lengthed. The uniforms are uniform.

The announcer calls out Kennitra Johnson's name. "She's got the most famous Band-Aid in Connecticut," he cries to knowing applause. Tattoos are also anathema, and KJ's, which says "KJ," is located on her left bicep. Almost half of the players on the team have tattoos, but only KJ's is visible when she is in uniform. Thus the Band-Aid to conceal it.

Geno does not coach today. He sits at the end of press row with Teresa Borton. Just the two of them. Marla Borton looks on, impressed that the coach is devoting his time entirely to Teresa but wary of the afternoon's affect on her daughter. "All the hype," Marla will later say. "It's not her."

During the weekend Teresa has bonded with the most hypephobic Husky, freshman Morgan Valley. Like Teresa, Morgan is introverted and a rural kid, from Colchester, Vermont. A 6'0" wing, Morgan is all bacon, no sizzle. At the Auriemma cookout the two talked to one another almost exclusively. In Morgan, Teresa sees a kindred spirit, a potential teammate with whom she knows she would get along.

Yesterday at practice Morgan, paralyzed by indecision, held on to the ball too long during an offensive possession. "What are you nervous about?" Geno asked her. "You're a freshman. I expect you to stink. You're playing pretty good. Why are you nervous?"

On the following play Diana, playing point guard, made a no-look pass to Morgan who, not ready for it, lost it out of bounds. "Hey, D, what are you doing?" he chided her. "She wasn't looking. She was still worrying about what I just said to her."

Morgan rooms with Diana. They are the most compatible roommates since Felix and Oscar, which is to say that although they are polar opposites, they really do get along. "We fight like sisters," says Morgan, "but five minutes later we're talking again."

"We roomed them together, hoping they'd rub off on each other," Geno tells the writers after the scrimmage. "It's not working out very well yet."

Is Diana a serious person?

"No, she's never serious," he says, "but is that bad? Morgan Valley's as serious as a heart attack. Is that good?"

In terms of absorbing Geno's comments, Morgan is quicksand and Diana cement. With Diana he can tell the scribes that "she's a typical freshman, with the added problem of being from California" and know that her zip code-size ego can handle it. With Morgan, well . . . she puzzles him.

It is nearly 6:00 p.m. now, and the New England sun has all but disappeared. In the lobby of Gampel Pavilion, all 15 players sit at rectangular tables, black Sharpie pens in hand. "We're going to make sure today that every single person in the building gets an autograph from one of the kids," Geno had promised the crowd earlier that afternoon. The line snakes more than halfway around the exterior of the building. The team will sign autographs for at least the next two hours. As Teresa Borton prepares to leave the premises and return with her family to the orchard, she gazes at the multitudes in awe. The past 24 hours has been a super show of UConn hegemony. Is it for her?

On the cross-country flight home, she barely says a word.

November

Friday, November 3 . . . The freshmen, fittingly, are made collective victims of the team's first prank of the season.

The Huskies have a set game-day routine for all games, home and away: a shootaround, which is a brief practice heavy on strategy, followed by a pregame meal, ideally devoured four hours before tip-off.

Today is a school day and also the first dress rehearsal of the season. EOS Malbas, a touring team from Sweden, has traveled to Storrs to play the role of sacrificial lamb. The shootaround takes place in the early afternoon. As the team is leaving the locker room, an upperclassman reminds the freshmen, "Pregame is in forty minutes. Remember, wear dress clothes."

Forty minutes later Ashley Battle, Maria Conlon, Jessica Moore, Diana Taurasi, and Morgan Valley enter the banquet room in dress slacks and sweaters. As they open the door, they are met by flashbulbs. The upperclassmen, clad in blue team sweats, have brought their cameras. Later, Jessica will recall that she should have figured something was amiss. "The five of us ran out of the locker room wondering if we'd have enough time," said the Alaskan, "and we should have noticed that we were the only ones running."

After the meal, most of the upperclassmen head back to their dorms for a brief respite. Shea Ralph and Christine Rigby, who live six miles off campus with Stacy Hansmeyer in a two-story house on Coventry Lake, walk over to Gampel. It is still three hours before tipoff when Shea walks into the locker room to find the five freshman sitting mute at their locker stalls, already dressed out in their uniforms.

"I thought I was bad," says Shea. "And I was. I am. But all five of them already dressed out, sitting mute, three hours before the game?"

"Well," says Morgan, "why change clothes again?"

The freshmen are good sports. Then again, the initiation was tame. This bodes well for the Huskies. In 16 seasons Geno's teams have rarely experienced problems with team chemistry, but when they have it has usually concerned the freshmen. More precisely, it has concerned the upperclassmen's resentment of the freshmen. Twice this has happened, two seasons that Geno would gladly forget.

The first time was the 1987-88 season, Kerry Bascom's freshman year. For perspective's sake, if you were to compare the principals of UConn's program to characters from the Bible, here is how it might look: the Old Testament matriarchs would be Peggy Walsh (now Myers), Kerry Bascom (Poliquin), and Meghan Pattyson. The savior would be Rebecca Lobo, surrounded by apostles Jennifer Rizzotti, Nykesha Sales, and Kara Wolters, all four All-Americans. The post-Salvation saints would be Shea and Svetlana, with Sue Bird, Asjha, Swin, and Tamika on the brink of canonization.

Peggy was a senior when Geno arrived. Kerry, a stocky 6'1" post player from Epping, New Hampshire, who came two years later, was the program's first blue-chip recruit. Her freshmen year was difficult. A few seniors, resentful of her prodigious talent which robbed them of their most precious commodity, playing time, addressed her only as "freshman". In the locker room before one game a senior demanded that Kerry exchange game shorts with her, since hers were newer and roomier in the behind. "You want 'em, come get 'em," Kerry replied. A pregame brawl ensued. The freshman won.

"My roommate was a senior that season," says Kerry, who is now married and living in Exeter, New Hampshire, "and she would lock me out of our room at night. I used to go down the hall and sleep in [sophomore] Kris Lamb's room."

Renee Najarian, a senior on that team and the squad's leading scorer, says the season provided few fond memories. "Even though we went 17-11, we should have won more games," says Najarian. "We never jelled. Coach was so sick of us that he canceled the postseason banquet."

Eleven seasons later, in 1998-99, Sue Bird, Swin Cash, Asjha Jones, Keirsten Walters, and Tamika Williams became by far the most talented freshmen class ever to enroll at UConn, perhaps at any school. Tamika was the Naismith National Player of the Year, Asjha and Swin were both first-team high school All-Americans, and Sue had been the point guard at Christ the King in New York City, the top-rated prep team in the nation.

Talented? Beyond a doubt. Audacious? Swin sent Geno her high school senior prom photo for him to display on his desk (he did) and, using the first-name initials of her classmates to form an acronym, nicknamed the quintet "The T.A.S.S.K. Force".

It was simple impetuousness, but it may have grated on the upperclassmen. Their skills grated more. The only one of the five to start fewer than fourteen games was Sue, who began the season as the starting point guard but suffered an ACL tear in practice on December 8. The frosh and upperclassmen were cultural opposites as well. The juniors and seniors were predominantly white and, as one former player says, "mall types". The frosh were more urban.

They would be Geno's only squad since 1993 that failed to win 30 games, winning 29.

Talent and chemistry. This year's freshman harvest is the most talented Geno's staff has reaped with the exception of the T.A.S.S.K. Force. Unlike that unit, however, he does not need these freshmen to play immediately. They know this and, it seems, accept it.

UConn beats EOS Malbas, 104-54. Midway through the first half, Diana makes a steal. She and Sveta lead the fast break, the freshman and the senior playing catch as they sprint upcourt. The ball never touches the ground. Finally Sveta, who can easily finish the play herself, sneaks a hook pass to Diana over the head of the lone defender. Diana scores on a left-handed layup. The senior rewards the freshman.

Wednesday, November 8 . . . The presidential election occurred yesterday and still no winner has been officially declared. The race between George Bush and Al Gore is, as the pundits are saying, "too close to call".

At Borton Fruit in Yakima, Washington, Teresa Borton's future is just as uncertain. Today is the first day of the weeklong early signing period for college-bound high school seniors. In the next seven days Teresa will make a decision that will affect the next four years of her life. She has eight days to choose between UConn and Notre Dame, her final two candidates.

She comes home from school and tells her father, "It's Notre Dame." Bill Borton hears the diffidence in his daughter's voice. "Make sure," he replies, "that you're choosing it not to avoid something."

Maybe it's not Notre Dame. Maybe Storrs is Teresa's destiny. But the Huskies already have three power forwards who will all be seniors—Asjha, Swin, and Tamika—when she will be a freshman. Playing time will be scarce.

Then again, they can teach Teresa so much. And maybe Geno really does think she can play for him. Hadn't he phoned her from Australia in September? That must mean something. Oh well, she does not have to decide today. She will sleep on it.

Recruiting. It has been a relatively soft summer and autumn of foraging for Geno and his staff. The Huskies already have five freshmen and an oral commitment from Ashley Valley, Morgan's younger sister. Besides, Geno has been away—far, far away—all summer.

"I spent more time in the Southern Hemisphere this summer," Geno says, "than I did in Connecticut."

In July Geno traveled to Argentina to be the head coach of the United States Junior National Team for the Qualifying Round of the World Championships, which will take place in the summer of 2001. Two of his incoming freshmen, Ashley Battle and Diana Taurasi, played on that team. Diana, the team's second-leading scorer, drained 26 points in the final game, a victory against Brazil. Geno liked to say that the bilingual 'baller was on the team "so that she could get us into all of the restaurants".

In August the Auriemmas spent two weeks at the south New Jersey shore, where each summer tens of thousands of Philadelphians trek to their second homes or summer shares in the dusty beach towns of Avalon, Sea Isle City, and Stone Harbor. Here, as he does every summer, Geno doted on his family and hung out with old buddies such as NBA referee Joe Crawford, Vanderbilt University women's basketball coach Jim Foster, and St. Joseph's (Pa.) University men's coach Phil Martelli. The latter two Geno worked with two decades earlier, coaching high school ball in Philly.

One evening Geno and Kathy dined out with Crawford and his wife. Geno reached for the check as he always does, but this time Crawford beat him to it.

"One of fifty-two in the whole world!" he proclaimed, denoting his elite status as an NBA referee as if it were a seat in the US Senate. "One of fifty-two!" he repeated, as if it were incumbent on him to pick up the tab. Geno let him.

The next morning in the newspaper Crawford read that Geno had signed a new contract at UConn, for $2.95 million over the next five years. He had overtaken Pat Summitt as the highest-paid coach in women's college basketball. Crawford howled. "That bastard!" he laughed. "He signed that contract, didn't tell us, and let me pay!"

In late August Geno departed for Australia and the Olympics, where he and Peggie Gillom of Texas A&M University served as assistant coaches for the USA women's squad under head coach Nell Fortner. He relished the Olympics. He felt honored as a naturalized citizen to march in the Opening Ceremonies behind the United States flag and to be in the company of the world's most superlative athletes of this, or any, era.

"There is nothing like when you are there and when you walk in the Opening Ceremonies and right next to you is Maurice Greene,and right in front of you is Alonzo Mourning," he would later tell Matt Eagan of *The Hartford Courant*. "When you walk through the Olympic village and somebody says, 'Hey, Coach,' and you realize that kid is the world-record holder in the 1,500 meters, that just can't transfer over to television."

Geno stayed in touch with his kids, with his players, with his coaches. He dispatched Chris Dailey and Jamelle Elliott, who in practice work with the post players, to Yakima to visit Teresa. He kept up on the news from the States. When someone informed him that Gore, who is from Tennessee, had chosen Connecticut senator Joseph Lieberman as his vice-presidential running mate, he could not resist a dig on the Tennessean who is his chief rival.

"Figures," Geno said, "that a guy from Tennessee would need a guy from Connecticut to get the job done."

At Olympic practices he held nothing back, but there were moments when he wondered if Team USA was not overpreparing at the expense of lost opportunities to enjoy heavenly Sydney.

In fairness to Fortner, the job of head coach of a USA Olympic basketball squad is a no-win proposition. Anything but gold in Sydney for the US would have been devastating to Fortner professionally. Plus, she had resigned her position as head coach of Purdue in 1998 in order to devote herself fully to this job for an entire year, and then the Lady Boilermakers had gone off and won the 1999 national championship without her. In case she was wondering if she had made the right career decision.

Fortunately, Fortner could now look back and say that she had chosen wisely. Team USA beat Australia in the gold-medal game, 76-54. Meanwhile, in Yakima, Teresa Borton sits and wonders which choice will bear more fruit.

Thursday, November 9 . . . They could sell tickets if they wished. UConn could sell tickets to watch practice. People would come.

Ten years ago the UConn athletic department poobahs met to discuss whether they should begin selling tickets to women's games. Now, if they wished, they could sell tickets to practice.

Leon Barmore, the Louisiana Tech coach whose .871 winning percentage is the all-time highest (Pat Summitt is second on that list, Geno third), said as much two days ago in a cover story in *USA Today*. "Geno's second team probably should be in the top ten," Barmore told writer Dick Patrick for a piece entitled "UConn Downright Scary". "In fact, their fans ought to go watch their scrimmages. They'll be better than some of the games."

They could call it *The Geno and CD Show*, the University of Connecticut's longest running program. Weekday afternoons live from the Gampel Pavilion. Geno and CD are in their 16th season together, longer than any coaching staff currently at UConn.

"Geno and CD play off each other well," says Howie Dickenman, the former UConn men's assistant basketball coach who is now the head coach at Central Connecticut State University. Dickenman's cramped office in the Fieldhouse was adjacent to theirs back in the Eighties before Gampel opened in 1990. "They're a good team. She's not afraid to disagree with him."

They are like Abbott and Costello, a morphologically dissimilar duo whose relationship is no stranger to amiable and respectful bickering. Geno is compactly, solidly built at 5'10". CD is a willowy 6'0".

They are an act. Acts use props. CD totes a plastic yellow broom that she paid $8 for at Target. She uses it to help post players develop an arc on their shots, holding it so that the whisk end is aloft. The players must shoot over the whisk. The broom is also somewhat of a talisman for CD, who considers it bad luck for the whisk to touch the ground.

Geno is not into props—he keeps his cordless whistle in his pocket and almost never blows it. He prefers monologues. "We stink," he declares today after the first team, which is always clad in blue mesh jerseys, surrenders an easy layup during a five-on-five drill. "We just do. We stink. There's no other explanation.

"Either that or we don't understand it and I gotta explain it better. We just don't understand that we can't give up a layup."

Geno wants—needs— the defense to communicate with one another, but that is easier said than done. "Nobody says anything back here," he says. "Nobody knows what the hell's going on. I don't know how the hell we're gonna stop anyone if nobody says anything. Just hope the other team stinks."

They could charge $5 per person, and no one would blink. Heck, fans have been mailing fives, tens, and twenties to the basketball offices for the past three years, ever since they learned that Sveta's parents, Oleg and Ludmila, could not afford to travel to the States to see their daughter play. All currency is returned so as not to violate NCAA rules.

They could put a live mike on Geno, but they might first wish to talk with Carol Stiff, ESPN's programming director for women's college basketball. Three years ago ESPN miked Geno for a game against Stanford that was played in Lakeland, Florida. Stiff was back in Connecticut watching the game when she heard "Shit!" followed a few minutes later by a concise review of Svetlana's performance. "She plays like a goddamn European!" cried her European-born coach.

"I don't usually like to call the [director's] truck in the middle of the game," recalls Stiff, "but that day I did."

She had them cut the mike.

They could sell tickets. They have what many keen-eyed observers are calling the best starting five (Sue, Shea, Svetlana, Swin, and Kelly Schumacher) in the game's history. They have a second team, the "white" team jersey-wise, that consists of Kennitra Johnson, Diana, Morgan, Tamika, and Asjha (two former Naismith winners and three more former prep All-Americans). They have Rebecca, Nykesha, and Rita, UConn icons all, practicing with them occasionally as well.

Sell tickets? People would scalp tickets.

People do visit, free of charge. As often as not, a high school coach or a family or a youth league team or, as happens today, a nursing-home group attends practice. Today a dozen senior citizens from the Brittany Farms Health Center in New Britain has made the pilgrimage. Among their number is wheelchair-bound Val Reed, 86, who is a recluse.

"He never, ever comes out of his room," says his daughter Marie, who accompanies him, "except for the Huskies."

Val has his own room and television. He prefers to watch the Huskies alone. He eats in his room and, with assistance, manages the remainder of life's vital functions in the adjoining bathroom. He could leave his room. He just never does.

"Before today," says Marie, "the last time my father left his room was for the championship celebration party the nursing home held in its day room."

That was more than six months ago. The Huskies are not only a basketball team, they are a remedy for agoraphobia. The Huskies help get the Val Reeds of Connecticut through the long, cold, lonely winter. Every winter.

"He sparkles when he watches them," says Marie of her dad. "You can see it in his eyes."

Geno, meanwhile, is not sparkling. During halfcourt offensive set work against a live defense, Sveta attempts a lob pass in to Kelly Schumacher that is stolen by Rebecca, who is coming off two ACL surgeries in the past two years and is painfully slow. For Rebecca to steal a pass from anyone, let alone the second-best player in the game (after Tennessee's Tamika Catchings) is astounding. Sveta, on the right wing, turns her back to the court and grins. Waiting for the storm.

"That's just so bad!" Geno barks, kicking the basketball. "That's just giving the team the ball."

When watching most half-court routines during practice, Geno and CD take the same positions. Geno kneels on one knee along the baseline while CD sits on the stanchion, one leg folded beneath her posterior, her lissome figure appearing to have as many foldable parts as a *Trivial Pursuit* board.

Kneeling, Geno continues: "When our two seniors are lousy, it's hard for us to be any good."

"Three," CD gently corrects him.

"Yeah, three," he says, "all three of you are playing lousy today."

Geno has good reason, actually two, to ride the reigning national champions today. First, the season-opener versus second-ranked Georgia is three days away. Second, in a scrimmage earlier in the week against a team of 11 male students assembled on the fly, the Huskies lost. Jamelle Elliot coached them. The game was split into four 10-minute quarters and thanks to some otherworldly three-point shooting by a student known only to the players as "Omar", the men overcame a one-point halftime deficit to win.

A rag-tag group of men had beaten the top-rated women's college basketball team in the nation. Somewhere Bobby Riggs was smiling.

"Coach was pissed, too," team manager Tom Tedesco recalls. He said, 'You're letting a bunch of guys beat you!'"

A bunch of guys.

Definitely, they should sell tickets.

Friday, November 10 . . . Autumn is over. A gloomy sky that spits soft rain hovers above Storrs. In two days the Huskies will play third-ranked Georgia in a nationally-televised doubleheader from the Hartford Civic Center.

Despite the inclement weather, Gampel is the epicenter of women's basketball today. Van Chancellor, the coach of the four-time WNBA champion Houston Comets, arrives at practice. Chancellor, a son of the Deep South with a bayou drawl and an easy manner, greets Rebecca, Nykesha, and Rita, whom he knows well. Their attendance at practice is permissible by the NCAA as long as any one of them is not present more than three days per week. UConn's coaching staff manages their schedules as carefully as Daedalus did flight. Everyone benefits. The WNBA players receive fantastic off-season conditioning which gives the league a better product, while the program accrues the dividends of its previous four-year investment into these players' development.

At this point in the season, however, it is Rebecca, Nykesha, and Rita who are being taken to school. One hour into practice, during a fullcourt press-break drill, Rita, who is tiny and lightning-quick, has the ball. She shot-fakes Shea Ralph, who is guarding her, then drives recklessly into the lane. She is hit and lands hard on her hip.

"You all right?" Geno asks. "That was an offensive foul, too. That was a charge on you, Rita."

Next Nykesha has the ball on a fastbreak. She jump stops, then, trapped by the defense, takes a second hop-step. The whistle blows. "What was that?" Geno asks.

"Travel," she confesses.

"Thank you," he replies.

He is grateful that they return. They provide a benchmark against which his All-Americans (Shea and Sveta) and burgeoning All-Americans (Sue, Diana, perhaps Swin) might measure themselves. They also validate the type of program that he and CD have endeavored to forge, a family. While none of the trio lives in Storrs, all reside close enough to attend practice. Their presence here is a testament to the program.

Rita drives the lane again, her 5'6", 135-pound frame a pinball ricocheting against mighty bumpers. She hits *Tilt!* and falls hard.

"Your player hit me in the back," she says.

"Who was it?" he asks.

"I don't care," she answers chippily.

Near the end of practice Geno's patience is tried on consecutive plays by Sveta and Diana, respectively. Unintentionally, they snare him in a coaching Catch-22. With the ball on the left wing, Sveta looks inside to feed Tamika Williams. However, she looks a moment too long. Morgan Valley reads Sveta's eyes, steps between Sveta and Tamika, and steals her pass.

"Put the ball in there like you wanna be a player, Svet," he says. "Nice bounce pass. Jesus! What do you think they're looking at? They're looking at what you're looking at."

On the next play Diana has the ball at the top of the key. She looks right then, spiritual daughter of Magic Johnson that she is, fires a one-handed, no-look bullet pass to Tamika, who is open under the basket. Tamika never sees it. The pass whizzes by her and hits Geno, who is standing next to the basket stanchion, in the side. Now whose fault is that?

Geno raises his eyes. Diana suppresses a laugh, then says, "Sorry." The team waits for a reaction. Will Geno go Vesuvius on Diana? Svet's pass failed because she fooled no one; Diana's because she fooled everyone. How do you tether Diana's virtuosity without clipping her wings?

He waits a beat. Then, with little conviction, he says, "I don't want to see any one-hand passes."

At 6:53 Geno calls Five Spots, and the players weave through their layup drill. Afterward, the UConn media assemble around him. The gang of writers who follow the men's team are known as the Horde, because they are so prolific in number. Connecticut is a well-read state of many minor cities; it has many newspapers, thus the profusion of writers. The women's beat writers are sometimes called the Horde, too, but that is a borrowed pseudonym. Let us give them a new one: the Herde.

The Herde assembles around Geno. He plops down in a seat in the front row of the bleachers, runs his fingers through his thick coif a time or two, then locks them behind his head. He rolls a lozenge around his mouth. Some college coaches (which is to say "most") despise sportswriters. Almost as many understand their influence and accommodate their needs. Still others, such as football coaches Lou Holtz (South Carolina) and Steve Spurrier (Florida) are so sharp-witted that they cannot help but be entertaining. They may not love the media, but they do keep its notebooks well-fed.

Then there is Geno. Surrounded by females all day—his coaching staff, his office assistants, his players, three of his four family members—he truly enjoys being in their midst. He loves the banter and says a zillion things that are off the record without preempting himself with, "This is off the record."

Geno knows them. Trusts them. Those who have covered him for some time—Carl Adamec and Randy Smith of *The Manchester Journal-Inquirer*, Mike DiMauro of *The New London Day*—treat him as they would a big brother. They respect him, sure, but they are not afraid to tell him he's nuts. That's why he likes them.

Carl Adamec asks him about Georgia, reminding him that two Southeastern Conference (SEC) teams, the Lady Vols and the Lady Bulldogs, are ranked directly behind UConn in the preseason poll. Carl is pushing Geno's buttons.

"Georgia," Geno says. "There's no love lost there. Georgia had seventeen hundred people at their exhibition game last week. The only time they ever sold out was when we played there [a 97-65 Husky win four seasons ago].

"They want what we've got," Geno continues, while enumerating Georgia's virtues. "They've got beautiful weather, a big campus, and football Saturdays. What do we have? Storrs, our campus, and our football team. Oh, and two national championships."

Saturday, November 11 . . . Michael Auriemma is 12 years old and wears size 12 sneakers. His feet are already bigger than his dad's. Michael is one of the few people you'll ever meet who acts his age and his shoe size.

Michael is 100% boy, "a real true boy", says his godfather Howie Dickenman. "The kid who brings his baseball mitt, bat, and ball to the park and is there all day."

Michael Auriemma's father is a real true boy, too. "We were at Michael's First Communion," Dickenman recalls, "and in the pew in front of me, Geno is drawing up a basketball play on a piece of paper. You gotta remember, a First Communion is when, May?"

Michael's "uniform" is a powder-blue pair of University of North Carolina gym shorts and a Jayson Williams #55 jersey. He adores the flashy Sacramento Kings point guard, which drives his father to distraction. *"Hey, Mike, if you really want to learn how to play point guard, watch Sue Bird."* You look at Michael and you think, maybe not every kid in the country is praying for a PlayStation 2 for Christmas.

It is 11:00 a.m. The Huskies practice at one end of the court at the Hartford Civic Center (HCC). Michael shoots at the other. He may love the game more than half the players on the team. He shoots three-pointers endlessly, as if he's resigned himself to the fact that he won't grow past 6'4" and so, if he's going to make a living in the NBA, it will be by shooting threes. Who knows, he may be right.

Dick Patrick of *USA Today*, who has known Geno for more than a dozen years, is seated courtside. Dick's wife, Jody Lavin-Patrick, was an assistant coach at Georgetown, a fellow Big East school, from 1986-1994. Lavin and Chris Dailey, in order to curb expenses, used to frequently room together when scouting players at AAU tournaments. "I remember once in New Mexico," CD will later recall, "[Georgetown coach] Pat Knapp phoned Jody about a player. We were both already in our beds. She looked at me and said, 'I'll see you in a bit.' She had to go outside and use the payphone so I wouldn't be able to hear her."

The Patricks have witnessed the evolution of Geno's empire as closely as any outsider. During the Big East tournament in 1992, held in Storrs, their four-month old son, Eamon, began crying from hunger. Lavin-Patrick found a vacant locker room and began breast-feeding her infant son. Kathy Auriemma walked in. "Didn't bat an eye," Lavin-Patrick will later recall. "She just started asking me questions about Eamon. She'd probably done the same thing there herself once."

Kathy is a hoops junkie who watches tapes of games while exercising in her basement. In 1991, on the night that UConn played in its first NCAA regional final, against Clemson in Philadelphia, Michael, then two, had developed a virus. He was too sick to attend the game so Kathy decided to stay with him in their hotel room.

"The game was televised," Kathy recalls, "but our hotel didn't get ESPN. This was our first chance to play for a trip to the Final Four. I had to know what was going on in that game."

Kathy phoned Geno's parents, who were then living in Norristown and who did not attend the game. "Nona," said

Kathy, "put the phone near the television set and turn on the sound."

There she sat for the next two hours, a phone cradled to her ear and her youngest child sleeping next to her. UConn won.

Much has changed in 10 years. The Huskies, who are playing 25 miles from campus, will stay in Hartford. While that is not particularly unusual for a Division I revenue sport, the Huskies are staying at the Goodwin, which is the Dom Perignon of Hartford lodging. Tomorrow, they will walk through the Goodwin's ornate lobby, through the front door and onto their bus, which will ferry them approximately 30 yards to the underground entrance to the Hartford Civic Center.

"That's just our gameday routine," says Sue Bird. "We always eat the same pregame meal (pasta, chicken, steamed vegetables), and we always bus to the arena."

Even if it is just across the street.

Sunday, November 12 . . . The word "Asylum" appears along the south side concourse of the 16,294-seat Hartford Civic Center. It denotes the name of the street that lines that end of the arena, a road sign to those who may have lost their bearings.

Asylum has two distinct meanings, "refuge" and "madhouse". This afternoon the Lady Bulldogs will discover the HCC to be none of the former and all of the latter. They will lose their way, yes, and their psyches will be in need of examination.

Georgia is led by the senior backcourt tandem of Kelly and Coco Miller of Rochester, Minnesota. The Minnesota twins are virtually identical in appearance: 5'10", lean and muscular, with dishwater brown hair that each ties in a ponytail.

Their togetherness is redoubtable: Kelly and Coco earned identical grades (all A's and one B) at Mayo High in Rochester, which is 75 miles south of Minneapolis-St. Paul (the Twin Cities). Until two years ago the dual pre-med majors had never spent a night apart. As sophomores both were assessed 79 fouls and came within one field goal of scoring the same number of points (628 for Kelly, 626 for Coco). Kelly and Coco Miller may be the world's first set of separated Siamese twins.

Kelly is a first-team All-American. Coco and the Lady Bulldogs' third perimeter player, Deanna Nolan, are also dangerous outside shooters. In UConn's pregame locker room,

48

Geno warns his squad of the trio's offensive potency. "Do not let the same kid of these three get on a little bit of a roll," he says, looking sharp in a gray suit and powder-blue tie. "The same one doesn't score twice. If 23 [Kelly] scores, she doesn't get the ball the next time down."

He turns his attention to offense and expectations. "We set a goal of scoring one hundred points," he says. "We can. It's going to be loud, people are going to be excited. It's their first opportunity to cheer for you since last year. Let's give 'em something to cheer about."

The Huskies have enjoyed a postcard summer, a Phileas Fogg respite from Storrs. They scattered to play basketball on five of the earth's seven continents: Sveta played with the Russian Olympic team in Europe and then Australia; Schuey, Shea, and Sue played in Asia on the United States Jones Cup team; Ashley and Diana played in South America for Geno on the US Junior National team.

Now they are all back together. Home. The capacity crowd stands as one as the five starters—Sue, Shea, Sveta, Swin, and Schuey—walk to midcourt. The crowd, in keeping with UConn tradition, stands. They will clap in unison and remain standing until the Huskies score. More than two minutes into the contest, they are still standing and clapping. Georgia has a 6-0 lead.

Then, with devastating fury, it is over. The Huskies outscore Georgia, 54-15 in the next seventeen minutes. Diana enters the game with 14:17 left in the half and promptly buries her first shot, a three-pointer. Except for Sveta's new, longer hairdo, the difference between today's Huskies and last April's is imperceptible. With one minute until halftime the Huskies lead the third-ranked team in the nation by 29 points.

Just before halftime Geno empties his bench, playing three frosh and senior center Christine Rigby, who has never entered a game in the first half. This unit gives up six unanswered points to end the half, allowing Geno to rant a little in the locker room at halftime.

"Six straight points," he barks at the Huskies' *de facto* third unit. "You're squandering what your teammates built up."

In the second half the Lady Bulldogs make a run, closing to 71-59 with eight minutes remaining. Georgia gets no closer. UConn plays a perfunctory second half, winning 99-70. When

Geno is asked about Georgia's second-half run, he smiles. "They got it to 12 points?" he says. "I wasn't paying attention any more."

Sveta has played luminously, with game-highs in points (18) and assists (11) and, more importantly to her coach, zero turnovers. "I'm in a state of depression right now because I don't have anyone to get mad at anymore," Geno jokes. "My whole reason for being has gone out the window. It's no fun if she's not going to turn the ball over, take dumb shots, and commit dumb fouls. It's taken all the joy out of coaching."

The expectations, already heady during the preseason, will with this win become stratospheric. Geno knows this. He has told his players, his family, and the entire state in fact that this is a season to be savored. Three days earlier Lori Riley of *The Hartford Courant* quoted Tennessee's Pat Summitt as saying, "We're playing for March," an allusion to the NCAA tournament. The comment rankled Geno.

"Everybody talks about 'Are we going to repeat?'" he says. "You know, they say 'You said it,' but I want to think in terms of what happens between now and then. Why would we want to skip right to that?"

Geno cannot stem the tide of public opinion, though, and he knows it. "When you get up tomorrow morning, we won Florida overwhelmingly," he says, alluding to the nation's disputed election tally. Then, sarcastically, "We're the biggest story in sports."

The team will eat out in Hartford tonight at Coach's, a sports bar owned by UConn men's basketball coach Jim Calhoun. They will then return to campus, and the five freshmen will head directly to the players' lounge inside Gampel for study hall, a Sunday evening tradition. Tomorrow, everything changes. It has to. The bar has been raised.

"They're not playing against the number three team in the country any more" Geno says, mindful of the superlatives his players will soon be reading about themselves. "They're playing against me, every day. Starting tomorrow."

Monday, November 13 . . . "I think I missed my calling," Chris Dailey, 42, tells an audience of some 400 adolescent girls and their moms. She is the keynote speaker at a career symposium in Waterbury entitled "Advancing Women in Sports". "I should have been a kindergarten teacher or a party planner."

Chris Dailey—CD— is the den mother of UConn women's basketball. She organizes games, conducts workshops on everything from etiquette to autograph signatures ("I have this thing," she says, "where I'd like them to sign a legible autograph"), and attempts, sometimes with great success and other times less so, to be the clearinghouse for team gossip.

She has rules. "CD's rules," Swin Cash sighs later this afternoon. "You are not to wear headphones in public places. No blue jeans, either. You must always say 'Thank You'. No tattoos. No fingernail polish is to be worn during a game. Jerseys must be tucked into your shorts at all times. Everybody wears white socks, all the same length. She's got a lot of little things like that."

"How we represent ourselves is important to us," CD tells her luncheon listeners. "Do you want to be like everyone else or do you want to be different?"

The game is much different than when CD last played it in 1982. As a senior at Rutgers, CD helped the Lady Scarlet Knights win the final Association of Intercollegiate Athletics for Women (AIAW) national championship. The NCAA inaugurated a women's national championship that same season.

CD had designs on becoming a Physical Education teacher and, in her senior year at Rutgers, student-taught at Spotswood (New Jersey) High School. "I had one girl," she tells the audience, "who tried to get out of class by telling me that she'd been having her 'friend' . . . for three straight weeks."

She taught Health as well, which required that she give a lecture on contraception. The school supplied a model of the female reproductive system as a teaching aid. On the day of the lecture someone swiped it. "Kids were walking the halls," she recalls, "asking, 'Has anyone seen Miss Dailey's vagina?'"

One day CD was coaching a girls softball game. One of her players struck out swinging, but the ball sailed past the catcher, meaning that the the batter could try to beat a throw to first base and be safe. "Run!" CD screamed.

The player ran—directly to CD. "I thought to myself, There's some power in this coaching job," CD recalls.

After a yearlong stint at Cornell as an assistant coach CD returned to her alma mater, helping her former coach, Theresa Grentz. After two more years of seasoning, Geno, who had been an assistant at Virginia and knew CD from the recruiting trail, asked her to be his assistant coach.

"He begged me," CD says ["I don't think so," Geno laughs]. "He asked me in May and called me all summer until I said yes at the end of July. I was his first recruit."

"I remember the day that Geno came to Rutgers to offer her the job," says Grentz, now the head coach at the University of Illinois. "When he was leaving the RAC [Rutgers Athletic Complex], I said to him, 'She's mine. You take care of her, or I'll come after you.'"

At the conclusion of her luncheon speech, CD opens up the floor for questions. None are immediately forthcoming. She knows why. There is one question that everybody always asks regarding CD, but rarely will anyone ask her directly. She is single—has never married—and so people wonder, if she is putting her career first—and she is—why she does not seek a head coaching job. Eventually, a student has the temerity to ask: "Don't you want to be a head coach?"

CD smiles. "I used to get really insulted when people asked, 'When are you leaving?'" she says. "Now I take it as a compliment. I think I have the best job in the country. I work in a state that loves college basketball, and I work with kids I want to work with."

Later this afternoon the Huskies have an abbreviated practice. They lift weights for half an hour—briefly but intensely under the sadistic direction of conditioning coach Andrea Hudy—and then Geno gathers them at midcourt in Gampel.

CD emerges from the southeast door leading to the arena all smiles. She is toting a large FedEx package. She opens it, and a dozen or so small jewelry boxes drop out. The coaches have sprung for rectangular gold necklaces for each of the players from last year's squad; an award promised at last spring's team banquet. The necklace has a miniature, gold Liberty Bell with a diamond clapper and says "National Champions 2000". The freshman receive candy necklaces.

As CD distributes the booty, Geno speaks with sincerity. "The Big East championship rings, the stuff that the conference or the NCAA gives you," he says, "we don't care if you want to give them to someone. You want to give them to your parents or a family member, that's fine. But we hope items such as this, things that we give you, we hope you keep those things yourselves."

Geno means it as much as he means anything. Around his own neck he wears the top half of a crucifix. His father Donato gave him the crucifix as a high school graduation gift. Later, when he worked at Allen Wood Steel in Conshohocken, Pennsylvania, the heat got so intense that one day the crucifix snapped in half. He still wears what remains, to remind him of his father and from where he came.

The necklaces are one of many fringe benefits of being a Husky. Immediately after receiving them, the players attack one of the incumbent duties of being a Husky. In the hallway outside the players' lounge 16 chairs are set up in a row behind three tables. Dozens and dozens of new basketballs are in boxes next to them. For the next 20 minutes the Huskies form themselves into an assembly line of autograph-workers, painstakingly signing each ball and passing it on. The signatures are legible.

"See that?" says Sue Bird, pointing to Svetlana Abrosimova, who is at the end of the line. "Sveta's nice. She goes to the back of the line because she has the longest name. She doesn't want to hold up the line."

Back in the basketball offices, Geno is being apprised of the onslaught of media headed his way by assistant sports information director Ann Marie Person.

"Fox Sports is here Wednesday," she says.

"What do they want?"

"To talk about women's sports."

"I'm sick of women's sports," he teases. "How about a story on men in women's sports? On Italian men in women's sports?"

"All about me."

"That's right, allaboutme.com."

Tuesday, November 14 . . . Geno was not kidding when he told the media two days earlier that his players would be "playing against me". The Huskies have been winning so often for so long that, a while back, the coaching staff created a list of 14 goals for the team to achieve each game. It is a matter of elevating the game from competition to art.

Winning is, save for a handful of games each season, a *fait accompli*. Since the 1993-94 season the Huskies' record is 248-17 (a .936 win percentage) with five of those losses coming to the Lady Vols. The lowest that they have finished in the final regular season Associated Press poll is fourth.

Thus the 14 goals, created with one goal in mind: to keep the Huskies sharp for those three or four games per season that do hang in the balance. They are as follows:

1) At least 17 offensive rebounds
2) At least 50% field-goal shooting
3) Less than 15 turnovers
4) At least 80% free-throw shooting
5) Hold opponent to 65 or fewer points
6) Hold opponent's high scorer to 20 or less points
7) Force 25 turnovers
8) Hold opponent below 40% field-goal shooting
9) Score the first basket of each half
10) Grab at least 58% of all rebounds
11) Commit 18 or fewer fouls
12) Attempt 15 more shots than the opponent
13) Attempt 20 three-pointers
14) Make 35 deflections and/or steals

Against Georgia the Huskies only attained three of the goals: they shot 56% from the field, held the Lady Bulldogs' high scorer, freshman center Christi Thomas, to 16 points, and held Georgia to 37% shooting from the field. They will not come close to attaining even half of the goals in any game this season.

"The point being," Geno tells them during practice, "that if you play a great game, you expect to get seven, eight, or nine of these things. We got three. That's not great. We spent a lot of time in the second half not playing great ball."

Geno is partially to blame. When he sent the third unit into the game one minute before halftime, he sent a message to his team that the game was over. What else was he to do? On national television the Huskies were routing the purported best team not wearing "UCONN" or "TENNESSEE" on its jerseys. He was embarrassing them and their coach, Andy Landers, who has led the Lady Bulldogs to the Women's Final Four twice in the past five seasons. It was bad for the sport for the Huskies to appear so insuperable.

Randy Smith, the veteran sports columnist for *The Manchester Journal-Inquirer*, believes that contrary to what most outsiders think, Geno is a softie. "He's a pussycat," says R. Smith (as Geno calls him), who told him as much in the wee hours of last April 1st. "Oh, I got mad at him that night. I told him that 'you can bet that the coach from Knoxville was probably back in her hotel room studying tape'. But he was more concerned with entertaining his family and friends. He's a pussycat. But if that's his biggest shortcoming, I can live with that."

Wednesday, November 15 . . . Teresa Borton has made up her mind. It's Notre Dame.

Thursday, November 16 . . . Larry Rifkin, 48, is a visionary. Nine years ago Rifkin, the executive vice president in charge of programming at Connecticut Public Television (CPTV), rented a video, entitled *Barney and the Backyard Gang*, for his daughter Leora, who was four at the time.

"I noticed how that video mesmerized my Leora," says Rifkin of the seven-foot tall purple dinosaur, Barney. "I called one of the co-creators and asked, 'Have you ever thought of putting this on public television?'"

The rest, as they say in broadcasting and paleontology, is prehistory. Rifkin brought Barney the Dinosaur to PBS and created a monster. Three years later Rifkin made another noteworthy find: the UConn women. "We began by broadcasting the 1994 Big East tournament," says Rifkin. "We had the serendipity of Rebecca Lobo and the 35-0 national championship season a year later."

Today UConn women's basketball is the most popular PBS program in the nation, on a local basis. The Huskies regularly get 7.0 and 8.0 ratings (each point equals approximately 16,000 viewers) in the Hartford/New Haven market. The next-highest-rated PBS program does well to register a 3.0. Six times in the past two seasons broadcasts of UConn games have ranked among the top three programs in prime time for the week. Besides a Ken Burns documentary, this is unheard of for PBS. "It doesn't matter who the women are playing," says Rifkin, who notes that the Huskies are 124-2 in their seven seasons on CPTV, "they draw well."

Larry Rifkin is a visionary. So is Geno Auriemma. In 1985 he accepted a job at the University of Connecticut, a school that had finished last in the Big East four straight seasons, for $29,000 a year. In those early days he shared an office with Chris Dailey and two assistants. The four of them had the use of two rotary phones. Their index fingers had calluses at the tips.

"I couldn't believe he'd take the job," says Charlene Curtis, who until then had been sharing an office with Geno at the University of Virginia. "From the outside it looked like a bad job."

From the inside, too. Practice was part of a three-ring circus: as track athletes ran on the indoor track that circumscribed the court, baseball players took batting practice, and football players lifted weights-all within earshot.

"I remember going up there to visit him," says Phil Martelli, "and it was like that old song, 'Is That All There Is?'."

His most valuable asset was his uncanny belief in himself and how basketball should be taught. "The first two weeks of practice," says Peggy Myers, his first captain, "all we did was defensive drills. None of us had ever worked that hard."

Peggy lived on the second floor of Watson Hall but was so exhausted from practice that she took the elevator to her room. She pulled her mattress from her sleeping loft to the floor so she could be spared the agony of climbing three steps up the ladder. She was spent. He thought she had more to give. "He called me into the office in the third week of the preseason, and he told me, 'If our season began tomorrow, you wouldn't start,'" Peggy recalls.

This was Geno's best player, his only decent shooter, and the team's captain. "That woke me up," she says.

Theodore Roosevelt saw less potential in the Isthmus of Panama than Geno did in Storrs. "He came in and told us everything he foresaw the program becoming," says Kerry Poliquin, "from Gampel to television coverage, and sure enough it has all come true."

"His standards were so high and he was so impatient," says sportswriter Teresa (T.C.) Karmel, the only one who has covered him from the beginning. "My impression was of a guy who was always looking at his watch."

Geno has arrived. Tonight CPTV is hosting a reception at its Hartford studios. The network's major donors have been invited and are mingling with the coaches and players in a cavernous yet crowded studio. At 7:30 p.m. Rifkin steps onto a small stage to introduce Geno. "This year," Rifkin proudly tells the audience, "every single UConn women's game will be televised, either on CPTV, ESPN, ESPN2, or CBS. That is a first for any women's college basketball program."

Geno then steps to the microphone, his players behind him. The crowd of roughly 150 cheer enthusiastically. "I didn't hear the players clapping very loud," he dryly notes. He stares at his team, grinning. They stare back, groaning, at least inwardly.

"Don't write me any letters about Svet," he says of his senior, who this week is being profiled in *Sports Illustrated* and is photographed in an alluring pose, "I'm sick of reading them. Especially now that she's modeling for *Sports Illustrated*. I don't know who's going to model for the swimsuit issue. Maybe me."

"Swin," he says, moving on to Swin Cash, "Swin's perfect. Except when she dribbles or shoots or passes."

"Keirsten," he says, motioning to junior point guard Keirsten Walters, an intense pre-med major who will miss the season after recently undergoing her sixth surgery since arriving in Storrs, "will be starring on *ER* the rest of the year. She's not as weird as she used to be, either. She comes by the office and says, 'Hi.' Last week I saw her teeth for the first time."

Not all the comments are barbed. "In all the time I've been coaching, twenty-five years, I've never been around anybody with Tamika's personality or sense of self-comfort around people," he says of Tamika Williams. "She was the high school player of the year a couple of years ago and she doesn't care about anything except winning, doesn't care if she starts."

He calls Sue Bird the team's most important player. His eyes rest on Kennitra Johnson, whom he had not played against Georgia as punishment for academic problems she has been having, and he stuns her. "If people say we have the best point guard in the country in Sue Bird," he says, "and I think we do, then we have the second-best point guard in K.J. Some days she's the best. If she could ever find a way to make me happy and get on the court . . . "

Meghan Pattyson is in the audience. She knows Geno better than anyone who has ever played for him. A 1992 graduate, she is a TV analyst for CPTV's coverage of UConn games and the host of *The Geno Auriemma Show*, whose first installment will be taped this evening. She is also a constant companion to the entire Auriemma family.

"I used to think that scholarships only lasted four years," Geno is wont to say, "and then I met Meghan."

"Blow it out your ass," is her stock reply.

Meghan may not have the national recognition value of Rebecca Lobo or Nykesha Sales, but in-state and among the current Huskies, no alum is more popular. She is a woman who never played like a girl.

Meghan understands Geno. If he gives you the business, you've gotta throw it back in his face. During the taping Geno and Meghan take phone calls, and one caller inquires about Jessica Moore, who is red-shirting.

"You know what my son Mike said about Jess?" Geno says. "After practice the other day he said, 'You know what I like about her? She's the same person every day. Always in a good mood.'"

"Nice that a twelve year-old would notice that," says Meghan.

"That's because he's the exact opposite," Geno counters. "Very moody."

"A lot of people say he's just like his dad."

You gotta throw it back in his face or take it, excuse the phrase, like a man. He used to ride Kerry Bascom about her horrible defense, and you know what she'd say? She'd look him in the eye and answer, "You knew I couldn't play defense when you recruited me," she'd say. "So why do you care now?"

The next caller asks about recruiting. Geno acknowledges its essential, if not primary, role in UConn's success. "Part of being a good coach is getting good players," he says, "and back in the 'Eightiess when we didn't get good players, we got good people. Like Meghan."

Blow it out . . .

Geno's recruiting trip to Meghan's home in Doylestown, Pennsylvania, had turned out to be little more than a day spent golfing with her father, Wally, and two of her brothers. At the end of the day Geno dined at the Pattyson's home and, after a few glasses of wine, had leaned back on the couch and locked his hands behind his head. "Meghan," he had told her, "go wherever you like. As long as you're happy."

Sunday, November 19 . . . There once was a barnstorming bunch of basketball babes known as the All-American Redheads. For fifty years, beginning in 1936, this distaff version of the Harlem Globetrotters traversed the US in a stretch Oldsmobile station wagon—four doors on each side—challenging and mostly beating men's teams.

The Huskies are off—on a commercial flight as opposed to a stretch Olds— to the West Coast. It's as close to barnstorming as UConn will come this season, playing Pepperdine University in Malibu on Tuesday, then heading north along the Pacific coast to play the University of Washington in Seattle the day after Thanksgiving.

I am reminded of the Redheads as I sit next to Christine Rigby and Kelly Schumacher on the Huskies' first and longest road trip of the season. Rigby, aka "Rig", aka "Rigga" and Schumacher, aka "Schu" or "Schuey" are easily paired on more than just seating arrangements. Rig and Schuey are both redheads and, at 6'6" and 6'5", respectively, big reds at that.

Both are from Canada, though Rig is a native Canadian, born and raised in Victoria, British Columbia (her father is a Royal Canadian Mountie), while Schuey moved to Quebec from Cincinnati with her mother when she was a teenager. Rig is a talented seamstress who is always making quilts and sweaters, what her teammates call "Riggawear". Riggawear is not available in any store, though as Husky players know, and Rig has learned, "When they ask me to teach them how to make a quilt that really means, 'Can you make me a quilt?'"

Rig lives in the cabin buried in the woods on Coventry Lake with Shea Ralph and Stacy Hansmeyer. From the outside it resembles the house of horrors in *Blair Witch Project*. From the inside, too, contends Rig. "It's haunted," she says resignedly, as if any ghost in its right mind would mess with Shea and Stacy. "No, really it is," says Rig. "I hear bumps and strange noises all the time when I'm there alone."

Rig lives out on Coventry Lake. Schuey, according to every-one on the team, lives in another galaxy. "Planet Schuey", they call it, referring to her penchant for flightiness. "She thought last Sunday's Georgia game was on Friday," says Chris Dailey.

Schuey has a regal carriage, her shoulders back and her chest forward. Her big, expressive blue eyes are as compelling as Geno's, and her smile is both infectious and mischievous. She is statuesque, glamorous even, with nary an awkward or dis-proportionate bone in her body. Yet there is definitely a fragility to her.

After last Sunday's game it was discovered that Schuey has a stress fracture in her right foot. Just last night the Huskies played an exhibition game against a team from the Ukraine—Dynamo Kiev—and Schuey, reduced to the role of well-heeled bench spectator, spent a portion of the game smuggling Reese's Pieces into her mouth. "That was a long game to have to sit through," she says of the Huskies' 89-35 win before a sellout crowd of 10,027. "I was hungry."

Schuey is a starter whose immense athleticism—Duke want-ed her to play volleyball and basketball—is disproportionate to her consistency. She played the game of her life in last April's NCAA championship, blocking a record-tying nine shots. In the first ten games of last season, she had a total of nine blocks. Rig is haunted by ghosts; Schuey by her talent.

And the media.

"There was a writer last year—he doesn't cover the team any more," Matt Eagan of *The Hartford Courant* says, "who asked to interview Schuey one-on-one. His first question to her was, 'Has your nose always been like that?'."

And to think athletes loathe sportswriters. I am hoping that, during our five hour flight together, Rig and Schuey will aban-don if not loathing, then at least circumspection about me. Definitely, they must be wondering what I am doing here.

In 1998 I was asked to coach the junior varsity girls team at Loyola College Prep on Manhattan's Upper East Side. The program was in its second year. The first inglorious season they'd finished 0-4, scoring a total of ten points. I enlisted an old buddy from both college and *SI*, Marty Burns, to coach the girls with me.

We soon discovered that coaching girls presented itself with new situations. During one game a player of ours was fouled from behind on a breakaway layup. She landed hard. I sprang from the bench, worried that she was seriously injured.

"Danielle," I asked, "are you okay?"

"Yeah, coach," she replied, still lying on the court, "but she knocked out my navel ring."

By the second half of the season Marty and I were scouting—scouting!—opponents. At one private school for sons and daughters of United Nations diplomats, where security is tight, we lied and said that we were uncles of a player. We must have looked like, well, you know what we must have looked like. Then Marty caught me taking out a notebook to diagram their plays.

"Put that away," he scolded. "We already look like a pair of jag-offs."

In our second season with the Loyola Lady Knights, I drove to Hartford to observe a UConn-Notre Dame game. It was like happening upon a distaff Promise Keepers revival. All these people are here for this?, I thought. But then I watched UConn play. All of their baskets, it seemed, came easily, the residue of smart, patient passing or Notre Dame turnovers.

The Huskies dissected the Irish, then the nation's 4th-ranked team, more than they defeated them. The only blight on the afternoon for the Huskies had been Svetlana Abrosimova, who had spent the entire game in foul trouble, the victim of a questionable whistle or two.

"Coach," Geno was baited during the postgame press conference, "do you think that referees discriminate against certain players?"

"Yes I do," he said. "I think they discriminate against players who commit stupid fouls."

In my mind I was already on the bus.

Monday, November 20 . . . "I got the feeling since the Georgia game," Geno tells the team as they assemble around him at the start of practice, "that our practices have been less than sharp. Let's have a good one this morning."

It is 10:00 a.m. inside the Firestone Fieldhouse at Pepperdine University. The Church of Christ-affiliated school is located at the intersection of the Pacific Coast Highway and Malibu Canyon Road. The campus is built into the canyon, providing California dreamin' vistas of movie star homes and the Pacific surf. Pepperdine is one university that takes an unbeatable college-brochure cover photo.

Pepperdine offers its students a tantalizing, frustrating paradox. Its MTV Beachhouse locale lures applicants like bees to honey. Then they discover its strict religious mores, where fraternizing between the sexes is limited to visiting hours and no alcohol is allowed on campus.

If any UConn player could adhere to Pepperdine's spartan code, it is Morgan Valley. Already the freshman's asceticism is legendary among her teammates. She drinks only milk and water and abstains from all types of potato chips, candy bars, ice cream and fast food.

"With one exception," Morgan confesses. "Taco Bell."

Morgan Valley will not eat after 8:00 p.m. unless she has not yet had dinner. Alcohol? No. How would she then be able to end each day by doing 200 sit-ups and ten push-ups? Or rise and shine before the sun does?

"Morgan's up at five a.m. every day," says Jessica Moore, who rooms with her and Diana Taurasi, "with her nose in a book."

Geno has a great line about Morgan. "She makes coffee nervous," he'll say. If she just relaxed, she would play so much better in games. But if she relaxed, would she be the same person who is the first to practice and the last to leave?

"Morgan Valley does the things you need to be a good basketball player," Geno says. "She can catch and shoot and pass."

This morning Morgan is doing it all. On one play she blocks Swin Cash's shot, inciting Swin to toss the ball in anger. Next Morgan steals a pass in the frontcourt and takes it in herself for a layup. On the ensuing inbound pass, an arcing toss toward the midcourt sideline, she lunges for a steal. She deflects it out of bounds, hurtling herself headlong into senior walk-on Marci Czel, who is standing on the sideline. The coaches exchange glances: She's playing awesome and pissing off the upperclassmen.

Good. Let *her* motivate them.

Shortly after noon the Huskies board their bus back to the hotel. There is no formal seating chart, but there may as well be. Be it bus or plane, it will not vary all season.

Geno sits in the front left row and Chris Dailey directly behind him. Jamelle Elliott and Tonya Cardoza sit across from them.

Next are the various support staff: administrative assistant Sarah Darras, team managers Kathryn Fieseler and Tom Tedesco, sports information director Ann Marie Person, trainer Rosemary Ragle, video assistant Aime Trzcienski, and ticket coordinator Scott Merritt.

This group gets one seat per person.

Behind them are the players, each of whom gets two seats, arranged as if by class: KJ, the lone sophomore, is first, followed by the juniors, then the seniors and, in the very back, the freshmen. The exception is Ashley Battle, who sits behind KJ.

The arrangement places Stacy Hansmeyer in an awkward position. She is a coach now, although more than half of the players on this bus were her teammates last season. She sits with the coaches up front. "Stacy," beckons Shea Ralph, who is seated in the next-to-last row, "are you not allowed to come back and talk to me?"

Stacy looks momentarily conflicted, then retreats to speak with Shea. The team is headed back to the hotel, to three hours of study hall together in a banquet room on this golden afternoon. Shea asks Stacy to ask Geno if the seniors can at least study in their own rooms. Stacy obliges and walks back to the front of the bus. She passes the request on to Geno, who looks back and raises a thumb in the air.

"And afterward," he says, "you can wear jeans out."

CD whips her neck around in mock-anger.

Dinner this evening is at the Pacific Dining Car, an upscale steakhouse in Santa Monica. As we enter, CD is stopped by a table of diners quite surprised at what they see. "What kind of budget do you have?" a man at the table asks admiringly.

The players sit at one long table. Geno, the coaching staff, and Ann Marie Person sit at another. The kids' table and the adults' table. At the kids' table Maria Conlon, who turned 18 today, is discovering what that entails as a member of the Huskies. The upperclassmen begin the birthday chorus:

> *"Skip around the room,*
> *Skip around the room,*
> *We won't shut up until*
> *You skip around the room."*

Maria sheepishly stands up and skips around the table. Geno excuses himself and returns a few minutes later wearing a grin. "I walked by their table," he says, "and Diana was speaking Spanish to the waiter. When she saw me she said, 'Don't worry, I'm getting us a deal.'"

Geno shakes his head. The kid has spunk. He lifts his glass of red wine and smiles. He has a habit of raising the glass and mechanically swishing the wine into a whirlpool. Is he contemplating the wine or something else? Or is he simply savoring it?

Diana's gregariousness triggers a discussion between Geno and CD regarding the freshmen.

"Morgan and Maria are *out there*," Geno says.

"Diana's a little out there, too," CD replies.

"Yeah," he says, reaching to spear an olive, "but I like her."

"You should really have a conversation with those two," she says, meaning Morgan and Maria.

"Fine, bring 'em over here," he says, lifting two olive spears before him. "First, stick these in my eyes."

Tuesday, November 21 . . . Enroute to tonight's game, Diana Taurasi peers out the bus window fretfully. From her seat she espies two classic southern California sights: the sun disappearing into the Pacific and bumper-to-bumper traffic on the Pacific Coast Highway. "We're never going to get there," she sighs.

Gradually the traffic dissipates. The bus turns off the PCH and onto the verdant campus just after the sun has sunk below the horizon. The coaches and support staff, all except Jamelle Elliott, exit the bus. She pops a videotape into the tape player.

Jamelle does this for every game, makes a two-to-three minute highlight video of the Huskies' previous game and sets it to music. The players watch themselves, enthralled.

By the time the players leave the bus, a small throng awaits them. The Taurasi clan is here: Diana's family and former teammates from Don Lugo High. Their coach, Larry Webster, canceled practice this afternoon so that everyone could make the 90-minute drive from Chino to see Diana play.

Lily Taurasi is at the top of the stairs that lead into the arena. Spotting Geno, she leaps into his arms and gives him a huge hug. If Roberto Benigni has a sister . . .

"Geno!" she cries happily. "Geno! Geno!"

"See," he laughs, motioning to Diana. "She's still alive."

Diana likes to say that Geno only mentioned this homecoming game "two hundred times" while he was recruiting her. Now she is back. A Firestone Fieldhouse record-crowd of 2,437 lines the bleachers. While UConn's appearance in Los Angeles is not the carnival come to Yazoo City, the Huskies have merited some attention locally. *The Los Angeles Times* wrote a brief preview of the game, acknowledging that UConn is "already being called by some the greatest team ever".

Watching this wave of attention crash onto Malibu's shores, knowing that, like all waves, it will soon recede, you get a sense of UConn's similarity to the UCLA men's basketball teams of the mid-Sixties. Women's college basketball today is quite similar to men's college hoops of that era. National television largely ignored the game during the regular season, picking it up during the NCAA tournament. UCLA players, like UConn's today, were more like rock superstars. When they visited your town they created a big splash but then they left and you forgot about them. Or, as Geno says, "The circus is in town again."

Inside the Pepperdine lockerroom, Waves coach Mark Trakh tries to relax his troops. "Nobody expects us to win," he tells his overmatched squad. "Nobody even expects us to keep it close. Go out and have some fun."

Trakh briefs his players on "key UConn personnel" and soon finds himself in the middle of a filibuster.

"Number ten, Sue Bird, excellent playmaker.

"Thirty-three, Shea Ralph, very strong guard. Likes to cut to the basket. You've got to play as hard as she does.

"Twenty-five, Abrosimova, likes to run the floor. Be physical with her.

"Thirty-two, Swin Cash. You've gotta box this kid out."

And on and on it goes. Tamika Williams. Asjha Jones. Diana Taurasi. Morgan Valley, et al.

The Waves take the floor. On UConn's bench Kelly Schumacher, in street clothes, peers keenly at Waves center Shannon Mayberry. "See that?" Schuey says, pointing to Mayberry's braids. "She has her hair in a 'diamond braid'. I originated that. Well, okay, first I saw it on *Buffy*, but I was the first player to do it."

The only suspense to this evening is how many points Diana will score in front of her hometown cheering section. They hold aloft cardboard signs that read WE LOVE U, DIANA.

Webster, her high school coach, recounts her performance at a national invitational high school tournament in Santa Barbara her senior year. "She made four buzzer-beater, game-winning shots," he says, "in four consecutive games. Never saw anything like it.

"She's a prolific scorer, obviously," Webster says, "but this is a kid who'd rather pass the ball. In the beginning, her freshman year, our girls had never played with anyone who could pass like her. She put a lot of tattoos on their heads that said 'Rawlings' or 'Wilson'."

You might think that someone as talented as Diana grew up amidst a litter of athletic brothers. She did not. In fact, Diana, Morgan, Shea, Sue, and Sveta each has one sibling, a sister. Only Morgan's sister, Ashley, is athletic. "Whenever you drove by Diana's house," says Webster, "you'd see all by herself, shooting the ball. Even after dark.

"She shot the ball when we needed a basket," Webster says, "but if we had the game won easily, she wouldn't shoot. She wanted to get her teammates involved."

Tonight Diana's scoring is not needed. The Huskies lead, 46-20, at the half. In the second half, with less than five minutes remaining, she has taken only three shots and missed all three. The second all-time leading high school scorer in California history is about to toss up her first-ever goose egg. It says nothing about how she's played in only her second college game, but a lot of folks, having driven a good distance to see her, are looking for an excuse to cheer for her.

Geno calls Diana over during a stoppage in play. "Hey," he tells her, "run a pick-and-roll for yourself so you can get a basket."

She does, but the shot misses. The game ends. If she is disappointed at not having scored, she does not show it. "I didn't play very well," she tells the media, which is not entirely true, "but we played well and got the victory, so I'm happy."

Lily Taurasi is happy, too. Geno has allowed her to take her daughter home to Chino until Thanksgiving morning. "I was saying all game, 'Just make one basket for mommy,'" says Lily. 'One basket! Two basket!'

"But it is okay, I have my baby," she says. "I told my husband, 'Tonight, you're sleeping in Diana's bed. Diana's sleeping with me.'"

Wednesday, November 22 . . . The team bus seems more like the family wagon each day. Tonight, as the Huskies head to the Staples Center to watch the Los Angeles Lakers play the Golden State Warriors, Shea Ralph has brought along Bopit Extreme, an electronic game that is more popular with this group than puppies.

Bopit Extreme resembles a steering wheel with two wedges excised. It is circular but has four ends and a center. At each end is a different knob and, in the center, a button that resembles a steering-wheel horn. The four different knobs can either be flicked, pulled, spun or twisted depending on the knob and the center can be pressed or bopped. To play you follow the audible directions ("Pull it!" . . . "Twist it!" . . . "Spin it!") and have no more than a second or two to comply. If you err, *e.g.* pull when you should have flicked or delay more than a second, the contraption emits a blood-curdling "YAAAAA!" as if it's just been kicked in the shin.

It is maddening. It is engrossing. A supreme test of both concentration and hand-eye coordination. If the police were to discover Bopit Extreme, they'd have the ultimate sobriety test. Shea passes the game around in the back of the bus. Up front the adults attempt to read books or talk quietly. It is no use.

"Flick it!"

"Twist it!"

"Flick it!"

"Pull it!"

"Bop it!"

"YAAAAA!"

Stacy Hansmeyer, sitting in the front of the bus with the coaches, looks back and smiles. "Dog just wants to play," she says, referring to Shea. "That's what she lives for."

Shea Ralph grew up in Fayetteville, North Carolina. The street perpendicular to hers was Player Avenue. Basketball was not her only sport. She was a state gymnastics champion at age nine. She was ripped even then. "They used to call her 'Muscles'," her mother, Marsha Lake, remembers.

Soon after Shea won the gymnastics title, she got into trouble at school for passing a note that contained profanity. Her stepdad, Bob Ralph, punished her by prohibiting her from doing gymnastics for a month. At the end of her internment Shea, who excelled at basketball as well, was a one-sport gal.

"Of all the relationships in my life," Shea has said, "basketball is the marriage."

She is a gamer, a fact that Geno exploits. He did not start her as a frosh, and still *The Sporting News* named her national Freshman of the Year. When he at last gave her a start, midway through her sophomore season, against Boston College, she scored a career-high 36 points.

In high school Shea battled anorexia, a disease she fights still. It began when an AAU teammate mentioned off-handedly that she looked "a little thick". Suddenly, Shea was issuing herself calorie challenges. How few calories could she ingest per day? 800 calories? 700? 600?

"Her sophomore year we played Pine Forest High," recalls Marsha Lake. "She had eaten one pear all day. During the junior varsity game that preceded hers, she did not have the strength to sit up in the bleachers. She had violent stomach cramps. We had to help her into the locker room before the game. She scored 30 points that night."

Meanwhile, Shea's weight had plummeted from 145 pounds to 108. Marsha was despondent. "I cried buckets of tears," she says. "I cooked weird stuff. Her favorite thing was a baked potato with nothing on it."

Oddly, Marsha Lake understood. She had been a high school valedictorian and then an All-American basketball player at the University of North Carolina. Yet she has always had tremendous battles with low self-esteem. "When I was nineteen," she says, "my boyfriend at the time asked me, 'How can somebody who's a valedictorian and an All-American have so little self-confidence?'"

So Marsha cooked baked potatoes. She prayed. Shea's AAU coach, John Ellington, was not so patient. After a game the summer before Shea's junior season, the team went out to dinner. Ellington placed a plate of mozzarella sticks and a $100 bill before Shea. "Eat these," he said, "and the money is yours."

She demurred. He upped the ante. "Gain weight," he said, "or quit the team."

The tough love worked. Shea began to eat more. She still exercised like a demon—running as much as ten miles a day— but gradually she gained weight. "I needed basketball," she says, "more than I needed to be thin."

"Shea is a lot like her mother," says Marsha's third husband, Roy Lake, who was also that boyfriend Marsha had when she was 19. "What motivates her most is a fear of failure."

When *USA Today* named Shea its High School Player of the Year, they featured her on the back page of their sports section. A thumbnail Q& A accompanied the photo, questions such as Food I Refuse to Eat ("hamburger"). Next to Greatest Fear she answered, "Having a career-ending injury".

Five years later, she has already suffered two, tearing the anterior cruciate ligament in her right knee twice. The first time was in March 1997, during the first game of the NCAA tournament, against Lehigh, her freshman year. At the time the Huskies were 30-0. Without her the rest of the way, UConn still advanced to the Midwest Regional Final, where they lost to eventual national champion Tennessee.

After the injury, which would require six months of rehabilitation, Geno was sanguine. After all she'd be ready by the start of practice next autumn. "I checked our schedule," he said, "and we don't have any games in July or August."

The mood was anything but morose. It was a setback, yes, but the program had been living a charmed life until then. In 12 seasons the Huskies had never lost a player to a season-ending injury. Fate was simply evening the score. A week or two before Shea went down, Jim Conrad, then covering the Huskies for *The Norwich Bulletin*, had even written an article about UConn's immunity to injury. Geno refers to what would follow as "Conrad's Curse".

On August 30 of that year, on the eve of Svetlana Abrosimova's arrival, Shea retore the ACL in a pick-up game. "It was the lead story on the eleven o'clock news that night," remembers Carl Adamec of *The Manchester Journal-Inquirer*.

"The only option that exists is for Shea to not compete this season [*i.e.*, redshirt]," Geno told the press. "This decision was not one she was happy with or easily agreed to. It took all of us combined to convince her this was the right way to go. She'll have to deal with it, and she'll deal with it head on like she does everything else."

The first ACL tear had been a body blow. The second was a sucker punch. To fix the first tear, cartilage had been grafted from a cadaver. The second time the physicians took cartilage from her healthy left knee.

"She couldn't bend either knee much after the surgery," Marsha says. "Whenever Shea had to use the restroom in her dorm, she'd walk in to the stall and then face the door. She'd grab the coat hook as long as she could and then she'd just have to plop onto the seat. You could hear her land from outside the bathroom."

Shea was miserable. She'd sit on the bench during games—not in street clothes but donning her UConn warm-ups—near Geno. She looked as if recess had just been canceled. "I need you to sit at the end of the bench," he would tell her, tiring of her lugubrious gaze, "because you are an incredible pain in the ass."

In late February of that season Nykesha Sales, the Huskies' senior All-American forward and leading scorer, tore her Achilles tendon. *Damn Jim Conrad.* The next day Shea walked into Geno's office. "I know what you're going to tell me," he told her, peremptorily refusing her offer to forgo the redshirt season to win a national championship. "Forget it."

Without Nykesha or Shea, UConn lost in the Mideast Regional to North Carolina State.

Had Geno taken Shea up on her offer, UConn might have at least advanced to the NCAA final against inevitable champ Tennessee. Then again, if he had accepted, she would not be playing for the Huskies this season. Her college eligibility would have expired last April in Philadelphia, where she validated all of the rehabilitation therapy she'd undergone by being named Most Outstanding Player of the Women's Final Four.

In Shea Geno sees the most heroic player he has ever coached. Why can't all kids be like her? "I probably think about Shea Ralph every day as much as I do about my own children," he has said. "Don't underestimate the will power Shea Ralph has."

Stacy Hansmeyer loves to play, too. She misses basketball. She had a tryout with the Phoenix Mercury of the WNBA last May but was cut. "I'd like to play in Europe," she says wistfully as the bus lurches along the Santa Monica Freeway toward downtown Los Angeles. "Maybe get another tryout with the WNBA next spring."

Stacy had been a starter for UConn until the T.A.S.S.K force arrived. Her heart was insuperable and her muscle welcome, but her talent was not equal to theirs. Geno called her Miss October, his point being that Stacy's best moments occurred before the regular-season began.

"In 1998," remembers Adamec, the Boswell of the UConn program, "Amy O'Brien of Holy Cross, who shot left-handed, lit up Stacy for 38 points [in an 87-76 UConn win]. At one point in the game Geno yelled, 'Stacy, her left, not yours!'"

Stacy's game has all the subtle grace of a sledgehammer. Her nickname is Bam Bam. Keirsten Walters, who is 5'8" and reed-thin, recalls a run-in she had with Bam Bam, a solid six-footer, in high school. "Stacy had the ball and was coming downcourt on a fast break," Keirsten recalls. "I was the only player back on defense. I stood at the free throw line, ready to take the charge. She never slowed down, never tried to avoid me. She knocked me from the free throw line to out of bounds."

"YAAAAAAA!"

Stacy, hearing Keirsten's version of the incident, smiles her county-fair, blue-ribbon smile. "Yeah," says Bam Bam. "I killed her."

Thursday, November 23 . . . Thanksgiving Day. A loneliness and a light mist hang in the Seattle air. Not only are the Huskies away from their families, they are as far from Storrs as they will be all season. The bus is quiet as it winds its way north on Interstate 5 from Seattle-Tacoma International Airport to the University of Washington,

Yesterday this trip was a family vacation in sunny California. Christine Rigby and Kelly Schumacher had gone to Venice Beach and rented a tandem bike, drawing stares, which is quite a feat there. Today it is a rock-and-roll tour, away from loved ones on the holidays and heading straight from the airport to the arena for a soundcheck.

Rock stars have groupies. So do the Huskies. As they enter UW's gorgeous new Bank of America Arena, which sports a retro-fieldhouse look, a young girl sits waiting for them. Her name is Carly Koebel. She is tall and blonde and wears a T-shirt that reads "Hoopaholics". She is tall like the Space Needle is tall. Carly Koebel is 6'3" and only in 8th grade. "My parents said it was okay to miss Thanksgiving," she says. "They know how badly I wanted to see UConn."

It has come to this: 6'3" middle-schoolers are blowing off major holidays to see the Huskies practice. "Oh, I'll be here tomorrow night, too," Koebel says. "I'm a ballgirl for U-Dub[Washington]. I sit right next to the basketball stanchion during the games."

Koebel, who currently plays on three different basketball teams, is clearly starstruck. On the greaseboard calendar in her room she has been circling each day as it passes, counting down to this day.

"My family went on vacation back East two summers ago," Koebel says, "and I begged my parents to make a side trip to Storrs. I wanted to see the campus in person."

There was a time, not too long ago, when just getting into the home of a 6'3" high school senior would be a major recruiting coup for Geno. With Rebecca Lobo's parents in 1991, for example, he felt about as welcome offering her a scholarship as if he'd ask her to take a ride on his Harley.

"My parents very much did not want me to go to UConn," says Rebecca. "They saw it as a second-class school."

Rebecca was 6'4", the most coveted player in the country, and a straight-A student at Southwich High School in south-central Massachusetts. Her parents, both teachers, made no bones about the fact that they hoped their daughter would choose a school with a more prestigious academic reputation, such as Notre Dame or Virginia. "My mom looked at Geno," Rebecca recalls, "and she said, 'We see UConn as a safety school,' and he was like, 'Uh, okay.'"

As practice ends Geno greets Koebel. College coaches are not allowed to have any contact with recruits until September of their junior year. However, the no-contact period does not begin until the player is actually in high school. This is kosher. He calls her over into the team huddle. She is taller than almost all of them, but in that group, she suddenly looks her age. She looks awestruck. They take photos with her and every player signs a notebook that she has brought. Will this be her family someday?

Friday, November 24 . . . Geno, Chris Dailey, Jamelle Elliott and Tonya Cardoza are eating breakfast in the second-floor coffee shop at the Madison Renaissance Hotel. CD peruses *The Seattle Post-Intelligencer*, specifically a preview of tonight's Huskies versus Huskies matchup. The headline of the story: "Is This The Greatest Team Ever?"

CD cites a quote by U-Dub senior Megan Franza, who has expressed a desire to score the first basket in her school's new arena. "Someone from their team really should do it," CD says.

"We could let them get the opening tip," offers Geno. "Tell the defense to ease up a little. But we'll only give them one crack at it."

"Don't want another Nykesha Sales scene."

On February 24, 1998, Nykesha, or "Keesh" as Geno calls her, fired women's college basketball's shot heard 'round the world, when she made a layup to open a game at Villanova. Some background: Nykesha Sales grew up in Bloomfield, Connecticut, just a few miles northwest of Hartford. She was a rare talent, a local kid with an open-court game and NORAD range. She was humble as well. "Nykesha Sales," says former teammate Kelley Hunt, "is the coolest person I've ever met."

Everyone loved Keesh, Geno included. He treated her so gently that behind his back the other Huskies called her "Precious". The press, too, lapped her up with a spoon.

"We started calling Geno 'Dean' after Dean Smith," says Carl Adamec. "The joke is that Dean Smith, Michael Jordan's coach at North Carolina, is the only person who could hold Jordan under twenty points a game. Geno was the only person who could hold Keesh under thirty points per game."

She scored a school-record 46 points against Stanford on a day when her sneakers had been lost and last-minute replacements were purchased at a local store. By mid-February of Keesh's senior season, Kerry Bascom's school scoring record of 2,177 points was well within reach. With two regular season games remaining—against Notre Dame and then at Villanova—Keesh had 2,149 points.

Against Notre Dame, on Senior Night, the final regular-season home game of Nykesha's wondrous career, all she needed was 29 points. She scored 27. With just under ten minutes remaining in the game, two points shy of breaking the record, Keesh missed a short jumper. Kelley Hunt grabbed the offensive rebound and fed her on the right wing. She took the pass, drove, jump-stopped—and crumpled to the floor. She reached for her right foot.

"I thought someone stepped on the back of my heel," Nykesha said. "I looked at the ref. He said, 'Keesh, there was no one around you.'"

Nykesha had torn her left Achilles tendon. The Huskies were devastated. "Fate has been very unkind to Nykesha," Geno said after the game. "I wish I could fix it for her."

Nykesha tore her Achilles on a Saturday. The Huskies would play on Tuesday at Villanova, whose coach, Harry Perretta, is an old Philly friend of Geno's. When Geno phoned his friend that Sunday, the first words out of Perretta's mouth were, "How can we make this right?"

Geno had an idea. First he wanted to square things with the one person whose blessing he felt was required. He phoned Kerry Poliquin in Exeter, New Hampshire.

"I have a question to ask," he told her. "What do you think of Nykesha making a basket to break your record?"

Kerry Poliquin is no pushover. She was as defiant a player as has ever donned a UConn uniform. Her nickname, as all UConn players know, is What the F___. "Geno would always call me into his office to give me suggestions about whom I was hanging out with," she says. "I'd say, 'I already have a father and a mother, thank you very much.'"

Geno's request was hardly the most bizarre blessing Kerry had ever been asked to bestow. Three years earlier when she was playing in France, her father, a widower, had phoned to invite her to his wedding. While she had been abroad, he had begun clandestinely dating Kerry's mother-in-law. "I want to invite you to our wedding," David Bascom told his daughter, "and I hope that you will be okay with this."

What the f___?

So when Geno asked Kerry if Nykesha could break her record, the matter was a trifle. "That's fine," she said. "It's only a school record."

The rest has been recorded *ad nauseum*. At Villanova the Huskies announced Kelley Hunt as a starter. Just before the tip-off, however, Keesh took Kelley's place and stood directly beneath UConn's basket. Geno and Harry Perretta had devised a plan in which UConn would win the opening tap. Rita Williams would pass the ball to Nykesha, who would score a layup to break the record. Then UConn would call timeout, subbing Nykesha out. Villanova would inbound by rolling the ball down the court (so as not to take time off the clock) to one of its players, who would in turn score an uncontested bucket. No harm done, score tied at 2-2, and Nykesha owns the UConn scoring record. Geno informed his athletic director, Lew Perkins, Big East commissioner Mike Tranghese, and the three game officials beforehand to be sure that no one would object to the scripted plays.

It was a sequence, like the opening volley on Lexington Green in 1775, that would last seconds but reverberate long after the moment had passed. ESPN led that night's 11 p.m. edition of *SportsCenter* with the shot. In *The Hartford Courant* columnist Jeff Jacobs, in a story headlined "What a Farce", had this lead:

Nykesha Sales didn't set the all-time UConn women's scoring record. Soupy Sales did.

Suddenly, Nykesha's drop in the bucket was anything but in terms of sports news. ABC's *World News Tonight* covered it. Mike and the Mad Dog, hosts of the most popular sports talk-radio show in New York City, on WFAN-AM, invited Geno onto their program and then criticized the way he ran his. Geno's apt rejoinder: "Why didn't you invite me on the show three years ago when we went thirty-five and oh?"

The *cause celebre* took the team by surprise. Keesh, who had undergone surgery the day after the Villanova game, phoned CD that night. "Can I just give the two points back?" she asked.

Within the Nutmeg State, the wagons circled around Connecticut's daughters. Jeff Jacobs received a phone call at home in which the caller threatened to behead him. Geno received support from his then eleven-year-old nephew, Donato, during a game at the Big East tournament the following week at Rutgers. Donato, seated a few rows behind the UConn bench, made a sign. On one side it read, *We Love You, Uncle Geno.* When the cameras found Donato and his sign, he flipped it so that the folks back in Connecticut watching on CPTV were able to read *Frig what the others think.*

The editors at *The Hartford Courant* wrote that "incredibly, no single event in recent memory, including the Persian Gulf War. . . has triggered so much reader response". To end an influx of mail only Mr. Claus could appreciate, they printed a 12-page supplement consisting entirely of letters.

While the Herde disagreed with Geno's gift, all were less caustic in their criticism than Jacobs. *The Manchester Journal-Inquirer's* R. Smith, for example, makes a salient contrarian point. "What's wrong with Nykesha finishing one point shy of the record?" he says. "She would have had heroic stature. One point shy. That's the stuff of legend."

The parting shot belongs to the two-time All-American. On the back of *The Hartford Courant's* 12-page letters supplement, Keesh is shown holding the ball, her right leg bandaged nearly to the knee. She is a moment away from the record, wearing her road-blue uniform and an expression of unfettered joy. It's difficult to disagree with any act that produced that smile.

Back in Seattle the mood at the noon shootaround is casual. CD and Geno sit on courtside seats as the first team, the blue team, runs the offense against the white team. They turn the ball over. Then they turn it over again. Geno says nothing. A third time in a row. A fourth. Still nothing. Then Svetlana Abrosimova attempts a skip pass that sails out of bounds.

"Five straight turnovers," Geno says from the bench, his right hand held above his head with all five fingers outstretched. "Five straight turnovers. Five! For *the greatest team ever assembled.*"

Geno is pleased. They suck right now. Tonight he will have their attention.

Eight hours later inside the Bank of America Arena Carly Koebel is rebounding for UConn during pregame warmups. Teresa Borton, whose family has driven across the Cascade Range to be here, watches from the stands. The Huskies, the visiting Huskies, are given a pregame standing ovation by the 6,098 fans. The circus is in town.

Sue Bird—not Megan Franza— scores the first basket in the the new arena but the first half belongs entirely to Sveta, who shoots 8-of-9 from the floor and makes myriad dazzling plays. With the Huskies leading, 36-18, Sveta runs down a pass that is heading out of bounds on the frontcourt baseline and dishes it across the lane to Sue Bird. She misses the shot, but Sveta grabs the rebound and converts the put-back.

Matt Eagan, the beat writer for *The Hartford Courant*, is incredulous. "Is she playing," he asks, "as well as anyone can play right now?"

At halftime UConn leads, 53-27. Send in the clowns. The starters sit for most of the second half. Swin Cash and Shea Ralph will play less than half of the game's 40 minutes. With three minutes remaining the U-Dub band, which is positioned directly behind the UConn bench, begins a "Put Shea in" chant. Sveta laughs while Shea, seated beside her, just grins. The final score is 100-54.

"You can tell a team that's a team," says Washington's Kellie O'Neal, whose 27 points were half her team's total. "They're a team. They play probably the best basketball that I have ever seen."

O'Neal's coach, June Daugherty, concurs. "They're the best basketball team that I have seen in twenty years."

U-Dub's 46-point loss is the second-worst in the school's history. Forty-six points. Four months from now they will advance to be one of the final eight teams in the NCAA tournament.

After the Huskies dress, they return to the court. The circus is also an autograph show and the players dutifully sign their names—legibly—for the dozens of mostly young girls who have waited for them. As Morgan Valley signs, Teresa Borton approaches her shyly. She was ambivalent about coming to say "Hi", was unsure of how she'd be received. Her mom insisted she do it, though, and sent her down to the court with a crate of apples. Morgan gives her a hug.

"I think Teresa was questioning herself," Morgan says later about why Borton chose Notre Dame. "Everyone who comes here questions themselves, whether or not they're good enough. I just wished her 'Good luck' and told her we'd see her next year."

Monday, November 27 . . . Swin Cash asserts that she introduced "Who Let the Dogs Out?" to the world. After last March's first-round NCAA tournament defeat of Hampton University, Swin did an impromptu performance of the song, originally sung by a group called the Baha Men, with the Hampton University pep band.

"Who Let the Dogs Out?" ("Who let the dogs out?/Who? Who? Who-Who?") soon became the Huskies' canine canon as they raced to the national championship six months ago. Then, says Swin, the whole world discovered it. "I never saw anyone do it or sing it before then," she says. "Besides, we are the Huskies. This song fits."

Swin Cash is an enigma. Everything about her screams "Baby, I'm a Star." Even her name is headline money. Be a little creative and Swin Cash becomes "$win Cash!" Her full first name is "Swintayla", which in the African dialect from which it comes means "astounding woman." She wears the name well.

"Swin wants the limelight," Geno often says.

She is the team diva, a beautiful young woman with delicate features, an AquaFresh smile, and a sinewy 6'2" frame. She modeled in high school and was student council president at

McKeesport (Pennsylvania) High. As a senior she took up the high hurdles. She used the men's hurdles at her first practice until the track coach, Lou Hegedos, showed her the lower women's barriers. "Those?" Swin said with disdain. "I've fallen off curbs higher than that."

Swin won the Western Pennsylvania Interscholastic Athletic League (WPIAL) title despite stumbling over the second hurdle in the final race. She finished third at the state meet.

Swin's teammates call her "Drama Queen" and have affixed a sign above her locker denoting that title. Trainer Rosemary Ragle has a lifesize photo of Swin, the patient who most tries her patience, on her office door. Swin put it there herself.

"Rosie, can I have an Aleve?" Swin will ask, or "Rosie, I need tissues." She has chronic shin splints. She is some HMO's future nightmare.

Swin is a priss. She is a warrior. She is a human pogo stick. She is always dramatic: Last season at UCLA she mistakenly shot at the Lady Bruins' hoop and scored. She is majestic, scoring 40 points, grabbing 21 rebounds, and blocking 10 shots in her last high school game. She is astounding.

"I went to watch her practice in high school when she was a sophomore," says Geno, "and I hate watching women's basketball practice. But when Swin was a sophomore, she may have already been the best high school player in the country."

Swin is always the most expressive Husky on the court. If she shoots and is fouled but the shot misses, she will clap her hands and grit her teeth. If the shot goes in, she simply lowers her arms to her sides and waits for the love that she knows is coming from her four teammates. She loves the stage.

Swin's athleticism and grace are reminiscent of a Kentucky Derby winner. The Drama Queen does yeoman's duties, grabbing rebounds and defending like a Doberman. She is not a natural scorer, like Sveta or Sue or Diana. She grabs the limelight by making herself useful.

After the Washington game on Friday night, Geno invited a few of the younger members of the staff to his hotel suite. He sat around talking shop with them, these twentysomethings whose age gives them greater proximity to his players: ticket office intern Scott Merritt, sports information director Ann Marie Person, Rosemary Ragle, and manager Tom Tedesco, a graduate student. As they sat around until the wee hours discussing players, it became very apparent that Geno understands Dr. Freud as much as he does Dr. Naismith.

"Svetlana's the best player in the country," he tells them, "but Asjha Jones is the best player on our team."

"So why doesn't Asjha start?" asked Rosemary.

"Because she doesn't need to start," he answered. "Swin needs to start. That's what revs her engine. And Tamika and Asjha are fine with that."

"How do you know that Asjha and Tamika are fine with that?" asked Rosemary.

"That week Swin was away for the funeral?" Geno said (Swin lost an aunt to cancer earlier this month), "Asjha took her place in the starting lineup. Swin's first day back, I just said 'Gimme five out on the floor,' and Asjha went in. The next day I said the same thing and Swin jumped in. Now who made that decision?"

Someone took a stab. "Asjha?"

"Exactly," Geno answered. "She knows Swin needs to start."

"So how do you keep everyone happy?" Scott asked. "How do you know which buttons to press on which people?"

Geno leaned back on the couch. He raised his arms in the air as a grin broke across his face. Then he mouthed a single word, did not even whisper it: "Coaching."

After today's late afternoon practice, most of the players eagerly rush toward the post-practice buffet that has been set up for them outside the players' lounge. Morgan Valley stays after practice, shooting free throws and three pointers. Geno watches.

Morgan, at least stylistically, is the anti-Swin. Swin changes hairdos weekly. Moe never wears makeup. Moe's game is all grim determination; Swin's is effervescence. Swin is aesthetic, Morgan ascetic. The Drama Queen can be a handful, but she is always ready when the curtain goes up. Morgan lives for rehearsals.

Half an hour later Morgan takes a seat in the players lounge. She watches as her teammates scarf down wedges of homemade sweet potato pie courtesy of Rita Williams's mom. Geno grabs the tin and a fork and takes a ravenous bite. Delicious.

"Moe," he asks, "how can you not eat this?"

"It's no good for you," she says.

"How can this not be good for you? It's got potatoes in it."

"The crust is not good for you."

"Then don't eat the crust."

"But that's the best part."

Tuesday, November 28 . . . "I hate dumbass passes. I hate 'em. I hate giving the ball away after we work our ass off to get it. I hate it!"

The Huskies are practicing a zone offense and everyone seems to have a case of the yips. Shea Ralph's poor pass has just been intercepted. Svetlana Abrosimova throws one away, too, prompting a more placid "Who was that to?"

He always corrects them. "He's a perfectionist," Kerry Poliquin will tell you. "That's just his personality. I compare it to Bobby Knight. When you're there you might not always like it, but when you leave you appreciate what he did for you."

There are some parallels between the two coaches. In fact a framed photo of them together, signed by Coach Knight, hangs to the left of Geno's desk. "He's great with other coaches," Geno says of Knight. "It's like being in the treehouse with your buddies: The worst guy in the treehouse is better than anybody else outside."

Geno does share some Bobby Knight traits. Both are perfectionists and military historians ("General Geno," some players call him behind his back whereas Coach Knight is universally known as The General). Both are extremely bright and sarcastic leaders whose moods, depending on their teams' performances, range from hilarious to mordant.

"Sue Bird, you were supposed to go in front of her, right?" he says after she goes the wrong way without the ball in the zone offense. "C'mon, you're not in eleventh grade anymore. I've already coached bad players. I know what they play like. I don't need any good players to play like bad players."

On the next possession the offense does a seamless job of passing the ball. As Shea drives to the basket, the zone collapses on her. Sue moves to the corner beyond the three-point arc, at a spot where Shea can see her and dish a pass back outside. She does, and Sue buries the three.

"That was a great play," Geno marvels. "That won't show up in the boxscore, how we worked on that to get you that shot in the corner."

After practice Geno pulls Sue aside. The two of them sit in the bleachers, talking for five minutes. Today the Herde, which is often allowed to watch the last hour of practice, must wait outside in the hallway. He takes advantage of a few private moments with his point guard.

Geno knows that they will ask Sue questions about her sub-par play in the first three games. The Huskies are 3-0 and three of their key players—All-Americans Shea and Sveta plus Tamika—are each shooting better than 70% from the field. Sue is the closest thing to a weak link that the stat sheet evinces. She has shot 33%, though nearly half of her shots have been three-pointers. But the Herde must be fed. Today's special is Bird.

Geno knows this, as does Sue. As he sends her off to answer their questions, he watches her walk across the court. Like a disproportionately high number of the Huskies, Sue exudes an enchanting quality that transcends her basketball skills. She is an avatar of UConn basketball, a hybrid of Geno's street-smart hoops savvy and Chris Dailey's feminine grace.

"She's the best," Geno says to no one in particular, loud enough to be heard clear across the court. "I always say, 'Sue Bird is the best. They don't come any better than that.'"

Outside in the hallway, the writers surround her. The Herde genuinely like the players. Even the tough questions are laced with concern. "Does it bother you when you miss?" Sue is asked.

"Does it bother me?" she repeats. "Well of course I want to make my shots."

No more than ten feet away, Geno leans against the painted cinderblock wall and, as usual, speaks candidly about his floor leader. "Yeah, there's the leaky faucet," he says looking across at her. "Her freshman year we also started three-and-oh and Sue was shooting eighteen percent but nobody knew what she could do then."

Diana Taurasi, who left practice 45 minutes early for a lab project, returns. As she passes Geno in the hallway, he asks, "You back already?"

"Yeah," Diana answers, "we just had a Psych project. Had to fill out a questionnaire."

"What was it about?" he asks. "How long you could hold onto something?"

She shoots him a look that says, *Whatever, wiseass.* Walks away.

Geno is forever picking the scabs of their flaws. During Kerry's sophomore year, the team was on a road trip. Geno visited her hotel room. They sat on opposite beds facing one another as Geno attempted to persuade his star player that if she could shed a few pounds, she'd be an even more imposing force.

"I'm thinking, What the ____?" says Kerry. "We must have argued for more than an hour that night. What I do remember vividly is that by the end of it my left hand was clutching his shirt and my right hand was balled into a fist."

He nags them for four years and what do they do? They take up the trade. Debbie Baer, Kerry, Carla Berube, Jamelle Elliott and Jennifer Rizzotti, all starters on various UConn Final Four teams, all coaches now.

"They're all doing it for the right reasons," Geno says, casting a glance at Sue, who will most likely make a terrific coach herself one day. "You give 'em a place to work out in the gym and get some meals for free, and they'll take the job."

Geno laughs with satisfaction. They get into coaching; then they understand. In her first year as an assistant coach at the University of New Hampshire, Kerry phoned him.

"Coach, this is Kerry," she said.

"Yeah, what's up?" he asked.

"Do you have a tape recorder?" she said. "'Cuz you're never going to hear this again: You were right."

Then she hung up.

Wednesday, November 29 . . . The Huskies taped a basketball instructional video this evening and disguised it as a basketball game. Before the usual 16,294 fans at the Hartford Civic Center, UConn defeated George Washington University, 90-63, playing as sublime a first half as any basketball coach could wish for.

The most provocative statistic: UConn had 20 first-half field goals and 19 assists, meaning that all but one basket was the product of a Husky finding a teammate who was (more) open. The lone unassisted bucket was a turn-and-pivot layup by Tamika Williams.

Minutes earlier, from the same high-post spot where this play started, Tamika had been a cog in the Huskies' most dazzling play of the season thus far. Diana Taurasi took an outlet pass from Asjha Jones. She dribbled up the right side, putting the ball behind her back to elude one defender and then, as she crossed midcourt, between her legs. Shading to her left, just beyond midcourt, Diana made a no-look backhanded bounce pass to Tamika who had flashed to the high-post on the left-hand side. As the "ooh"s and "ah"s were still pouring from fans' mouths, Tamika, without turning around, made her own no-look bounce pass 45 degrees behind her to Sue Bird, who had done a backdoor cut from the left wing. Sue grabbed the pass without breaking stride and hit the layup. It was the type of play that Hollywood directors choreograph in basketball films.

There were other plays like that tonight, none quite so spectacular, lending credence to the surging belief that the Huskies simply toy with their competition. 20 field goals, 19 assists! The Huskies also forced 18 first-half turnovers, and put together 15-0 and 12-0 runs in building a 52-20 lead at the half.

Georgia. Washington. George Washington. It doesn't matter. Subtract the Bulldogs 6-0 run at the end of the first half of the opener (against UConn's reserves), and the Huskies have doubled their opponents' first-half totals in all four games. They're lapping the field.

Diana has a perfect first half, shooting 4-4 from the field (3-3 on three pointers) and 2-2 from the free-throw line. She will play just 18 minutes tonight and still be the team's high scorer with 15 points. Watching the Huskies starters sit for most of the second half, you get the feeling that they cannot wait for practice where the scrimmages are at least competitive.

Afterward Geno, Kathy, Meghan Pattyson, and a few friends head out to Franklin Avenue, the main artery of the city's Italian section. Tonight the gang repairs to Sorrento Ristorante, whose owner, Robert DiPersio, looks a lot like Robert DeNiro. DiPersio adores his fellow *paisan* and lays out a spread of antipasto that befits a Roman orgy.

Geno is living *la dolce vita*. His team is a piece of art; he is surrounded on this night, as he is on most, by family and friends; and he earns more money than he ever might have imagined. The scene is in stark contrast to his early days at UConn, when such an evening would have seemed nothing less than a hallucination.

"We had four people in one office," Chris Dailey recalls. "We had two desks, two rotary phones, a chair, a couch, and a coffee table. Whenever we brought in a recruit, only one of us would be in the office with her. We didn't want her to think that all of us shared that space."

Everything seemed a struggle in those early years. CD ordered postgame sandwiches for the team once and was told that a batch of ham sandwiches would be on their way. She asked if the deli could make her a turkey sandwich instead of ham. No, she was told. She began to cry.

"Geno looks at me," CD recalls, "and says, 'Do you realize that you're crying over a ham sandwich?', and I said, 'That's not the point.'"

Times have changed. A dozen or so people sit around a big table, nibbling on hot and cold antipasto, and drinking wine as if they'll never see a bill. They won't. Geno always takes care of it.

As they sit and joke, Geno drawing from a seemingly bottomless reservoir of stories, the George Washington University coaching staff enters and sits at an adjoining table. Geno has invited them.

This season George Washington University is not the enemy. Nor is Miami, the next opponent, nor Holy Cross after them. The other team is not the enemy. Boredom is.

Thursday, November 30 . . . Diana Taurasi awoke today, peered out the window of her room in Belden Hall and saw snow. "Hell, no!" she cried, tossing the blankets back over her head.

"I have lived in this kind of weather my whole life," roommate Morgan Valley says later, "and I have one winter coat. D went out and bought five, plus she brought two from home."

Diana was born without a self-consciousness gene. On the bus during last week's road trip, she sang the rap group OutKast's song "Ms. Jackson" at the top of her lungs more than a few times. "She's driving me crazy," Shea Ralph would say from the seat across from D with a smile on her face. She envies the kid's spunk.

"SORRY, MS. JACKSON!" Diana would wail as the seniors around her stared at one another. Finally, after the Washington game, Christine Rigby and Kelly Schumacher tag-teamed D and shoved her in to the bus's lavatory for the ride back to the hotel. "Keep it up," Shea warned, "and you'll have the same seat on the flight home."

Maria Conlon rose to free Diana but Schuey, nearly a foot taller, stared her down. "I wouldn't if I were you," Schuey said. "We'll let her know you tried."

For the most part the freshmen have bonded. On Sunday nights they meet in the players' lounge at 7:00 p.m. for study hall ("study hell" Maria calls it). Of course, the players lounge also has a big screen TV, four computers (e-mail!), and close proximity to the Gampel court. Diana's high school coach, Larry Webster, called last week to inquire how his prodigy was doing. Moe answered the phone.

"Is she hitting the books?" Webster asked.

"Yep," said Moe, "she tosses them off the bed and they hit the floor."

Diana received a mid-semester grade report last week that perhaps only the gang from *Animal House* would covet. Instead of hiding it, she posted it in her locker.

Like Diana, Maria and Moe are 'ballers, pure and simple. When Moe's parents moved to their Colchester, Vermont, home in 1982, the very first thing her father, Jay, purchased—before curtains, before a couch—was a basketball hoop and pole. It was February. In Vermont.

Maria's backyard in Derby, Connecticut, is mostly a concrete court that has her numeral, 5, painted on it. An eight-foot cushioned fence abuts the baseline (saving both people and errant shots). When Geno went to offer her a scholarship, he noted that she had never missed a practice as a junior but had been tardy for 28 classes. "You miss one more class," he told her, "and I'm not giving you a scholarship."

Her attendance record was perfect after that.

Ashley Battle and Jessica Moore—AB and Jess—are different. Both prefer playing defense and are less apt to be found playing a shooting game or busting on people. AB is friendly but quiet. Jess is so open and gullible that, even at an athletically imposing 6'3," she has become the kid who gets picked on the most. Being so far from her Alaskan home and also being redshirted has also contributed to her homesickness. She finds comfort in phone calls home to her mom (her father died when she was four) and food.

"I have a little goodie cup for games," Jess says. "I give [manager] Kathryn Fieseler Reese's Pieces and M&M's before games, and she puts them in a goodie cup for me to munch on during the games. I've thought about filling up my water bottle with Sprite."

The five of them are adjusting to life away from home and with each other. "We do this thing every night called 'Our Time'," Morgan says. "It started in our [D's, Jess's, and her] room but now we've invited AB and Maria, too."

"It started out as 'Confessionals'," says Jess. "When we were all in bed about to go to sleep, we'd talk. The rule was you could ask any question you wanted and the person's gotta tell the truth. It lasts about an hour."

"Now it's beyond that," says Moe. "We still ask questions but it's also a chance for us to talk about what's going on with the team, how the upperclassmen are treating you, you know. It's our time."

DECEMBER

Wednesday, December 6 . . . Nykesha Sales ambles onto the court at Gampel Pavilion to find the Huskies stretching in silence.

"Why y'all so quiet?" she asks.

"Did you watch the game?" Swin Cash replies.

The Huskies played at the University of Miami last night. They won, 77-53 but, for the first time since last February, UConn played like a team that could be beaten. Also, Ashley Battle hyperextended her elbow diving for a loose ball in the second half, and no one knows how serious the injury is.

The Huskies left the gate in typical fashion, racing to a 16-4 lead in the first five minutes. Swin played like a velociraptor: stunningly quick, ferocious, and predatory. She would end the evening with 20 points and 12 rebounds.

However, after the initial burst the Huskies went flat. The Hurricanes outscored them for the next 13 minutes. UConn played too cute, as if they were more interested in feeding their genius than in winning the game. Even Picasso understood that there's a limit to how many pigs you depict floating against a clear-blue horizon.

"We said a hundred times to make the easy pass," Geno said afterward, referring to UConn's 24 turnovers. "We kept trying to pound it into a spot that's not open."

UConn had beaten Miami thirteen straight times. The crowd at Miami's Knight Sports Complex, though the second-largest ever to witness a game there, was only 1,516. It felt like a high school game. Minds wandered.

Afterward, the first disgruntled fan to harangue Geno was his wife, Kathy. She watched the game on TV and noticed that Geno, who habitually doffs his suit blazer two minutes into every game, was still wearing it almost midway through the first half. "The game was eight minutes old, and you still had your jacket on," Kathy said. "You looked bored. They take their cue from you."

Today at practice boredom is not an issue. "D!" he chides after Diana Taurasi fails to hustle back on defense, "I'm telling you, you better start thinking about how you wanna play this game instead of running around."

As practice continues, however, the Huskies look sharp. He calls for one of their favorite drills. Starting from halfcourt, the players form three lines and begin a pattern of the basic three-man-weave. After two passes, whoever has the ball attempts a three-pointer. A missed shot must be rebounded and put back in, which will count for one point. A missed shot that bounces before being rebounded sends the score back to zero. The goal is to score 35 points in two minutes. Fail, and they will run a suicide.

"Put two minutes up," Geno instructs manager Tom Tedesco, who handles the scoreboard clock. Suddenly the court is awash in enthusiasm. Hands are slapped, efforts are exhorted. Even the alumnae—Nykesha, Rebecca Lobo, Rita Williams—get into it because the goal is more challenging than a Big East game in December. The goal is to please him.

With 7.2 seconds on the clock, Sue Bird hits a three-pointer to make 35. Geno is satisfied. "Okay, ten free throws," he says, a signal for the players to pair off and shoot, two at a time, ten free throws each. "Let's step up and make these."

Next the two units, guards and big men, break off. Geno and Tonya Cardoza run a one-on-one drill where the player takes her defender off the dribble from the right wing. The defender must make two consecutive stops, and then she is allowed to go to the offense line. KJ, instead of stopping her man, Keesh, is beaten five straight times.

Geno, kneeling on one knee, hangs his head, and banishes KJ to the back of the offensive line. Now Sue guards Keesh and is fooled so badly that she falls onto her butt at the free throw line. "You don't want to be any good at this," Geno says. "'Cuz if you did, you'd try harder. You and KJ, you stink at this."

The next few players pass through the drill without incident. Soon KJ is on defense again. She guards Shea, who dribbles by her. Then Rita, who also beats her with ease. This is maddening. KJ is his quickest defender.

"They don't wanna listen," he tells Tonya. "They don't wanna get good at this."

The team comes together for four-on-four defensive drills. Before they begin, Geno elicits an observation. "We're an undisciplined bunch of guys," he says. "We win because we have a lot of talent and we play teams that generally suck. And that's the truth."

They play. The defense plays with a ravenous desire to force a turnover, to deny passes, to box out for rebounds. The mood shifts. He places Asjha Jones, Diana Taurasi, Morgan Valley, and Shea on the defense and says, "This is the slowest team we can put out there right now so we gotta be on our toes."

Shea smiles, waves Geno off dismissively. After a few more defensive stops, he subs in Christine Rigby for Asjha (*now* he has the slowest team he can put out there). They do the job as well, so he moves on to offense. The starting five run a halfcourt offense against a zone defense. On the first play, Svetlana Abrosimova's pass to Shea is stolen.

Geno, standing on the baseline, wears a look of disgust. "Are we just doing a bad job coaching here?"

"We know," says Shea.

"No, you don't know, Shea, because you keep making the same stupid plays," he says in a tone that is not hostile. "Someone in this organization is stupid right now. It's either you or us. Which is it? Sue Bird, do we not know how to do this?"

"We know," she says.

The prodding does its job. The zone offense looks smooth. After every few reps Geno subs players in and out on both offense and defense, with those not participating standing on the sideline. Shea, ever the gamer, roams a step or two out onto the court even when she is not in the drill. Keesh, playing defense, loses track of who is in and who is not; for two straight possessions she guards Shea until Chris Dailey notices.

"Nykesha," CD says, "Shea's not in."

The players chuckle.

"She was standing on the court," Keesh says sheepishly.

Geno waits a beat. "Nykesha actually did a good job," he says. "Shea hasn't scored in a while."

Thursday, December 7 . . . Holy Cross coach Bill Gibbons's breakfast was ruined when he read the sports page yesterday morning. "I woke up Wednesday morning hoping that UConn beat Miami by sixty," Gibbons says. "My worst fears were realized when I was eating my Cocoa Krispies and saw that UConn did not play well."

Eating cereal for breakfast, Gibbons knew that his Crusaders were already toast. "What's the only thing worse than playing UConn at UConn?" Gibbons asks after his team loses tonight's game by 60 points. "Playing UConn at UConn after they've played a bad game on the road."

Gibbons, 42, seems an affable guy and an even more realistic one. Holy Cross, located in Worcester, Massachusetts, plays in the Patriot League, whose athletic cachet is a rung or two down the ladder from the Big East. He knows that UConn, playing its first game at Gampel Pavilion since last March, is 115-3 here in the last seven seasons. He also knows that tonight's sell-out crowd of 10,027 (a half-season's worth of attendance at his school) is the Huskies' 39th straight.

This is David vs. Goliath. So why does Holy Cross play UConn? Because the kid with the slingshot has no chance of beating the giant if he does not attend the battle.

"We have two Top 150 recruits," says Gibbons, who started at Holy Cross the same year Geno arrived at UConn, "because we play UConn every year. I'm convinced of that. I'll play them every year."

Geno likes playing Holy Cross, too. Likes their spunk, their fans. When UConn visited Worcester last season, a 38-point Husky win, Geno was sitting on the bench when he noticed that the fans opposite the court from him were laughing. He turned around to find a student standing directly behind him holding a sign. The sign had an arrow pointing downward. Above the arrow were the words "HE JUST FARTED."

The Huskies led 24-2 after only eight minutes tonight. The lone blight during that stretch might have been that Diana Taurasi's first shot at Gampel, a three-pointer, was an airball. Then the Huskies scored 14 straight points, the crowd's blood-lust rising to a higher pitch with each incredible play.

It is becoming clear that Diana and Svetlana, the Spanish speaker and the Russian speaker, communicate telepathically on the hardwood. On consecutive first-half plays D found Sveta on no-look passes leading to layups, the latter a trademark Svetlana one-hander.

By halftime it was 50-19. Holy Cross scored only 13 in the second half. Some coaches take umbrage at being blown out. Providence coach Jim Jabir, after a 126-48 loss at Gampel in 1998, would tell the press (though not until returning home to Rhode Island) that he felt as if "UConn was kicking us when we were down in the fetal position".

Other coaches are sanguine. In December of 1994, in the midst of their unblemished 35-0 championship season, UConn beat Iona, 101-42. Iona coach Harry Hart not only thanked Geno for being merciful (yes, merciful) but invited him into the postgame locker room to address his team.

Gibbons, who phoned Geno yesterday morning to tell him that he was "really pissed that you guys played so lousy at Miami", is similarly gracious. "It just happens that we were playing two of the top three teams in the nation tonight," he says in the postgame press conference. "UConn's first team [is No. 1], Tennessee's number two, and then UConn's second team is number three. That's the best UConn team that I've seen."

At Gampel, the postgame press conferences are held in Room 117, a classroom on the concourse level. Unlike when UConn is on the road, or even playing at the Hartford Civic Center, there is a relaxed, jovial atmosphere. *This* is the Geno Auriemma Show. Here in Room 117, he is the hip professor come to lecture the mostly adoring class.

"After the Miami game," says Geno, "I must have heard the same thing from about ten different people. 'You looked lousy that night. You had a sourpuss on your face and you didn't take your jacket off. What a sourpuss you are.'

"And then I went into the locker room and made it worse. Then I came out and talked to you guys, and you know how you guys are. If it sounds good, you print it, and if it doesn't, you change it to make it sound better."

"Does playing a game like this teach you anything?" Rachel McLoughlin of *The Connecticut Post* asks.

He leans back in his chair at the front of the windowless room, folds his hands behind his head. "That's a good question, Rachel," he replies, "and it puts me in a bad position to have to answer that. We can't play the top ten teams every night because there's only nine of them.

"Right now there's just a big gap between us and a lot of teams. There just is. I hope it stays that way."

He is asked about Gibbons's comment, that he has the No. 1 and No. 3 starting fives in the country on the same bench.

"Who would be the other starting five?" he asks.

Diana and KJ at guard, Morgan and Tamika at forward, and Asjha at center, Geno is told.

"Hmm, they would be pretty good," he admits. "Who's coaching them? CD? Their shirts would be tucked in, but I don't know if they could top us."

Geno is the overdog. The 3-5 favorite. He can either tense up and contemplate all he has to lose or he can relax knowing that everyone would love to have his problems.

"What am I going to do?" Geno says. "I'm going to the Kentucky Derby with Secretariat and Man o' War."

Saturday, December 9 . . . A cold, drab morning greets the team on the campus of the University of Illinois, where speed bumps offer scenic vistas. If flatness can have a superlative degree, Champaign is its home.

The uninspiring landscape and 10-watt bulb sunlight have no effect on Geno. He is in a frolicsome mood at the Huskies' 9:00 a.m. practice inside Assembly Hall. During a one-on-one drill Sue Bird guards Marci Czel. The two are close friends and, as Marci drives, she steps on Sue's foot, inadvertently tripping her. Sue falls to the floor as Marci drives past her.

"Ooh, ooh," Geno coos at Sue.

"What?" she says, lifting herself up and slightly annoyed. "She stepped on my foot?"

"Ooh, ooh," he repeats. "She can't guard you, Marci."

During a halfcourt five-on-five drill Asjha gets a pass down low and converts the layup, though her feet barely leave the floor. "C'mon, Asjha," he chides, "you're jumping like a white girl."

On the sideline Shea Ralph and Kelly Schumacher, who is riding a stationary bike (she has not played since the Georgia game), mouth mild protests. Geno smiles in their direction.

You can credit much of UConn's success to what is happening right at this moment. Yes, they have outstanding talent, but they also as a team have a pretty good sense of humor. Everyone's a target, even Geno, and if you can't take it—and dish it out—you're in for trouble.

Everyone, everything is a target. Geno has even plumbed the infamous Nykesha Sales shot at Villanova for humor. "I thought about having Svet pass the ball to Nykesha instead of Rita," he has said, "but Svet probably would have taken the shot herself."

You gotta have thick skin to be a Husky. Otherwise, people stop speaking to one another. Almost everyone—even Chris Dailey—has gone a few days without speaking to Geno. Nykesha once gave him the silent treatment for two weeks because she was so upset with him. Before their feud Geno had ordered some compact discs with her from a mail-order music club. When they arrived in her mailbox in the UConn basketball office, she would not deliver them to him. Day after day they sat there, and day after day he waited for her to bring them to him. Finally, he took them himself. They were his, after all.

The next day there was a note on his desk. "Keep out of my mailbox," it read. "You owe me $45.00."

"The person I bought these from," he wrote back, "no longer exists."

Back at practice, CD, as someone intimately familiar with Illinois coach Theresa Grentz's methods, is organizing the scout team to run the Illini's offensive and defensive sets. Her preparation is, in a word, voluminous. After a short while Geno begins to wonder if she is conducting a practice or electing a pope.

"CD, today," he chides. "I know you got a 15-page scouting report, but it's not the national championship. It's just Illinois."

Marci Czel rolls her eyes. "Can someone turn him off?"

Sunday, December 10 . . . The game's local 2:00 p.m. start coincides with the last minutes of the NCAA men's soccer final between UConn and Creighton, which is airing on ESPN2. Minutes before their own game begins, the Husky coaches can be found watching the second half of the soccer match in a green room separate from the locker room. Today Geno is going after his 400th career victory, but he is just as interested in the Huskies' soccer match.

The UConn soccer squad leads 1-0 when the coaches finally depart for the court. During pregame warmups he dispatches a manager to provide soccer updates. As the referee tosses the opening jump ball, Geno shoots a quick look at his bench players and says, "Three minutes left, two-nothing."

If Geno or his team is distracted, no one in Assembly Hall can tell. Shea Ralph scores 18 first-half points, her trademark ponytail swirling like the tornadoes that frequent this part of the country. She misses just one of eight shots as the Huskies sprint to a 30-point lead by halftime, 55-25.

The Illini pose no problem for the Huskies, but an all-male cheering section calling themselves the "Illini Blue Crew" does. They notice that Tom Tedesco, who is a graduate student, is the only other male on the UConn bench. He is an easy target.

"LITTLE GENO!" (clap clap clap-clap-clap) they chant. "LITTLE GENO!" (clap clap clap-clap-clap).

"Hey, Little Geno," one of them yells, a mere 15 feet away. "Little Geno, do you ever date any of the players?"

At least they appreciate good basketball. With four minutes remaining in the first half, Tamika Williams grabs a defensive rebound and outlets it to Swin Cash, who passes crosscourt to Shea, who passes downcourt to Sveta Abrosimova for a layup. The ball never touches the floor. The Blue Crew, awed, begin a chant for mercy: "PUT IN MARCI CZEL!" Half the Husky bench cracks up.

In the locker room Geno confronts his most common halftime dilemna: How to help the other coach save face. The Illini are a young squad rendered even less inexperienced in the first half when their best player, Alison Curtin, suffered a severe ankle sprain. He certainly does not want to embarrass Theresa Grentz, who was a high school legend as a player in Philadelphia.

The Illini are also still licking their wounds from a whupping administered by Tennessee two weeks ago at a Thanksgiving tournament in Maui. The team from Knoxville beat Illinois 111-62. Afterward Lady Vol coach Pat Summitt said that it is her goal to score 120 points a game and hold the opponent to 50. That comment did not sit well with Theresa Grentz.

The loss was punctuated by 6'5" Lady Vol center Michelle Snow's second-half breakaway dunk. Snow's slam received plenty of media attention—it has become the most notorious basket in women's hoops since Nykesha Sales's.

Ever since 1998, when UConn beat Providence, 126-48, and their coach uttered the "kicking us in the fetal position" comment, Geno has become almost hyper-sensitive to any accusations of running up the score. Thus, none of his starters this season averages more than 26 minutes per game. Diana Taurasi and Tamika play less than 20 minutes, or less than one half, per game.

"Ridiculous, eh?" Geno has said. "Sometimes I feel like I'm being unfair to my players."

Two years ago UConn was in the midst of running away from Arkansas, 100-64, in a game staged in San Jose, Calif. At some point in the second half, a woman behind the UConn bench began imploring for Geno to play his subs. He tried to ignore her but she kept yelling at him. He turned around. "These are the subs!" he yelled. "You should be yelling for the starters to play."

Back in Champaign the Huskies' starters begin the second half with a 12-0 run. The score is now 67-25. Matt Eagan motions toward Christine Rigby on the bench and says, "We're going to see Rig-anomics awfully early today."

Sure enough Rig enters the game after the next whistle. Though Geno constantly upbraids Rig for her lack of passion, she actually has outstanding shooting touch. She scores 10 points, making all six free throws she attempts and both field goals as well.

Rig is also whistled for three quick fouls. She is so big and so immobile that even when she blocks a shot cleanly, referees are tempted to blow their whistle. After the third call the ever-passive Rig comes as close to losing her cool as she ever will.

"I don't foul people," Rig pleads to the referee. "I just roof 'em."

Hearing that, Geno laughs. Meanwhile on press row Mike DiMauro of *The New London Day* stares blankly at his blank computer screen. Another game, another blowout. "The real stars are the media," he says before writing up this afternoon's 97-53 win, "who have to come up with a different lead for the same story thirty-seven different times."

In the postgame locker room Grentz—who in the early Seventies was the cornerstone at Immaculata College, the suburban Philadelphia school that won the first three AIAW national championships—looks as if she has seen the ghost of her old team. "I don't particularly care to watch film, but watching them is a lot of fun," she says of UConn. "They play an extremely beautiful brand of basketball."

Sitting at a table in front of two dozen reporters, Grentz studies the stat sheet. It confirms her suspicions. Yes, it was a 42-point loss, which would seem to bear great resemblance to the 49-point loss against Tennessee. However, no UConn starter played more than 22 minutes this afternoon. Even Marci Czel, to the delight of the Blue Crew, played seven minutes.

"I would just like to say one thing," Grentz says at last, cryptically referring to Pat Summitt. "Geno Auriemma is a gentleman. Thank you."

When Geno takes the microphone, a Chicago-based writer asks, "Do your games often feel like a clinic?"

Geno stares at him thoughtfully, impressed. He locks his hands behind his head. "For only seeing us one time," he says, "that's a pretty good observation. We're not really looking at the scoreboard. We're not really looking at what the other team's going to do.

"So it is a glorified practice for us, and we either win or lose no matter what the score says," he says. "It's a mismatch, I know that. We're not here to embarrass anybody."

Downstairs, the UConn locker room has the festive air of a surprise party. Last night the Huskies spent three hours making decorations to fete their coach on his milestone win. Kelly Schumacher made a pair of paper bifocals in the shape of a 400. Shea, who was also around for win number 300, made a sign that would belong on her favorite programming, pro wrestling. "400 smackdowns . . . Bring it!"

"We got high on magic markers," Marci Czel says.

There is another sign hanging in the locker room. Its author is unknown, though to judge from the words, anyone might have done it. Even Geno. "Congrats on 400," it reads, "32 to go."

Monday, December 11 . . . Svetlana Abrosimova and Keirsten Walters are UConn's odd couple. Keirsten is a lean, blonde, 5'8" junior from Littleton, Colorado. Sveta is 6'2", brunette and muscular, a senior from St. Petersburg, Russia.

Keirsten has missed the last 45 games due to osteoarthritis that has required five knee surgeries. She also has torn right shoulder cartilage that was operated on six weeks ago. Sveta has never missed a game in her college career. "On February 20," says Sveta, "I am throwing Keirsten a party for the second anniversary of her rehab."

They are roommates. Sveta is the potential Naismith Player of the Year, the Huskies' leading scorer and, with the exception of his mortgage, the single-best reason Geno has for driving to practice each day. Keirsten sits at the end of the bench and may never recover sufficiently to play again. Her rigorous pre-med studies make her an enigma to her coach.

"I was going to get Keirsten one of those nerdy pocket protectors," Geno once said, "but she already had one."

Keirsten and Svetlana are best friends, though their basketball careers are diverging. Once upon a time they were both starters. When Sue Bird tore her ACL three years ago, Keirsten, Sue's classmate, took her place. The final initial in the T.A.S.S.K. Force and the final one to earn a start, Keirsten entered the lineup on January 7, 1999, at Pittsburgh. She shot a respectable 2-4 and had six assists.

The next game, a 91-82 home loss to Tennessee, Keirsten shot 3-14. Worse, she took a slew of ill-advised shots and committed three turnovers late in the game. She cried when the team reviewed the videotape of that loss.

"You lost your mind for three minutes," Geno told her. What else could he say?

"We became friends after that game," says Svetlana as the they sit in a booth at Willington Pizza, a rustic pizzeria five miles north of campus. "Keirsten was really quiet as a freshman, but we talked a lot after that game."

Keirsten is no more strange than your typical pre-med. Taking honors courses at Heritage High School in Littleton, she had a 4.68 grade-point average, though she had no idea.

"I don't check my grades," says Keirsten. "I never wanted to get caught up in that."

As a UConn freshman Keirsten regularly stayed in on Friday nights to study. "A few of the players would razz her," says Sveta, "but Keirsten wouldn't budge. I admired how she stood up for herself."

They are both geeks. Keirsten sleeps two to three hours per night, and it often shows on her face. Sveta would like to study more if she could find a place to do so. "I cannot study in the library or the dorm lounge," she says, "because people come up to talk to me. I cannot study in the room because Keirsten is always chatting with me."

There is another intrusion on her time, Keirsten points out. "What is that?" asks Sveta.

"You answer all of your fan mail," she says. Sveta shrugs. She does. Every last piece.

"Do your parents have any idea how famous you are here?" I ask Sveta.

"They have no idea," she says.

Wednesday, December 13 . . . Nykesha Sales arrives at practice looking like the reason coffee was invented. It's 10:00 a.m. and her baggy attire and red bandana (or 'do-rag) suggest that she has not made a costume change since waking up.

She doffs her 'do-rag as she crosses the baseline. Geno notices her and wonders if Ashley Battle, Sveta Abrosimova, and Tamika Williams, who are nowhere to be seen, will soon be here.

"Where are those other guys?" he calls out.

"Rita's outta town, Rebecca left," she answers. A few players chuckle. "What? Those are the only guys I know."

Rebecca Lobo is in Europe. Last Friday she left for the Canary Islands, where she will play on a Spanish League team with former Husky Paige Sauer.

"How about the guy who does your hair?" Geno asks Nykesha.

"Outta town."

"Outta town? Been dead for a few months."

The levity is short-lived. Turning in toward the circle, Geno, dressed in a white turtleneck and blue corduroys, addresses the team: "I'm really concerned with the mindset of our team," he says as they encircle him underneath a basket. "We have some guys who don't give two shits about anyone but themselves. Every time I go into the lockerroom it looks like a pig stye. It shows that you don't care. What else could it mean? What else could it mean?"

"When I have to tell someone fifteen times to talk, it shows they don't care. What else could it mean? That's why we ask you when you come out onto the floor to tuck your shirt in EVERY DAY! Every day. Not every other day. *Every day.* To show you care."

Geno has three children, he knows the drill. You can warn kids until your face turns blue, but some lessons only experience can teach. "There are things that are important," he says, "and to me our reputation is most important. Anything that you do on campus takes on more importance. What Rebecca Lobo or Jen Rizzotti did to establish us, you can tear down. The next kid following you has to overcome that."

Geno is irritated by separate incidents involving Swin Cash and Shea Ralph. On the Illinois trip Swin lost a laptop computer that belongs to the athletic department. Upon returning to campus very late Sunday evening from Illinois, Shea discovered that her pickup truck had been towed from an on-campus parking lot. She had parked illegally.

"This is serious," Geno says. "And I want all of you to take it seriously. Am I clear with everybody?"

He looks around, meets each player eye-to-eye. "Let's go," he says, rounding them up. "Together!"

If Geno's lecture was intended to light a spark beneath his team, it is clear after a few drills that it has failed. Finals are looming. The next game, against Wake Forest, is nine days away. Their heads are elsewhere. Perhaps they've been pilfered, like Swin's laptop, or towed.

"Rig, we're missing Schuey and Tamika right now," Geno says. "Is there any difference in your intensity today? No, I didn't think so. And you wonder why you're sitting on the end of the bench. I should have my head examined."

At 10:50 a.m. Geno instructs Tom Tedesco to put two minutes up on the scoreboard. They must score 35 points doing the three-man weave drill, with three-pointers worth three and putbacks counting as one. If they fail, they must run one full-court suicide. This they must complete in 32 seconds.

In the first session the Huskies score 30 points, falling five short. "On the baseline," says Geno.

They hustle to the baseline and then wait. Geno is clearly irritated with their lack of effort "I got guys who don't call people's names out," he says. "Who are they, Stace?"

Stacy Hansmeyer fingers her housemate. "Rig is one of them," she says.

"Who else?"

"Maria."

"Who else?"

"KJ."

"Put thirty-two seconds up," he tells Tom.

They're off. The Huskies are in outstanding condition, though unlike many coaches, Geno rarely devotes practice time to conditioning for conditioning's sake. "The only time they ever run without a basketball," Chris Dailey has said, "is for a lack of effort."

Or for failure to listen. Kerry Poliquin, for example, will never forget the day that she arrived at practice to find a garbage can at each of the four corners of the court. "He had told us that you can't go to Ted's [the popular on-campus dive]," she recalls, "and somebody went."

That day Geno lined them up on the baseline, and they ran suicides. And then they ran a few more. And the three players who went to Ted's realized earlier than anyone else had why the garbage cans were there—because each girl vomited into one of them.

After the suicide, in which Sue and Swin finish first, the players pair off for free throws. After everyone shoots her 10 she reports her scores to Tom or Kathryn Fieseler, who quickly tabulate the team average. If the Huskies shoot 90% or above, they do not run. This is standard procedure at UConn practices.

Tom reports that the team shot 84%.

"Put thirty-two seconds up," Geno says. They run the sprint. Rig, slow afoot, finishes last. She usually does.

"Let's go again. Everyone on the free throw line. Different basket this time."

After the shooting stops this time, Tom reports, "Eighty-one percent."

Geno shakes his head. They stand on the baseline, each one of them staring straight at him.

"You went from eighty-four to eighty-one," he says. "How did I know that? How many'd you hit, Rig?"

"Seven," she answers.

"Seven. Great. You come in last then you only make seven? What is it? Are you tired from studying? Is that it? We don't have a game for nine days, and it's only Wake Forest? 'Cuz when you're the greatest team in the history of college basketball, all you have to do is show up?"

"Put thirty-two seconds up."

Again, they run. After finishing they stand on the baseline, hands on hips, sucking air.

"You'll get your wake-up call on the thirtieth," Geno continues, referring to Tennessee's visit. During this entire interlude he never raises his voice. If his players feel at all threatened, it is only a fear of disappointing him.

"You'll get your wake-up call when the Lady Vols come in and start dancing on your floor. Then you'll come into the locker room and be all pissed off. But you don't know about that, do you, Maria? Or you, Rig, 'cuz you won't be out there. You won't be the one [Michelle] Snow dunks on. That will bother you, but nothing I say can bother you."

A third time, they shoot 10 free throws apiece. Either their shooting improves or their capacity for duplicity (or Tom's) improves. "Ninety-two percent," Tom announces.

Geno isn't finished.

"You know when it will show up?" he asks, walking toward midcourt. "When we play somebody that's pretty good. You're just lucky that we play so many teams that suck. But that'll change. That'll change."

Monday, December 18 . . . One of the shortest days of the year is, for Geno, the longest of days. He awoke at 4:30 a.m. for a 6:15 flight to Madison, Wisconsin, with a stopover in Detroit. His final destination is Janesville, Wisconsin, about 45 miles south of Madison, to see a recruit.

Her name is Mistie Bass. A 6'2" junior at Janesville's Parker High School, she is already among the two or three best post players in the nation. Because the the Huskies lost out on signing Teresa Borton, they will have only one true returning post player—Jessica Moore—two seasons from now. If Teresa Borton is the one that got away, Mistie Bass is the catch of the day.

She is being raised by her mother. Mistie's estranged father is singer Chubby Checker, who met Mistie's mom when she was working as a maid at a Janesville hotel at which he stayed. A twist of fate, you might say.

"You know how Chubby Checker got that name?" Geno says. "His real name is Ernest Evans. He was just starting out in the music business, and Dick Clark's wife suggested the name. 'There's already a Fats Domino, so he'll be Chubby Checker.'"

Geno's plane landed in a blizzard in Madison, and by the time he arrived in Janesville, he was in the midst of a winter wonderland. Under the byzantine rules of the NCAA, Geno cannot speak with Bass today. This visit is nothing more than a Hallmark card to her: UConn cares enough to send its very best. If the coach of the number one team in the nation flies halfway across the country through a blizzard just to see you practice, he must be interested.

The temperature is below zero as Geno drives to a local sports bar, Spirits, for lunch. "I think," he chatters, "that this is where they came up with the concept of layering."

He is the coach of the top-ranked team in the nation, a team that has won 25 consecutive games, the longest active streak in men's or women's college hoops. Christmas Day is a week away. Yet here he is up against Jack London weather, just to observe a player who will not play in a college game for 23 months. That's how you win national championships.

"The most important part of being a great coach," Geno will tell you, "is having great players."

After practice he chats with two of Mistie's coaches, Tom Klawitter and his female assistant. They discuss baseball

(Klawitter briefly pitched for the Minnesota Twins in 1985), and the coaches pick Geno's brain a little about practice techniques.

"I never like to practice more than four days in a row," Geno tells them. "I like to give them a day off. That way I can make them feel guilty the day before—'Come on, you're off tomorrow, give some extra effort'— and the day after—'You just had a day off, you should be working harder.' I get 'em feeling guilty coming and going."

The female coach gives a low whistle of admiration. "Oh," she says, "you understand women."

From Janesville it is a three-hour drive down an icy Interstate 90 to Chicago, where Nike is hosting the Tournament of Champions, a showcase for some of the top high school teams in the nation. In Chicago Geno dines with Doug Bruno, the head coach at DePaul University. Bruno is an instantly likeable guy. Wiry, dark-haired, and in his mid-forties, he has a voice that sounds like rocks in a blender.

They swap stories. "The first time we ever played at Tennessee," Bruno tells his old friend, "they beat us by sixty-three. In the second half the game was way out of hand. I felt embarrassed, like we weren't keeping our part of the bargain. So I jotted a note right there and had someone give it to Coach Summitt."

"What did the note say?" asks Geno.

"It said," replies Bruno, "'*What would you like to work on?*'"

Wednesday, December 20 . . . Shea Ralph and Keirsten Walters walked into their 1:00 p.m. animal physiology final this afternoon knowing it would be tough. They took their seats nervously and grew more anxious when they heard the proctor direct the class to "Put your section on top of the paper."

Shea turned to the male student seated across from her. "What does he mean by 'section'?" she asked.

"For your discussion group," the student replied. Shea and Keirsten looked at each other. Animal physiology has no discussion group.

"What class is this?" they asked.

"Linguistics."

Meanwhile, half an hour before practice on this pristine blue-sky afternoon, Geno is reclining on his couch, desperately

hoping that the next few minutes pass like days. Like his players, sleep has eluded him this finals week. He stayed in Chicago
another day to watch the Tournament of Champions and hang
out with Doug Bruno and Katie Post, the women's basketball
representative from Nike. Last night the trio dined at an Italian
restaurant. As Geno drove them back to the Hyatt Regency, he
received a traffic ticket.

"I wasn't sure if I was allowed to make a left-hand turn into
the entrance of the hotel," Geno says, "but Mr. Chicago [Bruno]
sitting in the backseat says, 'Oh yeah, you can do that.' So I
turned and the next thing I know, the cops stopped me."

Both officers were females. As they walked back to their
patrol car, Geno turned toward his buddy in the back seat. "Just
my luck," he said to Bruno. "Two women for cops."

Today Jack Eisenmann sits in on practice. Jack and Geno are
old friends, having played basketball together at Bishop
Kenrick High School in Norristown.

"Geno was a soccer player," Eisenmann says. "He wasn't on
the basketball team as a freshman. One day after school he
played in a pickup game with us. Our coach, Buddy Gardler,
saw him and asked me, 'Who is that guy?'"

Later Eisenmann told Geno that Gardler had asked about
him. "Geno's eyes just bugged out," says Eisenmann, who is the
men's coach at the University of Ottawa in Quebec. "You gotta
understand, Buddy Gardler was a legend to us. He had been the
sixth man [*i.e.*, the first player off the bench] at St. Joe's."

Buddy Gardler, who now coaches the boys team at Cardinal
O'Hara High School (Theresa Grentz's alma mater) in
Philadelphia, is Geno's mentor. His surrogate dad. Before prac-
tice today Geno and Eisenmann are sharing favorite Buddy
Gardler tales.

"Once we were up by eleven with two minutes left," Geno
says. "I haven't shot all game long, but I wasn't supposed to.
Well, I'm open at the top of the key. So as I'm going up to shoot,
out of the corner of my eye, I can see Buddy pulling someone off
the bench to take me out of the game. I hit the shot. He sits the
kid back down."

Gardler was a hoops fundamentalist as is Geno, his prodigy.
What frustrates Geno is players who can do spectacular things,
things that he never had the talent to do, yet are incapable or

unwilling to consistently perform the game's menial tasks. Players such as . . .

"D!" he yells about an hour into practice after one of Diana Taurasi's no-look passes sails five feet wide of Shea. "D! What is this shit? You've got her wide open, but you've got to no-look pass and fake them out. They're *already* faked out! She's wide open!"

Players trying to do too much. Making "dumbass" plays. At Keirsten's very first practice her freshman year, she had the ball deep in the left corner and attempted a cross-court no-look pass to the right wing that sailed beyond its target and bopped the timekeeper in the head. Geno thought then, *This* is going to be a long year. Which it was.

They progress to a full-court scrimmage. Diana is wide open for a three but passes instead. "Hey, yo," he says, "shoot the damn ball."

Next time downcourt, Diana nails a three. Then she steals a pass, takes two dribbles, and flips it to Sue Bird on the fast break. Sue dribbles to the top of the key and returns it to D on the left side. Again, she rains down a three.

"Good!" Geno cries, "but next time make that pass to Sue earlier. You know when you want to make that pass? Right when you stole it. Then you fill the wing. We want to run what you call a 'fast break'."

Geno is standing behind her as he says this, and so he cannot see as she sticks her tongue out. But she is smiling.

"Remember," he says, "the only things acceptable on a fast break are a wide-open three or a layup."

Quickly, the worm turns. Sue has her layup blocked by one of the two male student practice players. Diana commits a turnover. Sue does the same.

"We're a team that feeds off each other," Geno says. "Turns into a brain hemorrhage where everyone starts making mistakes, one after the other. Just once, after two or three straight turnovers, I'd like to see someone make a really simple play to stop the hemorrhage."

Alas, on the next fast break, Diana's no-look pass flies out of bounds.

"That's unbelievable!" says Geno, speaking directly to Diana. "That's unbelievable. I've been coaching twenty-five years and I've never seen, as often as I've seen the last three days, how many new ways you can find to turn the ball over on the break. You continue to try to prove that you can make this pass [he takes the ball, chucks a one-hand pass, from two feet away, at her feet] after I tell you all I want is a wide-open layup that a guy can have a heart attack and still make or a wide-open three. After I tell you anything else is unacceptable. It's unbelievable!"

For the first time since Diana donned a UConn jersey, or maybe for the first time ever on a basketball court, her face is flush with embarrassment. He excuses them to shoot ten free throws, then walks over to Jack Eisenmann. "See," he confides, "that was good for me so that I can see what their breaking point is."

Svetlana Abrosimova, Diana's hoops soulmate, is having her problems with Nykesha Sales. In one sequence Keesh steals the ball from Sveta off the dribble, then beats her on a backdoor play for an easy two.

"Hey, Svet," Geno asks, "what are you doing?"

Svetlana looks at him, pouts. A while later she again tries to dribble past Nykesha, which is like trying to play "Gotcha!" with a cobra. Again, Nykesha picks Sveta's pocket as she dribbles past, this time with Svetlana tripping over Nykesha's foot and sprawling to the floor.

"That's a clean steal," Geno says. "Every time you dribble by Nykesha, she steals the ball. Every time. Not every other time. *Every* time. Because you're careless with the ball."

Sveta fumes silently. Jack Eisenmann is fascinated. You could sit on the top post of a corral fence and not see a better display of a maverick colt being broken. She is a senior, and she still resists the bridle.

"Similar thing happened at a practice last year," Eisenmann says. "Svet was being ridden all practice long by G. Then she hit a three-pointer and stared at him. He kicked her out of practice. Instead, she just walked over to the sideline. He looked at her and said, 'Do I have to carry you off?'"

Sveta left. "When I saw her after practice," Eisenmann says, "she was still in tears."

Thursday, December 21 . . . The final day of practice before Christmas finds everyone in a better mood. It has been a long 11 days. The ceaseless torment of finals and basketball practice is almost done. The next time they go this long without playing a game will be after the season.

Scrimmaging. A scout-team defense guards the first team and, on the first play, Sue Bird, the premier point guard in the nation, beats Marci Czel, the walk-on, for an easy bucket. Marci Czel stamps her foot in anger, which amuses Geno.

"Hold it," he says. "Marci Czel is pissed. She knew that play was coming."

Marci Czel smirks at him. Today is her 22nd birthday. She is Marci Czel to everyone at UConn, never just Marci. "My freshman year we had Marci Glenney [since transferred to Clemson] so I was 'Marci-the-walk-on'," she will tell you. "Then she left, and I became Marci Czel. Look around. Do you see any other Marci's on this team?"

At 5'7", Marci Czel is the shortest player on the team and arguably the least talented. A Connecticut kid, she led Guilford High School to a 24-1 record her senior year and was second-team All-State. She fielded a few offers from Division II schools but decided to attend UConn. Marci Czel's conversations with family and friends that summer pretty much went like this:

"What are you doing next year?"

"I'm going to UConn."

"So you're not playing?"

"Yeah."

What could Marci Czel say? She called the basketball offices expressing her interest in trying out. Jamelle Elliott told her when the team ran the timed mile and for Marci Czel to be there.

"There was another walk-on," Marci Czel recalls. "She ran right off the track after half a lap. Just kept on running."

Marci Czel made the 6:15 cutoff time for guards—"It had to be the adrenaline"— and was allowed to try out, where she never gave Geno a good enough reason to cut her.

"If you keep doing what you're doing," Chris Dailey told her after two weeks with the squad, "we'll have to get you a uniform."

Still, Marci Czel understood the caste system between scholarship players and athletes. "I walked into the cafeteria one night," she says, "at a time when we had a lot of players getting hurt. Paige Sauer was talking to people, and I heard her say, 'We got so many injuries the damn walk-on's gonna be starting.'"

Marci Czel has never started, but as the years passed she has found her niche with this team. When a Husky hits a three or a big shot, Marci Czel hops up and down the bench, giving two-handed high-fives to all of her teammates. That she has to leap to reach many of the Huskies raised hands only makes the scene more charming.

"One of my things is to get along with everyone on the team," Marci Czel says. "CD always pumps me for information because she knows I'm the insider. But I can't tell her everything."

The Herde greets Geno after practice and the mood, matching the season, is merry. Although the Wake Forest game is tomorrow, the sportswriters are anxious to talk about Tennessee. The Demon Deacons are stocking stuffers. The Lady Vols are that mysteriously shaped present that does not fit under the tree, the one you cannot wait to open.

"Any new wrinkles for Tennessee?" someone asks.

"We're not going to put something in just for Tennessee," Geno says, then has a mischievous thought. "We're going to put four or five things in offensively. Make sure you write that, they'll see it."

He retreats to the players' lounge, where the team is doing a Christmas gift exchange. Many of the presents are inspired: Schuey gives Jamelle Elliott a sketch of the two of them while Rig gives Tonya Cardoza a beautiful homemade quilt, 100% Riggawear. Shea Ralph gives Diana Taurasi a bottle of Gas-X, which brings appreciative applause from the entire squad.

Finally, Geno presents everyone with books. All the freshman receive the children's classic *The Polar Express*, while the upperclassmen are given Anna Quindlen's *A Short Guide to a Happy Life*. He also gives them a homework assignment, their last of the semester.

"I want a one-page interpretation of what you think the book you've been given is all about," Geno says. "Doesn't have to be deep, doesn't have to be silly, just first impressions. I don't even want your name on it."

Diana cannot resist a jab at her roomie. "Morgan," she says, "will probably get a tutor for this."

Friday, December 22 . . . Last night CPTV taped *The Geno Auriemma Show* at Sorrento, the cozy Italian bistro on Franklin Avenue in Hartford, as part of a 400th-victory party. Rebecca Lobo (back from the Canary Islands for the holidays and looking quite tan), Jennifer Rizzotti, and Kara Wolters were among nearly two dozen former Huskies who came to show their support.

After the taping Geno threw a small feast for his inner circle of friends, people whose names don't make the paper: his agent, Sol Kerensky, and his wife; Jack Eisenmann and his younger brother, Phil; and a few others.

Geno was at his best on this evening. He hosted, toasted, and roasted those who are closest to him. Looking at his wife of 22 years, Kathy, he said with more than a trace of sarcasm, "Oh, yeah, I owe everything to you. I'd be nowhere without you," as she waved her arm in a keep-it-coming gesture.

Phil Eisenmann has vivid memories of Geno, four years his senior, when both were younger. "I remember Geno and my parents sitting at our dining room table having these long conversations," says Eisenmann, 42. "Grown-up talks about stuff like paying the bills, taking care of the kids. My mom would tell us, 'Geno has responsibilities you kids couldn't dream about.'"

Geno Auriemma, by the age of eight, was the man of the house on 815 Kohn Street in Norristown. His parents never learned to read. His father, Donato, never spoke English and his mother, Nona, knew only the most basic words back then. Donato walked or hitched rides to his job seven miles from home at a cinder block plant where he earned $65 a week. Nona woke up at 4:30 a.m., prepared lunches and then walked two miles to a rug factory where she worked. At the end of each month Geno would make the rounds in Norristown, paying the various bills.

"It was all up to him," says Phil. "He was in the second grade at St. Francis of Assisi, his first year in the country and he had to teach himself English. The nun said, 'If you can do this by June, then you can go to the third grade. If not, you stay in second grade."

Geno advanced to the third grade. "He used to tell me, 'I'm never going to get married,'" says Phil. "'I'm already doing all that stuff now.'"

By the time the coach at Bishop Kenrick, Buddy Gardler, handed Geno the point guard job, he had a Ph.D. in responsibility. "He was like a coach on the floor," recalls Phil. "He was the leader in his own family before he was ten. How could you not turn out like he did?"

Kerensky is, like Geno, an immigrant. He was born in Russia and has made a very successful life for himself in the States.

After UConn won the national championship last April, Kerensky obtained copies of the contracts of the two highest-paid women's basketball coaches in the country, Pat Summitt of Tennessee and C. Vivian Stringer of Rutgers University (both are state employees; their contracts are public record). Summitt and Stringer earn approximately $500,000 and $400,000, respectively. Kerensky and UConn athletic director Lew Perkins agreed that Geno's new contract should be the new standard.

Perkins told the media that he wanted to make Geno the highest paid women's coach in the land. Geno's response to that: "That's exactly what I'm thinking!" He now earns from UConn alone (in base salary plus various other amenities related to speaking engagements, summer camp, etc.) $590,000 per year through 2004.

Geno is now the best-paid coach in women's collegiate hoops. He is also the winningest coach in the sport the last seven years, and his team's home attendance is second only to Tennessee's (the Huskies, however, generate more ticket revenue than the Lady Vols).

Last night at Sorrento Geno saw himself as less blessed with dollars than with what they enable him to do. "When I was a boy, we didn't have a home that was big enough to do things like this," he told the group. Then he raised his wine glass. "I just want to give thanks that we can do something like this tonight and that all of you can be here."

This afternoon's matchup with 7-2 Wake Forest has a weekday matinee feel. The Friday afternoon 2:00 p.m. start disrupts fans' last-minute Christmas shopping plans. Nevertheless Gampel Pavilion is, with the exception of the student section, full.

Geno had not been in a festive mood at this morning's 8:30 shootaround. The players, finished with finals and in their minds already home for the holidays, were in a state of torpor. Disgusted, he walked off the court for 20 minutes.

Whether the wake-up call was merited, the Huskies put on yet another ethereal performance. Fifty-three seconds into the game Wake Forest coach Charlene Curtis calls a timeout after UConn scores two quick buckets off a blocked shot by Swin Cash and a steal by Sue Bird. The defense, as usual, sets up the offense.

Curtis has set a personal goal for this game. She does not tell her players, but her hope is that the Demon Deacons will hold UConn to under 100 points.

They do not. UConn goes on a 21-2 run early in the first half, culminated by a halfcourt no-look assist from Diana Taurasi to Svetlana Abrosimova for a layup. Midway through the second half, with the Huskies leading, 63-31, Asjha Jones grabs a defensive rebound and throws a length-of-the-court pass, a home-run pass, to Sveta, who is streaking down the right side. The pass is overthrown.

The ball takes a bounce a few feet before the baseline. As it sails out of bounds, Sveta leaps after it. With her right hand she scoops it and tosses it underneath the basket and past the arms of two defenders to Shea Ralph, who is standing in the left corner. Shea takes the pass (as Sveta sprawls out of bounds) and feeds Asjha, the play's initiator, with a pass as she sprints into the lane. Asjha hits the layup and is fouled.

All this with a 32-point lead.

The Gampel fans, momentarily dumbstruck, emit a roar. Even Sveta and Shea are smiling at the deed as they envelop Asjha in a hug. On press row Mike DiMauro of the *The New London Day* and Randy Smith of *The Manchester Journal-Inquirer*, bored by the grandeur, are already talking about next season.

"Diana will start at off-guard," says DiMauro, "and they're going to need KJ to play better."

"You're right," agrees Smith. "There'll be some depth concerns next year."

Yes, and Michelle Pfeiffer doesn't look quite as heavenly as she used to.

UConn wins, 107-52. The fans cheer raucously. UConn followers have a bloodlust for such outcomes.

"I don't know what the answer is," says Carl Adamec, who has sat through almost as many of these blowouts as has Geno. "At West Virginia last year they won, 100-28. He emptied his bench, but it didn't make a difference. Some guy on crutches began yelling, 'Hey, Geno, put me in.'"

Curtis has no enmity about today's outcome. "Their second or even third teams could beat most teams in the nation," she says. "In terms of how far ahead of everyone else they are, this may be the best team ever."

When Geno enters the classroom, he is in a garrulous mood. The Herde, which obediently and patiently has refrained from asking about the next opponent, feel a sense of liberation. Nobody even says the word "Tennessee" or "Summitt." Up here they are simply "the team from Knoxville" or "the coach from Knoxville".

"Do you have an agenda for your game with the team from Knoxville?" somebody asks.

"Everybody's gotta go into this game with their own agenda," he replies. "Ours is, we got a game on the thirtieth against a team we don't like."

Next he is asked about Diana, who from her guard spot led the team in rebounds with five and was second in scoring and assists. From one favorite topic to another. He grins. This is batting practice.

"I tell my kids, if you're running downcourt, and D has the ball, and she's looking *at* you, forget it, go get something to eat," he says. "'Cuz you're not getting the ball.

"You can tell Taurasi anything, it won't phase her," he says. "I say, 'You're the worst player I ever recruited,' and she comes over and puts an arm around you and says, 'Coach, what are you doing tonight? Tell Kathy I said hello.' She's impossible not to like. That's the sign of a con artist."

It had been suggested to him when he was in Chicago, earlier in the week, that Diana may become the best player he has ever coached. Ridiculous, right? With three former National Players of the Year on his resume (Rebecca Lobo, Jen Rizzotti, Kara Wolters), plus Nykesha Sales—not to mention Svetlana.

And someone wondered if Diana had the potential to surpass all of them?

"Diana Taurasi," he answered, "might already be the best player I've ever coached."

Monday, December 25 . . . Christmas morning. Svetlana Abrosimova awakens to discover that she cannot bend over to put on her socks. "Shea, something is wrong," she says to teammate Shea Ralph, at whose Florida home she is staying. "Will you put my socks on?"

This is Sveta's second Christmas staying with Shea, Marsha, Roy, and Ryan (Shea's younger sister). The Russian émigré cannot afford to go home for Christmas and, besides, the recess only lasts four days. Last year, when Marsha Lake heard that Sveta planned to spend the holiday at the Quality Inn, the hotel where the team holes up before school resumes in late January, she ordered Shea to tender an invitation to their home in Satellite Beach, Florida.

"Sveta was so tentative last Christmas," Marsha Lake recalls, "so we thought that we'd have a little fun with her."

As a joke Ryan gave Sveta a Chia Pet. "Ah, this is so nice," said Sveta, truly grateful.

"Svet, it's a gag gift," they told her. "A joke."

She did not see it that way. Sveta toted the Chia Pet back to Connecticut. When the Huskies went on the road last January, she asked the maid at the Quality Inn to water it for her.

Last Christmas Shea's family had urged her to call her parents back in St. Petersburg on Christmas morning. When she did, Roy, Marsha, Shea, and Ryan gathered around her. After a minute or two, Sveta stopped talking and eyed her hosts curiously. She felt self-conscious.

"Go ahead, Svet," they urged. "We just want to hear you speak Russian."

Yesterday Roy Lake, Marsha's husband, took Shea and Sveta to play basketball at an upscale, indoor athletic complex in the town of Merritt Island. The trio waited awhile to get in a game—nobody recognized them—but once they got on the court, they did not lose the rest of the day. On one play Sveta, positioning herself for a rebound, was shoved from behind. At the time she thought nothing of it, but this morning Sveta is Florida's newest invalid.

This afternoon Roy, who manages the Florida Marlins spring-training facility in Cocoa Beach, takes Sveta to the Marlins' chiropractor. By now she is experiencing back spasms. He works on her back for two hours.

A gnawing uneasiness begins to take root. Should they phone Geno? On Christmas? Let the coach in Manchester enjoy the day with his family. It's probably no big deal, anyway. Sveta most likely will wake up tomorrow feeling good as new.

Wednesday, December 27 . . . Last September 16 was an absolutely gorgeous day for college football. Pat Summitt stood on the sideline at Neyland Stadium in Knoxville as the University of Florida and the University of Tennessee engaged in one of the sport's most satisfying rivalries. On that brilliant afternoon, Coach Summitt was entertaining both a recruit and thoughts of the school's other monster rivalry, her team's feud with UConn.

Earlier that morning Summitt had reviewed the tape of last April's NCAA championship debacle, the 71-52 loss to the Huskies. She stepped onto her elliptical exercise machine at home and watched the entire game straight through for the first time since April 2. "There wasn't an answer to why we lost on that tape," she would say later. "Not one that I could see."

Summitt had nothing to apologize for. In the previous six seasons the Lady Vols had won three national titles and made it to the championship two other times only to lose to UConn. Only during the 1998-99 season did Summitt fail to coach in the title game. That year two of the Lady Vols' three losses were to Duke and Purdue, the teams that played for the national championship.

Autumn would take Summitt and the Lady Vols on a strange odyssey. A week after the football game she found herself in Thousand Oaks, California, part of an historic meeting. Her 1976 US Olympic coach, Billie Moore, who also coached at UCLA from 1977-93, arranged for Summitt to visit John Wooden. The Wizard of Westwood, as Wooden is known, is 90 years old. He is the Yoda of college hoops, its peerless epitome of grace and wisdom, its strongest link to the past.

Wooden's and Summitt's successes are remarkably similar. His ten national championships, in a 12-year span from 1964-75, are the most by any Division I college basketball coach. Her six national championships are the most among women's coaches and second-most overall after his. His Bruins won 88 straight games in the early Seventies, still the benchmark in college basketball. Her Lady Vols won 69 consecutive home games from 1991-96, an NCAA homecourt record that was ended by UConn.

Thus Summitt's meeting was in essence a summit meeting of college basketball's king and queen of coaching. In fact two years earlier Summitt was featured in a cover story in *Sports Illustrated* entitled "The Wizard of Knoxville". On the cover the question was posed, *Is Tennessee's Pat Summitt the best college basketball coach since John Wooden?*

The tall, athletic, 48-year-old coach, along with Moore and Tennessee associate head coach Mikki DeMoss, piled into one car as if they were children on an epic adventure. Which they were. They were off to see the Wizard.

"It was heaven," Summitt recalls. "I was in basketball heaven."

The foursome spent two and a half hours together. "Mostly, we talked about managing egos," Summitt recalls. "His best advice: the bench is your greatest ally."

Talent Summitt has. Forward Tamika Catchings is the reigning National Player of the Year, and the one player whose heart and courage Geno admire as much as that of any player in the nation. "She's what Shea would be," he has said of Catchings, "if Shea were built like Svet."

It is just a matter of getting everyone to play together. Something they had failed to do last April 1.

"There's one thing all players love to do," Wooden told Summitt. "Players love to play."

Before they left, DeMoss asked Wooden to compare his sideline demeanor, which had always appeared so placid, to her boss's. He considered the question for a moment. Then, peering over his eyeglasses at Summitt, the Wizard said, "I didn't yell."

The rest of the autumn had been a suitcase semester for the Lady Vol coach. She was in Springfield, Massachusetts, for the Basketball Hall of Fame induction dinner on October 13. In her speech she mentioned that in her first season in Knoxville,

1974-75, she earned $3,000. "I'm sure some people thought I was overpaid *then*," she quipped.

The Lady Vols' traveled to Maui to play in a tournament, the site of Michelle Snow's dunk. They ventured to Ruston, Louisiana, and Austin, Texas, where Summitt had squared off against women's basketball's all-time winningest coach (Louisiana Tech's Leon Barmore) and its all-time wins leader (Texas's Jody Conradt). Summitt, second in both categories, inched closer to the top as the Lady Vols won both games.

Which brought them to this evening, to Phoenix, Arizona, for a quirky, historic moment in the history of the women's game. The Lady Vols are playing Arizona State University outdoors on a court laid over the infield of Bank One Ballpark, home of the Major League Baseball Arizona Diamondbacks. 16,282 curious fans—among them ESPN's dean of men's college hoops, Dick Vitale—have come to see what is believed to be the first outdoor women's college basketball game.

Arizona State makes the most of its opportunity, trailing the Lady Vols by only four at halftime. In the second half the temperature cools considerably. On the Tennessee sideline DeMoss, looking miserable, dons an overcoat. The Lady Vol players pass handwarmers to one another, gazing enviously at their teammates working up a sweat out on the court.

Nobody feels more chilled than Summitt, exacerbated by her squad's sluggish play. In the second half a referee whistles Arizona State for a foul. "Best call you made all night," Summitt chirps. The ref blows his whistle again. Technical foul on Summitt, only the sixth in her career. Arizona State plays Tennessee dead even in the second half, losing 67-63.

"It was a unique setting," Summitt says afterward. "Our basketball team had some challenges that they probably won't have the rest of their career."

The Lady Vols will board a red-eye flight and land in Hartford tomorrow morning. Forty-eight hours later the coach from Knoxville will have the rematch that she has waited nine months for. The Lady Vols are 11-0 but tonight's effort left Summitt feeling somewhat left out in the cold. Someone asks if the cross-country flight, accompanying jet lag, and one full day of preparation will be sufficient time to prepare for the Huskies.

Summitt is quick with a wink and a smile, the kind that engenders comity between herself and sportswriters. With just one facial tic she appears to be saying, "We're all on this train together. It's a great ride, eh?"

"Enough time to prepare for UConn?" the Wizard of Knoxville says. Wink. Smile. "How many years would it take?"

Saturday, December 30 . . . Shea Ralph is spending her fifth winter in Storrs. Earlier in life she spent six summers in Knoxville. Each July, from the time she was 12 until she was 17, Shea attended Pat Summitt's basketball camp at the University of Tennessee.

"I had phoned Pat [Summitt] when Shea was eleven because we're old friends," says her mom, Marsha Lake, who played on the 1973 World University Games team with Summitt. "I said, 'Pat, I think my little girl may be something special.'"

Summitt, then Pat Head, had played at the University of Tennessee-Martin. Lake, then Marsha Mann, had been an All-American at the University of North Carolina (the school would later retire her number, 44, which still hangs in the rafters at Carmichael Auditorium). When Lake called her old World University Games teammate in 1990, Summitt invited her little girl to attend her camp in Knoxville.

The first time Shea suited up for a UConn-Tennessee game as a freshman, on January 5, 1997, at the Hartford Civic Center (HCC), she saw the players in the orange uniforms and was in awe. In awe of the Lady Vols. Shortly after Geno sent Shea into the game that day he yanked her right back out.

"You're scared," he told her.

"No, I'm not," she said.

Shea begged him to put her back in. Geno relented, saying, "Okay, two minutes."

She returned and scored the game's next eight points. Shea would play thirty minutes. UConn won, 72-57.

Two years and two ACL surgeries later, in 1999, the Lady Vols returned to Connecticut for a 2:00 p.m. game at Gampel Pavilion. Geno scheduled a 10:00 a.m. shootaround. When he arrived at 8:30 a.m., he peeked inside the arena. There was Shea, already on the court shooting baskets. Lake was rebounding for her.

"If it's possible," says Geno, "Shea used to want to win too badly."

She still does, though she cannot play the way she used to. Her knees will not allow it. Before she walks out on the floor, she tapes the area just below each of them as if applying a tourniquet. She has never worn knee pads—not that they would have prevented the ACL tears—because she was afraid of comparisons with former Husky star Jen Rizzotti, who did. She tapes below the knees, however, for support. She is a 22-year-old woman with 66-year-old knees.

"You walk with her," says Lake, "and sometimes you'll hear a sound like a hammer hitting wood. I truly don't know how she plays."

When Shea awoke this morning, it was a toss-up whether anyone would play today. A nor'easter is in the midst of dumping eight to 12 inches of snow on Hartford, the worst blizzard since an April Fool's Day 1997 storm. The roads, while not treacherous, are unfit for driving. But on the last weekend of the millennium, the deluge seems only to lift people's spirits.

The HCC is at a fever pitch by the 4:00 p.m. tip-off. More than 15,500 fans have conquered old man winter to be here. All of them could have stayed at home and watched the game, which CBS is broadcasting nationally. "Ever hear the saying that it never rains on a golf course?" Lester Baum, a 72-year-old retiree from Vernon, Connecticut, tells *The Hartford Courant*. "Well, it never snows when UConn plays Tennessee."

The Lady Vols, who only three nights earlier were shivering outside in the desert, acclimatize well. Four minutes into the game they lead, 8-4. After the first media timeout, however, UConn foments a blizzard of its own. In the next five minutes six different Huskies score as UConn goes on a 19-2 run against the number two team in the nation. Swin Cash's layup with 10:19 remaining in the first half makes it 23-10 and, as Pat Summitt motions for a timeout, the din is deafening. Jogging over to the UConn bench, Tamika Williams nudges Diana Taurasi. "This," she says, acknowledging the cacophony, "is why I came here."

For the next 20 minutes of game clock the Huskies lead comfortably. Svetlana Abrosimova, who started but did not score in the first half, is a non-factor. Back spasms have haunted her since she woke up on Christmas morning and asked Shea, "Will you put my socks on?" Sveta and Shea waited two days to give Geno the news about Sveta's injury incurred during the pickup game. His reaction: "Well, did you win?"

"Yeah," said Shea, "we won."

"Okay, then."

Sveta will score only four points today, all free throws. Shea and Diana bear the burden of the Huskies' sled. Shea plays 37 minutes and, with Sue Bird, leads the team in scoring with 15 points. But it is one shot by Diana Taurasi that is both the game's imprimatur and the portent of her shoot-first, answer-questions-later style. It happens late in the game. Tennessee has gone on a 16-4 run, capped by Tamika Catchings's three-pointer taken right in front of the Tennessee bench. Suddenly, with 5:27 remaining, the Lady Vols trail by two, 69-67.

UConn inbounds to Sue Bird, who dribbles upcourt. She passes to Diana on the left wing, who is standing eight feet behind the three-point line. Catchings, last season's Player of the Year, is standing right in front of her, staring her down. Diana doesn't flinch, launching what must be a 30-foot jumper without even taking a dribble. Swish.

Summitt, who had turned her back to the court momentarily to peruse her bench and mull a substitution, never sees the shot. Seizing her assistant, Micki DeMoss, she asks incredulously, "Was that from downtown Hartford?"

"No," DeMoss answers, "it was from Storrs."

In the final minute Diana's impulsiveness almost wrecks UConn, as she airballs a three-pointer that did not need to be attempted. On the next play, however, with the Huskies ahead, 77-74, Catchings is whistled for an offensive foul while setting a pick. It is a dubious call and ends the team from Knoxville's chance of a comeback. UConn hangs on to win, 81-76.

Before leaving the court, Geno approaches the scorer's table and takes the microphone. "Hey, before everybody leaves," he says, addressing the throng, "we just want to thank everyone for coming out on a day like today. We really appreciate it."

Afterward, in the catacombs of the HCC, there is a charged residue of the lightning just seen. The press, who would have paid to watch this one, may anticipate the postgame comments even more. Geno Auriemma and Pat Summitt are the twin titans of this sport, but they also generate its best quotes.

Summitt is aglow about Diana. "Four years of that," she whistles in admiration. "I don't even want to think about it."

Jeff Jacobs asks Summitt about the offensive foul that was called on Catchings in the final minute. Among the coaching and media vanguard in women's college hoops, the most oft-heard bleat is that the refereeing is a barnacle on the hull of the sport.

"Oh, I saw it," says Summitt. "I was sitting right by you. Did you see it?"

"When do you suspect," asks Randy Smith, "the officiating will catch up to the game?"

Summitt smiles at him. Winks. "You know," she says, "I really cannot comment on that."

When Geno takes the podium, a twentysomething male TV reporter in a black leather trenchcoat asks him if it was satisfying to beat a team that he hates. The question has a "Senator, when did you stop beating your wife?" tone, exacerbated by the fact that the Hartford-based reporter is no regular at UConn games.

"I don't think it's hatred," Geno says contemptuously. "I think the phrase was 'don't like'. I think it's good to have a healthy unlike for your opponent. Any other questions?"

"From me?" the reporter asks.

"Yeah," Geno replies. "Because you got an angle, and I want to know what it is. 'Tennessee got screwed,' is that what it is?"

The reporter is nonplussed—this is a side of the coach few reporters ever see—but answers. "It's just that call late in the game," he says. "You wanna see players decide it."

"You do wanna see players decide it," Geno agrees. "The players did decide it."

Someone restores the amicable mood, asking a question about Shea. "I thought Shea was tremendous in the leadership department," he says, "and we needed that without Sveta."

The 37 minutes represent the most Shea, whose knees are now packed in ice, has ever played in one game at UConn. She actually asked to come out for a breather in the second half "and she never asks to come out", Geno says.

Shea has come full circle in this series.

Two hours later Geno, the team, and a few close friends are dining at Hot Tomato's, a popular Italian eatery near the HCC. There's a 'Baby, it's cold outside' warmth to being here, to peering out at the frosty white night and knowing that you're warm, well-fed, and satisfied with a job well-done.

Katie Post of Nike is here again, with her husband Josh. In fact, Post who is based at Nike's headquarters in Beaverton, Oregon, has been a frequent and corporately conscientious visitor to the Nutmeg State since the very first day of practice.

In September Nike assigned Post, 27, to be its women's college basketball field manager. A former player at Division II Portland (Oregon) State, Post's duty is to foster Nike's relationship with the 100-plus Division I schools in its fold. Katie Post was at the first practice. She was, in fact, the first person there on that October Saturday morning after Shea Ralph. She returned to Hartford for UConn's first game, against Georgia. She was in Seattle over Thanksgiving for the Washington game. She was in Chicago ten days ago.

Tonight Post is sporting a pair of retro plaid slacks that garner much attention. "You look like Jack Ramsey," Geno says, referring to the former Portland Trail Blazers coach renowned for his garish outfits in the Seventies. "Where can I get a pair of those Ramseys?"

"Coach," Post good-naturedly protests, "you're killing me."

Katie Post's easy demeanor only amplifies the teasing. Earlier she told a few people at the table about her own playing days; about playing in the Division II championship game in Fargo and losing to the University of North Dakota. Afterward she and a few of her underage teammates visited a liquor store to curb their woes, and the proprietor said, "Hey, I know you. You're the girls from Portland State," and sold them the beer anyway. It was a funny tale but all anyone at the table seems to retain is that the game had been played in Fargo. Soon Katie Post has a new nickname.

"Hey, Fargo," Kathy Auriemma says, "pass the garlic bread."

"You're killin' me," Post objects with an air of cheerful resignation.

If you were walking past Hot Tomato's on this frigid night, you would see some strange sights. Across the street Rita

Williams's car is in the process of being towed. The team bus, filled with the Husky players and Rita, are in the midst of a comical, low-speed pursuit of the towtruck. Just outside the restaurant entrance, the twentysomething TV reporter in the black leather trenchcoat stands sentry in the blizzard with a cameraman, in hopes of getting a live interview with Sveta. Inside you would see a table filled with laughter, and people blithely unconcerned about how they will find their way home this evening.

At the head of that table is a youthfully handsome middle-aged man. He muses about the past year, a period in which he coached on three different continents. The various teams with which he was associated won a national championship in North America, a Junior World Cup Qualifying Tournament in South America, and an Olympic gold medal in Australia, while achieving a combined record of 46-1. His current edition of Huskies is 9-0 and ranked number one. He is exactly where he wants to be tonight and in life. He grins the grin of someone who has had a very good year.

Sunday, December 31 . . . If Kathy Auriemma has one complaint about her husband, it is his chronic tardiness. This morning he was reading the newspaper in his kitchen 20 minutes before practice. Gampel is roughly a 20-minute drive from the Auriemma home in Manchester.

"G! Go!" she ordered.

He left. "Geno," sighs Kathy, "has no transition game."

The calendar and the millennia are in transition. Svetlana Abrosimova is excited because in her homeland New Year's Eve is a more anticipated holiday than Christmas. "It is a big deal, New Year's," Sveta will tell you. "When the clock strikes midnight, it is tradition to jump into the new year."

So it is that on 11:59 p.m. Sveta, Morgan Valley, Keirsten Walters, and manager Kathryn Fieseler all find themselves perched on Sveta's queen-size bed at the Quality Inn in Vernon. They are about to leap to the floor and into 2001. Sveta, who has reluctantly been popping muscle relaxant pills four times daily since returning to Connecticut— "I don't like taking them," she says. "They make me drowsy"—has temporarily forgotten her back woes.

"This is what we do in St. Petersburg," she tells them. "It is a big celebration."

For the members of the UConn Huskies, the Quality Inn is their home away from home away from home. The University of Connecticut does not begin its spring semester until January 24. Like many schools in New England, the university hibernates during January.

The dorms and cafeterias shut down as well, necessitating a move off-campus for the school's winter sports teams. For the past few years the women's basketball team has been lodged about 15 miles off campus at the Quality Inn, known affectionately by the players as "The Qual".

"I love The Qual!" says Morgan Valley, echoing the sentiment of the freshmen. "I get my own double bed and I only have to share my bathroom with one person."

The Qual is, more than anything else, a litmus test of team chemistry. For nearly a month it places all of the Huskies within close quarters (all reside on the same floor) with no academic obligations. Basketball is the only scheduled activity, and the temperatures rarely climb above freezing. Indoor distractions must be found. The nearby Buckland Hills Mall becomes a favorite destination as does a local multiplex theater.

Back inside Sveta and Keirsten's room, the clock strikes midnight. All four of them leap off the bed and into a new year. The trio of players have a uniform reaction: "Ow!" It's as if all of a sudden they remember that they have injuries. Keirsten has an injured shoulder. Morgan tore the medial meniscus in her right knee two weeks ago and has missed the last two games. And Sveta has her back problems.

"That was not smart to do," says Sveta, as they lay on the floor, laughing and groaning.

A few minutes later, Keirsten disappears. She has a surprise in store for Sveta. Outside in the hallway a few Huskies are lingering.

"It's time," says Keirsten, rounding everyone up. They had hatched the plan a few days earlier for all of them to contribute to a cash gift for Svetlana. Her parents, who earn the equivalent of approximately $1,700 annually, have never seen their daughter play for UConn in person.

Sveta's parents will come for the first time in late February, for Senior Night. For years Sveta has scrimped and saved. As a scholarship athlete, she cannot work but she can hoard the meal money that she receives when the Huskies go on road trips. Fans have sent in hundreds of dollars to assist her, but that is an NCAA violation. What is not against the rules is for an athlete's teammates to present her a gift.

Thus Keirsten enters the room followed by the rest of the Huskies. Sveta looks up in surprise, wondering what is up. "Here, this is for you," says Keirsten, handing Sveta an envelope.

Inside the envelope is a wad of cash. Tears well up in Sveta's eyes. They have gotten to her. Svetlana is so incomparable on the court and so confident off it that many of her teammates, talented as they are, find her difficult to get to know well. She is the team's DiMaggio. She is to them what they are to the rest of the state: an icon.

Sveta hugs her teammates. She cannot believe what they have done for her. Neither can her parents, whom she phones to share the good news.

"Eighty-five dollars?" Ludmila asks in Russian. "Eighty-five?"

"No," her daughter responds, also in her native tongue. "Eight hundred and fifty dollars!"

JANUARY

Monday, January 1 . . . Rosemary Ragle is a woman in need of an assist. Ragle, the team's athletic trainer, is treating four players who cannot practice today and a fifth, Svetlana Abrosimova, who is running very gingerly.

Morgan Valley is mending her torn medial meniscus. Ashley Battle, who tore her left elbow versus Miami, will not return this season. Keirsten Walters, with her right shoulder, is a longtime regular. The latest player to dock in sick bay is Maria Conlon, who has mononucleosis.

If you were to ask Ragle which one of her five current patients tax her the most, she would name a sixth. "Swin," she says.

"Swin's the kind of patient," remarks Keirsten, the aspiring orthopedic surgeon, "to whom I'd say, 'Come back in an hour.'"

Swin is high-maintenance, but she is high-performance, too. A French poodle trapped in a Dalmation's body. She leads the Huskies in rebounds and is second in scoring, and for all of her neediness—a box of tissues is set on the scorer's table each practice for her—she never misses a practice or a game.

You have to know how to handle her. Marci Czel roomed with Swin one year and called it "a miserable experience". But Sue Bird, who now rooms with Swin, has a better understanding of the Swin Rules. For example, Swin prefers the room to be hot. Sue does not argue. But most nights when they go to sleep, Sue takes the remote thermostat control to bed with her, slowly and steadily turning down the heat as she snuggles beneath her comforter.

Tamika Williams combats Swin with humor. If Swin starts yapping too much about something that's bothering her,

Tamika puts a hand above Swin's head and mimes that she is sprinkling fairy dust on it. The joke is a reference to the film *Beetlejuice*, in which a mute tribesmen sprinkles magic dust onto the heads of people whom he finds tiresome. Their heads shrink to walnut-size.

"Are you Beetlejuicing me?" Swin asks in mock anger—but she gets the message.

Geno has no want of *Beetlejuice* dust for this afternoon's practice. Tomorrow the Huskies play Georgetown, against whom Geno has a career record of 27-3. He takes his players through their regular drills, including one called "Eleven Spots." The Huskies react to the words "eleven spots" the way first-graders do to the word "recess."

Here is how the drill works: Five minutes on the clock. Three-pointers are worth two points, two-pointers are worth one. The team as a whole must score 25 points. The drill is full-court transition chaos, a series of back-and-forth, three-on-two situations.

If this were a squad of something less than A-type personalities, a coach would have to guard against the fact that the defense may relent in order to help the offense score 25 points (the 25 being the sum of hoops scored at both baskets). However, the players know that Geno watches them even more intently on defense.

Nobody lets up. Today, in the final few seconds, the score is stuck on 23. Sue Bird finds the ball in her hands as she dribbles past midcourt. Arriving above the three-point line at the top of the key, she jump stops then launches a three. Basket, 25 points.

"Sue usually hits the big shots," says Maria, who is watching from a first-row seat.

Next the Huskies do free throws, hitting 79%, so they run. After everyone shoots another ten, Kathryn Fieseler announces the tally to Geno. "Ninety-seven percent," she says.

"You guys are lying," he says with a sly grin. "Now you're going to run 'cuz you piss me off. You shoulda' got ninety-seven before."

In fact, they were lying. On the preceding set, Marci Czel had shot 5-8 and reported that she had made eight. Sue had shot 7-8 and reported nine. The UConn Huskies cut corners occasionally, too. Geno is too keen an observer not to notice this duplicity, but he lets it slide.

The day ends with a scrimmage. With all the wounded unable to play, Stacy Hansmeyer is pressed into service. She misses playing with her former teammates immensely. The feeling is not mutual. Once she steps onto the court, Stacy disappears and Bam Bam emerges.

Thrice this afternoon Bam Bam bangs Kelly Schumacher to the floor. After the third collision Schuey chucks the basketball at her coach's legs.

A few minutes later Sveta, who has been receiving electric probe treatments to combat her back spasms, has the ball on a breakaway. Bam Bam gives chase and knocks Sveta to the ground as she attempts the layup. Sveta gives Stacy a withering look as if to say: I'm an All-American. Was that really necessary?

Stacy is no longer a player, a reality that is difficult to face. "I'd like to play in Europe if I got the chance," she will tell you, but the likelihood is that her playing days ended when the Phoenix Mercury cut her last May. Her enthusiasm, personability, and UConn pedigree have paved a fine future for her in coaching. But she longs to play. Stacy is struggling with her transition game.

Tuesday, January 2 . . . Matt Eagan played Little League baseball while growing up in Wolcott, Connecticut. He was a pitcher. Once a batter stepped up to the plate to face Eagan unaware, or worse, unconcerned, that he was standing on home plate.

Noticing the *faux pas*, young Eagan stepped off the mound and motioned to the home plate umpire, who did nothing. "But his toes are on home plate!" young Eagan cried.

"You worry about the pitching," said the ump, "and I'll worry about the umpiring."

Eagan walked back to the mound. Toed the rubber. And beaned the hapless boy.

"What was I supposed to do?" Eagan asks.

Eagan, 32, is in his second season on the Husky beat and is one of the sharper minds in the Herde. There are as many writers who regularly cover the Huskies as there are Huskies, a unique situation in women's college basketball. Because of mismatches such as tonight's 107-45 annihilation of Georgetown,

Diana Taurasi: only her brunette mane is wound tightly. Number 3 converted a team-high 71 threes during her freshman season.

Sveta and Shea wait to hear their names called at the Hartford Civic Center in January. It would be their last home start together.

"I'd take Sue Bird and four others," said ESPN basketball commentator Mike Patrick in 2000— during a men's game, "and go to war any day." The junior from Syosset, N.Y., is the two-time winner of the Nancy Lieberman-Cline Award honoring the nation's top point guard.

Asjha Jones puts up a shot between two Colorado State University defenders in the second round of the NCAAs.

Svetlana Abrosimova, before and after her injury. When the Russian native enrolled at UConn in August of 1997, her English was suspect. Four years later she could often be seen tutoring her freshman teammates while still finding time to respond, in English, to all of her voluminous mail.

In his first game as UConn's coach in 1985, Geno received two technical fouls. More than 400 victories later, he is more judicious though no less animated on the bench:

Exasperated--"D! Who was that pass to?!?"; in control of the situation; and worn down from the trials of a tougher season than he expected.

Proudly greeting Marci Czel as she walks off the Gampel Pavilion court— to a standing ovation—for the final time.

Geno hugs Tamika Williams as she jogs off the court. A former USA Today National High School Player of the Year, Tamika rarely starts and never complains. She is the embodiment of one of Geno's favorite mantras: "Know your role, shut your hole".

The 2000-01 University of Connecticut Huskies women's basketball team: (front row, left to right) Associate Head Coach Chris Dailey, Maria Conlon, Kennitra Johnson, Keirsten Walters, Svetlana Abrosimova, Shea Ralph, Marci Czel, Sue Bird, Ashley Battle, Head Coach Geno Auriemma; (top row, left to right) Assistant Coach Tonya Cardoza, Diana Taurasi, Swin Cash, Asjha Jones, Kelly Schumacher, Christine Rigby, Jessica Moore, Tamika Williams, Morgan Valley, Graduate Assistant Coach Stacy Hansmeyer, Assistant Coach Jamelle Elliott.

Svetlana leads a high-five ring that includes (from left) Morgan Valley, Tamika Williams and Swin Cash (#32).

Swin Cash strikes like lightning in the low post. On February 20th she had 20 points and 20 rebounds in just 26 minutes versus West Virginia. Here, against Colorado State, she reaches for one of her game-high 11 rebounds.

Shea Ralph stares down opposing players as a means of intimidation. "I look them in the eye," says the fifth-year senior, "and they usually look in the other direction."

there is ample time during the games themselves to get to know these people.

Randy Smith, for example. R. Smith is a Runyonesque character. He is the wordsmith and, at 51, the senior member of the Herde. R. Smith has been writing for *The Manchester Journal-Inquirer* for 30 years. He'll never forget his first day of employment, February 1, 1971. "I arrive into work at 5:30 a.m.," he says, "and there's a sign on my desk that says 'WELCOME ABAORD.' I thought to myself, I can help these people."

The Herde are a chummy gang. Road trips find them making dinner reservations for tables of twelve to eighteen. Their amity is the product of a few factors: first, it's always more fun to cover a winner; second, they enjoy the players.

"Debbie Baer [class of '92] was as adorable as they come," says Carl Adamec, speaking of the former brunette point guard who played on UConn's first Final Four team. "We'd ask her questions like, 'Debbie, are you smarter than the average Baer?' and she would just giggle."

Most of all, though, they enjoy Geno. This phenomenon that he has created, well, it's unheard of in women's hoops. "When he [Geno] leaves," says Carl, "I'm leaving."

Swin Cash jumps center to start tonight's game at Gampel and taps it to Shea Ralph, who finds Sveta Abrosimova streaking downcourt with a bounce pass. The score is 2-0 Huskies. Seven seconds have elapsed. Nykesha Sales's final UConn basket was as well-defended.

Georgetown has not come to play. Shea has. In the first three minutes of the game she scores nine points and collects two assists and steals each. The Herde on press row, who believe that her best days are behind her, nevertheless cherish this moment. She is playing like the Shea of old.

"She was the best freshman I ever saw," says R. Smith during the game's first timeout. "She invented the 70-foot drive to the basket. Shea had star written all over her."

"She had balls," says Scott Gray, who does play-by-play on WTIC-AM radio.

"That's it," agrees R. Smith. "She had balls."

At halftime the numbers tell the by-now mundane tale of a squad that seems peerless. The Huskies have virtually doubled the Hoyas on the scoreboard, leading 59-30. Their 22 field goals have come via 20 assists. They are shooting 64.7%. And yet nine players played at least nine minutes, or virtually half, of the first half.

With eleven seconds remaining the Huskies lead, 105-45, and Diana Taurasi has the ball on the break. For the entire second half she has heeded Geno's warnings to slow the pace of the game (*i.e.*, score less), but you cannot ask Seattle Slew to trot forever.

Diana dribbles to the top of the key, hesitates, then drives left. Reaching the left elbow of the free throw line, she puts the ball in her left hand and spins backwards, counterclockwise. Ninety degrees into her turn, facing the left sideline, the ball leaves her left hand and floats across the free-throw lane, hitting Kelly Schumacher in stride at chest level. Schuey catches it and makes the layup. The fans—heck, Geno, too—are still shaking their heads in disbelief as the buzzer sounds.

"It's fun to watch, even for me," Geno says afterward. "I enjoyed watching tonight, I really did."

"You're trying to build the perfect team, the perfect season," says R. Smith, "and you're amazed by this?"

"Yeah, I really am," Geno says. "You don't expect to be playing all that well, but this is a really unique group of kids."

He may be the last convert in the building. But he is beginning to see the light. "I actually have said, 'We're the greatest team ever,' but always in sarcastic ways," says Geno. "All I've said sincerely is, we have set out to become one of, if not the, greatest team ever."

Two-thirds of Florida's unbeatable three-on-three team, Shea and Sveta, enter the interview room. Tonight Rutgers and Tennessee, both Women's Final Four entrants last season, are playing in Madison Square Garden. As Shea and Sveta make their way into the classroom, T.C. Karmel of *The Willimantic Press* wonders aloud, "Who won the Rutgers-Tennessee game?"

"Rutgers," answers Sveta as she passes the reporter, "by five points."

Karmel's eyes become saucers.

"She's lying," Adamec says.

Sveta giggles mischievously. Shea, who in her last two games is averaging 17 points (she had 19 tonight) and zero turnovers, answers every question patiently. Shea may inwardly bristle at the questions she receives, but she is unfailingly polite and respectful. As opposed to Sveta, who had only been in the United States for a month when she said to Chris Dailey of the press, "But they ask such stupid questions," to which CD replied, "I knew you were smart."

Tonight should be an easy interrogation for Shea, given her stellar play over the last month. She battles the knee pain constantly. Marsha Lake had brought some prescription pain killers with her from Florida, handing them to Kathryn Fieseler after the contest with the admonition, "These cost a hundred and twenty-six dollars. Tell Shea if she loses them, she's dead."

Shea can battle the pains and ills to a stalemate, but there is one foe she cannot shake: the Herde's memories of her younger self. She grows weary of the comparisons, of fighting a battle that is impossible to win.

"The last two games," asks one reporter, "have you felt like the old Shea?"

"You're like the eighteenth person to ask me that question," she says.

Mike DiMauro tries a different approach. "You played thirty-seven minutes on Saturday," he says. "Did you feel it in the knees?"

"Thirty-seven minutes is more than I'm used to playing," Shea replies.

"So that's a . . . "

She stares at him for a moment. She knows what they want, but they will never get weakness or pain from her. Will never get that admission.

"That's my answer."

Wednesday, January 3 . . . Stacy Hansmeyer hails from Norman, Oklahoma, home of the University of Oklahoma Sooners. Stacy's former high school coach, Sherri Coale, now coaches the Sooners' women's basketball team. Tonight Stacy and her younger sister, Crystal, who is visiting, are parked in front of the TV at The Qual, as the top-ranked and undefeated OU football team plays Florida State in the Orange Bowl for the national championship

"It's just," says Stacy, "the biggest night of my life."

Shortly after 9:00 p.m., with the Sooners nursing a 3-0 lead, Diana Taurasi enters and says, "Shea's sick."

Stacy goes to check on Shea Ralph, who is lying on the bathroom floor, shivering. Tamika Williams is holding her, covering her with blankets in an effort to raise her body temperature. Shea is freezing and weak, having vomited or suffered from diarrhea much of the last few hours.

"Stacy," she says, "I'm scared."

Earlier that day Shea and Stacy had gone to Buckland Hills mall to kill a few hours. They lunched on sushi. Now Shea believes that the raw fish has given her food poisoning.

Kathryn Fieseler is dispatched to go to a drug store and get Pepto-Bismol. She sprints down the hallway at The Qual, a frantic look on her face. Swin Cash, unaware that Shea is sick, spots Kathryn running toward the door. "Kathryn," Swin says, "can you get me some chocolate chip cookies?"

Kathryn ignores her, keeps running. When she returns, Shea looks no better. Stacy ponders whether to phone Geno, who lives nearby. Meanwhile players are milling outside Shea's room. "Eating sushi from *the mall*? Damn, what was she thinking?"

At 11:30 p.m. Stacy finally relents and phones Geno. He tells them to meet him at the hospital, where Shea is given intravenous fluid and is prescribed antibiotics. It is only a scare, but the players will not forget what they saw.

"Shea is the strongest person on the team," says Sveta Abrosimova, "and she looked like she was dying."

Friday, January 5 . . . Stacy Hansmeyer is playing Pygmalion with Morgan Valley. Stacy, who can go from Bam Bam to glam with ease, is intrigued by the freshman from Colchester, Vermont. Morgan does not wear makeup or style her hair beyond shampoo and a brush. She owns more pairs of sweats than she does skirts, and if ESPN's *SportsCenter* did not exist, she probably wouldn't watch television.

Stacy has taken Moe under her wing, though, and is determined to turn her into a lady. "It all started when I realized that Moe had taken my number [20]," says Stacy, "and that really brings it home that you're history. But Moe has my locker, too. She even stretches in the same spot on the floor where I used to stretch. It's eerie."

In Morgan Valley Stacy sees her past. "When I started college, I was set in my ways," she says. "But by the end of my freshman year I realized how much fun I'd had. It's all about trying new things."

Last night Stacy and her sister, Crystal, gave Morgan a makeover. Stacy applied the make-up, and Crystal did her hair. Stacy lent her an outfit. "They tried to get me to pluck my eyebrows," says Moe, "but that's never going to happen."

When they were done, Stacy called the rest of the team to her room to witness the transformation of Morgan Valley. "You look good, girl," Swin Cash said, and that made Morgan feel good.

After Geno, nobody makes more of an impact on a player during her years in Storrs than the upperclassman who takes her under her wing freshman year. "I will always feel like a freshman when I'm around Rebecca Lobo," Kelley Hunt, who was a freshman during Lobo's celebrated senior season, will later tell me. "She'd always stop by my room before she went out, would always include me in anything she was doing. She taught me a lot."

Before today's 1:30 p.m. practice Shea Ralph can be found slumped on the floor in Rosemary Ragle's increasingly crowded training room. She will not tell the media about her bout with food poisoning nor will any of her teammates ("Know your role, shut your hole" is a popular Geno mantra). She only hopes that she quickly recovers.

Though Shea is at practice, she is not vocal today. Shea Dog, as they call her, or just Dog, looks sick as one. Geno, with a game looming on Sunday at Louisiana Tech, the Little Big Horn of women's college basketball outposts, picks up the slack. On a fastbreak drill Diana Taurasi dribbles to the top of the key and makes a rare I'm-looking-right-at-you pass to Sveta Abrosimova, who drains the three-pointer. "That was great," encourages Geno, clapping. "Good job. Really good."

On the next play Sveta gets the ball on the right wing beyond the three-point line. She pump fakes, drawing her defender into the air, and drives right by her. Sveta pulls up for an eight-foot jumper, but her shot falls embarrassingly short, barely grazing the bottom of the rim.

"I like that move, Sveta," he says.

"Thanks."

"Just make that shot. Make a great move like that, that was a shitty shot."

Sveta smirks. After four years she can anticipate the wise-cracks.

The team breaks for free throws. Today Kelly Schumacher and Sveta are put under surveillance. Both shoot 7 of 8 but both report nine. After practice sports information director Ann Marie Person asks the media if they need any one-on-ones with players. "I need Morgan," says Rachel McLoughlin of *The Connecticut Post*. "And then I'll need a backup in case she does-n't talk."

The Herde gather 'round the quote trough that is Geno. He has a healthy level of anxiety about the visit to Ruston. It will be UConn's third nationally televised game of the season, this time on ESPN2. The Huskies played at Louisiana Tech (or "La. Tech") once, in 1999, and lost 90-76. It is their worst defeat of the past six-plus seasons. And as for the southern hospitality . . .

"The last time we played there, they [the Huskies] heard things they've never heard before, in a way they've never heard before," Geno says. "People are nasty down there. I just hope one of the refs looks familiar."

Saturday, January 6 . . . Sarah Darras, the Huskies' highly reli-able administrative assistant, is the first person to arrive at the charter-flights terminal at Bradley International Airport this morning. Never mind that Sarah lives furthest from the airport and is four months pregnant.

Sarah Darras is a chronically prepared woman. When, for example, she drove 100 miles from her then home in Fairfield, Connecticut, to UConn for her job interview in 1994, she stopped at a McDonald's a few miles from campus, changing from sweats into a business suit. "My suit would have gotten wrinkled during the drive," she says, "and I didn't want to look sloppy."

Shortly after 2:00 p.m. the Husky plane touches down in sunny and warm Monroe, Louisiana. The tiny town of Ruston, home of Louisiana Tech, lies 30 miles west. The team buses directly from Monroe to La. Tech's Thomas Assembly Center, an intimate (capacity 8,000) arena whose hardwood floor was laid directly on top of cement. La. Tech's legendary coach, Leon

Barmore, retired at the age of 56 last April in part because of chronic back pain attributed to the floor.

Barmore's retirement lasted 17 days. It had been assumed that Kim Mulkey-Robertson, his assistant for the past 15 years and a Women's Basketball Hall of Fame inductee as a Lady Techster player, would succeed him. However, La. Tech offered Mulkey-Robertson a four-year contract when a five-year deal would have vested her for a pension. Feeling betrayed, she accepted the vacant head coaching job at Baylor University in Waco, Texas.

"They were willing to sacrifice the future of Lady Techster basketball," said clearly miffed former La. Tech president F. Jay Taylor, "for one additional contract year."

Or maybe they, the administration, gambled that Barmore cared too much to walk away. He received more than 50 phone calls pleading with him to stay. One was from Pat Summitt, the only coach with more Final Fours—12—in her past than his nine.

"Pat Summitt called," says Barmore, "and told me I still had too much to give to get out."

Barmore, a graduate of Ruston High School and a three-year starter on La. Tech's men's team as a walk-on, was loath to see his life's work come unhinged so quickly. So, 17 days into his golden years, he retired from retirement.

"I enjoyed it but you can only play golf so many days in a row," says Barmore. "But everyone should try it for two weeks at least."

Mulkey-Robertson, meanwhile, made a good choice. She has the Lady Bears of Baylor undefeated thus far.

Inside the arena Geno addresses the players before practice. "It's always a challenge when you come here to play," he tells them. "Last time we weren't up to the challenge."

The girls begin stretching, and Geno heads over to the scorer's table, where Keirsten Walters is talking to Rosemary Ragle. "Keirsten," he says, leaning over the table, "I need a minute."

"I need a minute" is Husky code for "shoulder massage, please". Many of the players and coaches indulge in this, Geno not the least of them. Unfortunately for Keirsten, also a fan of the shoulder massage, she gives better than she gets. Her magic fingers are frequently pressed into service.

"I'm going to start charging for this," Keirsten sighs as she begins kneading his deltoid muscles.

As Geno succumbs to relaxation, Tom Tedesco enters the arena looking very tense. "We can't find coach's travel bag," he confides to Sarah. "I know we put it on the plane but we can't find it in the bus's cargo hold."

Geno is an impeccable dresser—he has his own tailor—and Ruston's only department store is a Target. It is after 5:00 p.m., too late to ship a suit from home. Plus, tomorrow night's game is on national television.

Geno handles the news with grace. After practice he finds the one men's store that is still open. A sale is about to be made when Tom, who had been scouring the cargo hold, locates the wardrobe bag behind a stack of metal trunks bearing video equipment.

"I've got it," Tom cries, sprinting down the quiet street toward the men's store. Ruining one salesman's day, but salvaging his.

Sunday, January 7 . . . Pat Babcock is UConn's associate athletic director and women's senior administrator. She is also a woman who is not afraid to admit she was wrong. "I wanted a woman to coach the team," says Babcock, who cast the lone dissenting vote among the six-person search committee entrusted to hire a women's basketball coach in 1985. "I still would like to see women coach women. But I do think we have the best coach in the country."

Babcock sits in the stands at the Thomas Assembly Center on this drizzly morning during the Huskies' shootaround. For the past 16 seasons, she has enjoyed being along for the ride on which Geno has taken UConn. She is the lone person from the search committee still employed at the school.

"In the early days there were never more than fifty people at a game in the Fieldhouse," says Babcock, "and it's true, the roof leaked. For the women's game, they'd put a bucket in the corner [just out of bounds] to catch leaks in the roof. For mens' games, though, they stationed someone with a towel to catch each drop that hit the floor."

If it sounds as if Babcock is sensitive about the disparities between men's and women's college athletics, she is. "If it weren't for some of Geno's successes," she says, "we wouldn't even be employed. Because of women's basketball, all but two of our women's sports are fully funded."

The success of the program still astounds Babcock. "Where else," she asks, "do you see people line up an hour and a half before the doors open for a game when they have reserved seats?"

Out on the floor, practice has ended. Kelly Schumacher is entertaining her teammates by attempting to dunk. There seems little chance of that, though, as she is still not fully recovered from her stress fracture and this court has no bounce. Being Schuey, she dunks it.

Geno just shakes his head. "How come she can't jump that high with a jump shot?" he asks, generating laughs.

Babcock takes it all in. "If he were oh-and-twenty every year," she says, "he wouldn't be very funny."

There are five truly intimidating venues in women's college basketball. They are UConn's Gampel Pavilion and Hartford Civic Center (where the Huskies are 162-15 and 19-2, respectively), Rutgers' Louis Brown Athletic Center (aka the RAC), Tennessee's Thompson-Boling Arena (home of the record 69-game win streak), and the Thomas Assembly Center, where La. Tech has won 35 of the last 36 games.

What separates the Thomas Assembly Center from the other four is that the Huskies have played and won at the other sites. Here, the Huskies are 0-1.

This game has the recipe for an upset. National television, a congested arena and a spirited student cheering section whose behavior belies the fact that Lincoln Parish is a dry county. The opening tip lands in Svetlana Abrosimova's hands in the front-court. She passes it to Sue Bird, who is standing in the back-court. Turnover, backcourt violation, UConn. The Huskies quickly get the ball back, but Swin Cash travels. Two turnovers only 30 seconds into the game.

Geno refuses to get rattled. But as the half continues the Huskies appear frustrated, less by their own errors than by La. Tech's deliberate, half-court play. The Lady Techsters' strategy is to concede the rebound on the offensive end to UConn, sending three guards back on defense with every shot attempt. At half-time La. Tech has only five offensive boards but trail only by eight, 37-29.

Only Swin looks unstoppable, scoring 14 points and grabbing 10 rebounds while putting the defensive clamps on Tech's leading scorer, Ayana Walker. The second half features the same plodding play. La. Tech's commitment to a halfcourt game is exacerbated by the officials' commitment to calling fouls. A sum of 40, or one per minute, will be called tonight.

"Do you realize that the number one team in the country traveled all the way down here to play on national television," Geno tells referee Robyn Ensminger after she whistles a foul on UConn away from the basket, "and you're making an embarrassment of yourself?"

Unable to run, due to both La. Tech's three-women-back scheme and the stoppages in play from foul calls, UConn's three ballhandlers—Shea Ralph, Sue and Sveta—seem stifled. Sue particularly so. With five minutes remaining and UConn leading, 58-49, the nation's premier point guard has no points or assists. She finishes with one assist and six points via a pair of inconsequential three-pointers. But UConn has a 71-55 victory

When Barmore enters the interview room, he looks spent. "Our assistant coaches usually keep track of fouls to try to get someone on the other team to foul out," he says in response to a question about Swin. "I told them not to worry about that tonight. They got eight others on the bench who can play.

"I feel like Richard Widmark," Barmore says, an acceptance of the defeat seeping into his words. "You remember that movie, *The Alamo*?"

Geno is grateful to be the last man standing in this duel. He's leaving Ruston with his boots on, and in his own suit. Two Louisiana writers approach Geno to thank him for bringing his team to Ruston. "You're always welcome here, coach," one of them says.

"Thanks, thanks a lot," he replies.

It is an ugly victory, but the Huskies are 10-0, and the possibilities are still limitless. As the team buses back to the Holiday

Inn, they pass a Pizza Hut. "Look," Sue announces with longing in her voice, "a Pizza Hut."

Geno does not motion for the bus driver to stop. Sue's response to the silence is to wait a few seconds before saying, "Oops, we passed it."

Up in the front seat, Geno gets the last word. "That," he says in a low growl, "is about the only thing Sue passed tonight."

Monday, January 8 . . . Roy and Marsha Lake arrive in Syracuse, N.Y., shortly after the Huskies do. UConn has flown directly from Ruston for a Big East conference game tomorrow night against Syracuse University. Roy and Marsha have traveled from their home in the Sunshine State to the city that, according to the U.S. Weather Service, receives less sunlight than any other in the country. For Marsha this is her second visit to the frigid northeast to see her daughter play in less than a week.

Shea Ralph has magnetic properties. She brought Roy and Marsha Lake here. She also brought them together five years ago. The very idea of her, however, was what originally repelled them from one another more than 25 years earlier. In the early Seventies both were students at the University of North Carolina. She was Marsha Mann, No. 44, a 6'0" All-American. He was a 5'8" hellraiser. They dated for a year and a half.

"As we got closer to graduating," says Marsha, "I knew that I wanted to get married and start a family. I said, 'Roy, it's time to make decisions.'"

Roy decided to move to Hawaii. Marsha wed Perry Lewis, a tennis pro six years older than her. Lewis is Shea's biological father. Marsha divorced him after two years and moved to Fayetteville, North Carolina, where she earned a master's degree in mathematics and then taught at a local community college. There she met and wed another teacher in the math department, Bob Ralph.

That marriage soured when Shea was a sophomore in high school. Marsha and Bob were divorced. To this day Bob Ralph keeps in touch with Shea. As for Shea's biological father, "Perry chose not to be a part of our life," says Marsha. "He saw her play twice in high school, but he hasn't seen her since."

Roy Lake also saw Shea play in high school, though he did not realize it at first. Living in Florida at the time, he was watching the Sunshine Network, a Florida-based cable sports channel. A girls' high school basketball game was being shown, and he was about to flip the channel when he realized that it was being played in Carmichael Auditorium, the University of North Carolina's fabled basketball arena.

Lake kept watching. Then he saw this blonde, pony-tailed girl step to the line to shoot free throws. He saw a ghost. That must be Marsha's daughter, he thought. Has to be.

It was. Shea was a sophomore at Terry Sanford High, which was playing for the state championship. Roy did some digging and obtained Marsha's phone number.

He called. They spoke. Then she wrote him a letter, saying "My husband is a dud." Roy thought it read, "My husband is a dude." He did not reply.

Two years passed. Roy got divorced. One day he was perusing USA Today and spotted the full-page photo of Shea Ralph in which she was being hailed as the National High School Player of the Year.

Roy phoned once more. Shea answered. "Shea, my name is Roy Lake, and I'm a friend of your mother's," he said. "I just wanted to congratulate you on being named player of the year."

"Thanks," she said. "Okay, 'bye."

Roy assumed that Shea would tell her mother that he had called. She did not. Marsha never knew Roy had phoned, and Roy felt sheepish about phoning again. Six months passed, and once again Roy spotted Shea, this time on television in her first game at UConn. She played terrific, scoring 13 points in 24 minutes against Western Kentucky. Roy was moved to phone Marsha. One last time.

This time he got her. By the time they finally reunited in person, Marsha, who had just driven Shea home from Connecticut for the Christmas holidays her freshman year, was in no mood for a long courtship. "Roy," she told him that night, exhausted from an 18-hour drive, "I'm too old to play games."

Six months later the two college sweethearts, now in their forties, were wed.

Tuesday, January 9 . . . In the trophy case at Manley Field House is the game ball from when Syracuse defeated UConn 62-59 in 1996. It is one of only three Big East defeats the Huskies have suffered in the past six seasons. In the six games since that defeat UConn has beaten the Orangewomen by an average of 38 points.

Manley Fieldhouse is reminiscent of the Huskies' former homecourt. A track encircles the court, and pullout bleachers accommodate the 2,024-plus fans, half of whom appear to be girls' high school teams en masse. A bearded blond man looking the part of the eternal graduate student sits right behind press row. "C'mon, Syracuse," he exhorts, "let's make these idiots rewrite their stories."

Syracuse, despite its 7-5 record, seems up to the task. Late in the first half the Orangewomen trail only by three, 22-19, when Shea is whistled for her second offensive foul. Geno, already choleric from a half in which the Huskies will shoot just two free throws in the first 19 minutes, rises from the bench and says something to referee Nan Sisk. She rewards him with his first technical foul of the season. Chris Dailey quickly rises and blocks Geno from advancing further. CD is 8-0 in games that she has either finished for Geno or coached herself due to his absence. She has no want of testing that streak this evening.

Only last night Geno told the story of the last time he was ejected from a game, during last year's home opener versus Kentucky at the Hartford Civic Center. What made the tale comical, as Geno retold it, were the visitations he endured in the locker room as if he were Scrooge and it were Christmas eve.

First Lew Perkins, the athletic director, followed him into the UConn locker room. "All you want to do is scream at the top of your lungs," Geno said, "and there's big Lew [Perkins is a colossal 6'5] sitting across from you asking, 'Are you all right?'"

Next Geno's two younger children, Alysa and Mike, ventured in. "What are you doing here?" he asked them.

"Everybody in our section was saying you were nuts," said a tearful Alysa, "so we left."

"Why are you crying?"

"Da-ad," she replied, "you embarrassed me in front of my friends."

Finally, the ghost of Christmas journalism, Randy Smith, entered the locker room. R. Smith, as a member of the media, had no right to be there but by this point Geno had lost the will to protest.

"Randy's saying, 'This isn't good, oh, this is not good,'" Geno recalled, "and I'm like, 'How the hell did *he* get in here?'"

It was funny last night. Nobody is laughing this evening. The Huskies enter halftime with a ten-point lead, 35-25, but they are struggling. Svetlana Abrosimova is scoreless. Whatever malaise infiltrated the Huskies in Ruston has accompanied them north.

UConn opens the second half on a 26-8 run and look to have redeemed themselves. The Huskies have a 28-point lead, led by Diana Taurasi's 14 points, with around nine minutes remaining. That's when Geno begins emptying his bench. And the trouble begins.

Rig allows an entry pass to hit her in the belly. KJ throws a soft pass from the point to Marci Czel on the left wing, who inexplicably allows it to roll through her fingers and out of bounds right next to Geno, who is leaning on one knee. As the ball slithers past, he is a statue, not even moving his eyes to glance at the ball or Marci Czel. His disgust is palpable.

The Huskies win, but Syracuse outscores them by 15 in the last eight minutes. The final score is 76-63. When asked about Syracuse's late surge, their coach, Marianna Freeman, is joyful. "That almost made me cry," she says. "That may be the finest moment in my coaching career."

When Freeman leaves, Geno, Diana, Shea Ralph, and Sveta enter the tiny classroom where the media is encamped. To see the trio of UConn players' anguished faces, to see how they cannot even look at their coach, you'd never know who won.

"We're not playing very well right now," says Geno. "We rely on our talent and I hate that. I hate that. We're just content to run up and down the floor. Just like everybody else. If we're going to be like everybody else, don't call us the best team in the country. Call us the most talented team in the country."

A middle-aged Syracuse-based writer sits no more than five feet from the UConn contingent. He is among the last writers to leave the room and seems to be asking questions more out of his fascination with what he's seeing—a despondent group of winners in women's athletics—than out of a need to procure a quote. "How about you, Diana?" he asks. "Are you enjoying this?"

"Oh yeah, it's wonderful," says Diana. "I mean, everybody goes through a slump. We're going through a slump right now."

The writer chuckles. "You guys define slump a little differently than we do."

"You're right," says Geno. "You're absolutely right. See, if you cover us, the only story you've got is if we play bad or if we lose [*Let's make these idiots rewrite their stories*]. Other than that, it's the same old story."

Afterward, the players return to the court where dozens of schoolgirls await them for autographs. It is nearing 10:00 p.m. and the Huskies are eager to return to The Qual after four days on the road. Still, they graciously sign the items handed to them.

Shea, who scored a career-low three points tonight, is the last one to depart. As she exits the arena into the swirling blizzard, a handful of girls still trail her. She does not know if these girls want an autograph and are afraid to approach her, or are just gazing at her. "Is everyone taken care of?" she asks. "Anybody need me? Is that it?"

Shea waits a moment. Satisfied at last that no one who wanted her signature will go home unhappy tonight, Shea boards the bus. Safely inside, she reaches for a giant stuffed pig and squeezes it to her chest. She is asked about the two offensive foul calls, which were more a by-product of her overpowering her defender than of fouling her. "You know what it is?" says Shea, still angry. "It's punishment for work in the weight room."

She may very well be right. Meanwhile, nearly 3,000 miles away in Yakima, Washington, Teresa Borton's sister, Valerie

Rubright, is giving birth to a baby girl. Valerie's husband, Jason, has already picked out a name for his daughter. They name her Shea.

Thursday, January 11 . . . Geno had given the players Wednesday off—they all needed a break from one another—but on this crisp, clear morning the Huskies are clustered inside their locker room at Gampel at 9:30 a.m.

"I don't know if you know what it means to be champions," Geno tells them before running through the tape. "You gotta knock people out. People aren't going to be knocked out because you walk into the gym. You gotta give a knockout punch or else it's going to be a very long year."

The locker room is located behind the players' lounge. Both rooms are entered through one door that connects to the hallway that circumscribes the court level of Gampel. Inside the players' lounge it is not uncommon to find a parent of a player or Alysa or Michael Auriemma. The lockerroom, though, is sacrosanct. It is a refuge within a refuge for the Huskies.

"We've got people on our team," he continues, "—and I'm not talking about off the court, this is strictly between the white lines—that when things don't go your way, you pout. You pout, and it affects the whole team. And if you were to ask me right now, Who are the people who no matter what happens are consistent and stable? Diana . . . Asjha . . . Sue Bird's getting better at it. Tamika sometimes.

"Swin keeps playing hard, but it's written all over her face," he says. "Svet keeps playing hard, but it's written over *her* face."

He doesn't mention Shea, but by not including her, he has spoken to her the loudest. "You gotta ask yourselves, 'What's our frustration level?'" he says. "If you're going to get frustrated because we don't knock somebody out early, then we're setting ourselves up for a bad fall at the end."

On the back of the lockerroom door are three short sentences. They are the last words that each Husky reads before she strides onto Gampel's court for a game or practice. "Play Hard," "Play Smart," and "Have Fun", they say. At Louisiana Tech and

Syracuse, the Huskies only obeyed the first of the three rules, and even that is open to debate.

"If you're content to be a talented group of players who play well once in a while, then we're just a bunch of talented guys who, when their ankle isn't hurt and they're not having their period and they haven't had a fight with their boyfriend . . . then fine, I'll come to practice with those expectations. But then you better hope we don't have a day like that in March, because the season will be over, and this team will have not played up to its potential.

"Yeah," he reassures them, "we're the most talented team in America. But that may not be good enough. My guess is, after today and tomorrow, we'll be back where we want to be. After two good days of work, we'll be right back where we want to be."

At practice Geno tells them that they need to be conscious of attempting more three-point shots. "Hey, hey, hey, listen up," he says before one shooting drill. "I don't think we shoot enough threes. I think we gotta be the kind of team to shoot twenty to twenty-five three-pointers. Number one, we're athletic enough to get the rebounds and number two, it'll speed up the game a little bit."

UConn's obsession with the three-point shot began shortly after the troubled 1987-88 season. Kerry Bascom, then a freshman who had attempted just three three-pointers that season (and missed 'em all), was shooting around in the Fieldhouse. Geno was watching her, and suddenly he had an idea. He asked her to give him the basketball and told her to go to halfcourt.

"Now run like you're running on a fastbreak," he said, "and I'm going to pass you the ball when you get to the top of the key. I want you to make six out of ten from there."

Kerry made eight of ten.

A month later, back home in Epping, Kerry began a summer fling with the three-point shot. Every night she and her dad, who served as her rebounder, went to the gym. Kerry would pick seven spots around the three-point arc, which is 19'9" from the basket. From each spot she had to make seven of ten shots and, if she failed, she had to start again.

"If I started out oh-for-four from one spot," she recalls, "I'd still have to shoot six more before I could start over again from the same spot. I shot a lot of three-pointers that summer."

The following season, after hitting zero three-pointers as a freshman, Kerry made 60. Ever since the Huskies have been in love with that shot.

To instill a heightened three-point-attempt awareness this morning, Geno has his players scrimmage four-on-four for five minutes at a time. Subtracting a player from each side opens up the court for drives to the basket and/or kick-out passes to players who spot up beyond the three-point line. "What are we going to call this?" he asks. "'Let's Kick their Ass With Threes and Drives'."

The Huskies play to five minutes. With :33 left Diana Taurasi has the ball at the top of the key. She pulls up for a shot but, once airborne, decides to pass. Alas, no one is open. She turns the ball over, tossing it to Nykesha Sales, who races downcourt for an uncontested layup.

"The best high school player in the history of the world," says Geno, "and she costs us the game."

Diana takes the criticism stoically. Her teammates respect her as much for her unflappable nature in the face of Geno's daily barbs as for her prodigious talent. Diana is this season's whipping post, and she handles it with aplomb.

Diana had thrown away three consecutive passes during a practice before the Tennessee game. "I kicked her off the court," he said, "and I look over at her, and she's laughing. I didn't know whether to be angry or to laugh, so I put her back in."

Diana gets along with everyone, but cliques are inevitable on any team. Do they hurt team chemistry? When the Huskies returned to The Qual after the Syracuse game, the players called a meeting to ask one another that very question.

"We talked about it: Are there too many cliques?" Marci Czel says later. "Tamika and Sue were sort of the ringleaders for the meeting."

Shea Ralph was chastised for spending too much time away from the team. "Shea just sat there, not saying much, looking pissed," says Marci Czel.

Morgan Valley was also criticized. "I got called out for hanging out with Stacy too much," she says. "I don't think the meeting did much for morale."

Today Chris Dailey has a less emotionally exhausting idea to forge team unity: a top-secret field trip. After practice all of the players are herded into two vans and driven blind-folded to a secret location (the Basketball Hall of Fame, in Springfield, Massachusetts). Each van is its own team. To keep them occupied during the excursion, CD provides both vans with a list of trivia questions and challenges to answer and fulfill.

One of the challenges the players must execute is for one of them to walk into a McDonald's and order a Diet Coke blind-folded. Swin Cash volunteers. She must make quite a sight as she enters: tall, athletic, her eyes wrapped. "Is that Swin Cash?" patrons wonder. "Can she sign an autograph for me if she cannot see?"

Swin is gone only a few minutes and returns with a soft drink in her hands. "I'll tell you," she says, clambering up into her seat, "I really feel bad for the blind-folded now."

Saturday, January 13 . . . Renee Najarian, at the age of 35, still looks as if she could play 30 minutes per game for almost any team in the country. She is a coltish, 6', pony-tailed woman with a youthful glow, whose 17.1 points-per-game average is second all-time at UConn behind only Kerry Bascom. Most fans, however, have no idea who she is.

"I was Geno's first pain in the ass," says Renee, who played two seasons for the Huskies (1986-87 and 1987-88). One night a year she escapes her anonymity by playing in the Alumnae Game, which precedes tonight's contest against the Providence Lady Friars.

The most renowned ex-Huskies, such as Rebecca Lobo, Jennifer Rizzotti, and Nykesha Sales, do not play because of stipulations in their WNBA contracts. Meghan Pattyson cannot play because she is broadcasting the Providence-UConn game that will immediately follow. Carla Berube, an assistant coach for the Lady Friars, and Jamelle Elliott prefer to focus on their bench duties this evening. Stacy Hansmeyer has coaching duties tonight as well, but the gravitational pull of playing in front of fans at Gampel is too strong for her to resist. She plays.

Stacy and Renee jump center for the tipoff. The referee tosses the ball in the air. As Renee coils her legs to jump, Stacy punches her in the face. "Not a curled-fist, break-your-nose punch," Renee will say later, "but enough to make my eyes water."

"You gotta do," Bam Bam later confesses, "what you gotta do."

Renee Najarian has a long history of on-court physical abuse. "In my first practice with the Huskies," she says, "I took a shot and Peggy Walsh flattened me. Nobody blew a whistle."

Peggy Walsh was a senior captain that season (1985-86), and Renee was a transfer from the University of South Carolina who had to sit out a year before her eligibility could be restored. "I was at Geno's first practice," she says proudly. "I just remember how dark and dingy the Fieldhouse was. It was a pretty grimy place."

Renee remembers one practice in which the Huskies were doing the layup drill, the one in which every player must make her layup or the drill starts from scratch. "People would keep missing them," Renee recalls, "but I didn't. All the misses were really beginning to frustrate him."

Instead of punishing the players who missed, Geno pulled them out of the drill. One by one the number of players on the court dwindled until the only one remaining was Renee. Her teammates stood on the sidelines and watched as she dribbled downcourt and hit a layup, then dribbled down to the other end of the court and made another. And on and on and on.

"He just let me keep going and going," Renee says, "and of course I got angrier and angrier. Angry at my teammates and angry at him. And tired, too. Finally I dribbled up to the basket and just threw the ball off the backboard as hard as I could.

"And that was the end of the drill," she says. "I realize now that he was just seeing how far I could be pushed."

She was a team captain as a senior, when the Huskies lost seven games by seven or fewer points. Geno refers to it as his least enjoyable season. Renee remembers a particularly frustrating moment at St. John's University late in the season, a 62-55 loss. He subbed for her in the second half and, when she took her seat on the bench, he approached her.

"I quit!" he said.

"*You* quit?" she said. "You can't quit!"

Geno just didn't know where to turn, though, and each loss branded a new scar on him. After that loss, in the locker room, he was more contemplative. "You know who sucked tonight?" he asked his players. "I sucked tonight."

There is a wistfulness to Renee as she recounts her playing days, a sadness almost. Today she is the assistant athletic director at E.O. Smith High School, which abuts the UConn campus as a garage does a home. Besides Jamelle Elliott, who coaches, and Peggy Myers, who works in the basketball office as an assistant, no former player is so physically close to the UConn program as Renee is. Yet she never visits. Never. Except on this night.

"They always tell me to come by," Renee says, "but I've got a lot going on here. And I'm not sure how comfortable I'd feel."

Renee has all the qualities Geno admires. She is self-disciplined, motivated, genuine, and likeable if not extroverted. She wants to be a college coach. No. She wants to be a college coach in Storrs.

"Sure, I'd love to be a part of the program," says Renee, who will lead all scorers in tonight's Alumnae Game with 18 points. "Geno has told me that he just doesn't have any openings."

Hers is an unrequited love story. There is a force inside of Renee telling her to move on, but she cannot bring herself to leave.

"I loved playing for him," she says. "I'd love to be involved with them again."

When Renee played in the late Eighties, Providence was the class of the Big East. Indeed, many of the women who play in tonight's Alumnae Game never defeated the Lady Friars. From 1976 through 1987 Providence beat UConn 16 straight. Geno started out 0-5 against them, but since 1994 his teams have compiled a 13-game win streak against their conference neighbors.

Tonight is another victory for inertia, as the Huskies leap out to a staggering 58-22 halftime lead. UConn officially broke out of its two-game funk with a 28-0 jailbreak three minutes into the game. Svetlana Abrosimova even scored on a layup, her first first-half bucket since the Louisiana Tech game.

It has been an unusual new year for the Russian senior. During the Christmas break she decided that she wanted to know what it was like to work in an office. She arranged with Geno's agent, Sol Kerensky, to work at his law offices.

So the Naismith Award candidate became a legal clerk. For two days. Then the coaches got wind of it, and Sveta's 9-to-5 job was 86ed. "I really enjoyed it," says Sveta, who was never paid because that would have constituted an NCAA violation. "I remember feeling so nervous. I thought, What am I going to wear to work today? But I also did it to cure the boredom. I didn't want to stick around The Qual or go to the mall every day."

Sveta's legal career ended abruptly. Her basketball career is in doldrums. Since injuring her back on Christmas Eve she has averaged just eight points per game. Unbeknownst to the media, she suffered a scratched cornea against Syracuse. "I have to wake up in the middle of the night to take eyedrops," she says. "I have to put the eyedrops in every hour. I am not sleeping very well."

Nobody knows this, however, and nobody cares. Not tonight. Other Huskies step up in the 104-49 win. Shea Ralph, who scored a total of eight points in last week's two road games, gets 14 points in the win. Diana and KJ each score a team-high 16.

"How good did you guys look tonight?" Mike DiMauro asks Geno afterward. "Really good? Really, really good? Really, really, really good?"

"You shouldn't have to give a State of the Union address after every game," says Geno. Minutes later he is gone. It has been a long day of basketball. Earlier in the afternoon he watched his son's undefeated Police Athletic League (or PAL) team play in Torrington, 50 miles northwest of Storrs. Michael's team suffered its first defeat and Geno, stuck in traffic on Interstate 84, arrived only half an hour before tipoff.

Now he unwinds with Kathy and a dozen or so friends at Cavey's, a tony Italian bistro in Manchester. It has been a long day of basketball. It has in fact been a very long week, the longest he has had in quite some time. A visit to Notre Dame, now the only other undefeated team in the nation, looms on Monday. But that is tomorrow. Tonight the Huskies are 13-0 and have the nation's longest win streak, 30 games. Tonight is an evening to savor.

Sunday, January 14 . . . "South Bend," Kathryn Hepburn says in the 1940 classic *The Philadelphia Story*, "it almost sounds like springtime."

Almost, but not quite. South Bend, the address of the University of Notre Dame, is buried in snow. On the eve of tomorrow's contest, Connecticut's second No. 1-vs.-No. 2 tilt in 17 days, the Huskies are dining in what once was the Studebaker (yeah, the automobile folks) mansion, which is now an upscale restaurant called Tippecanoe Place.

At the moment the Huskies are turning fine dining on its ear. Diana Taurasi raps her fork on Morgan Valley's plate. "Attention," she announces, standing up in front of the team and holding Morgan's flatware as if it were a prize pelt. "The plate is clean."

The proclamation is met with giddy cheers. Earlier in the season Diana noticed that the word "leftover" is not part of Morgan's vocabulary. She never fails to finish every morsel on her plate. So D has taken to announcing "the plate is clean" in the same way the military plays "Taps" before lights out.

"I don't understand what the big deal is," Morgan will say. "I was raised to finish the food that's on your plate."

In Connecticut, which is known as the Land of Steady Habits, Morgan, a creature of habit, is welcome. Besides always cleaning her plate, she forces herself to make twenty consecutive free throws before she will walk off the court after practice. And do 10 push-ups each night before she goes to bed. And 200 sit-ups.

Christine Rigby bites her nails. Assistant coach Jamelle Elliott collects anything that has Winnie the Pooh on it. Chris Dailey drinks two Diet Cokes each game (one for each half), from the fountain, with plenty of ice.

"When we go on the road," says CD, "the first thing the managers have to check is whether the arena serves Coke or Pepsi. If it's Pepsi, they go to a fast-food joint that serves Coke."

Winning is a steady habit. The Huskies have won 30 straight and are 11-0 all-time versus Notre Dame. The Fighting Irish, however, are fostering some special customs themselves. They are 16-0 entering tomorrow's game and have won 31 straight at the Joyce Athletic & Convocation Center (the JACC). Tomorrow's game, a nationally televised matinee on Martin Luther King, Jr., Day, is gathering buzz around the nation.

Geno is not at dinner. He is in the habit of eating a great meal (Italian food or steak) on the eve of a game and having a glass of wine with the Herde in the hotel lounge. But it is not to be this evening. Geno is in his hotel room at the South Bend Marriott, bedridden by flu-like symptoms.

"What's wrong with him?" CD asks Kathy Auriemma, who is traveling with the team for this game.

"It's not a pretty picture," Kathy answers. "I'd rather not ruin your appetite."

After dinner a small party of Huskies venture to the tranquil, snow-covered Notre Dame campus. The second semester does not begin until Tuesday, and most students are enjoying the last wisps of Christmas break with their families. The players walk over to the Grotto, a re-creation of the cave in Lourdes, France, where it is believed that the Virgin Mother appeared to a few children over a century ago.

At Notre Dame the Grotto holds special significance for students as a haven to escape the pressures of studying. Before a big exam it is tradition among students to visit the Grotto and light a candle. Either for yourself or for a friend. Svetlana Abrosimova, upon learning of this habit, enters and lights a candle.

"I didn't light candle for team," she says cheekily, "I lit it for myself."

Monday, January 15 . . . By 9:30 a.m Notre Dame coach Muffet McGraw's day is already made. "I came in for our shootaround," says McGraw, "and one of the ushers said to me, 'Did you hear? It's a sellout.'"

McGraw has coached the Fighting Irish for 14 seasons. None of the previous 173 home games has sold out. This afternoon's game, however, features the last two unbeatens in women's college hoops (Baylor lost last week).

The Irish have never beaten a top-ranked team and have never been No. 1 themselves. They enter today's game a combined 0-24 versus UConn and Tennessee. Many around the game believe that Notre Dame's biggest obstacle is its own self-doubt. "They were a Final Four team last year," says Rutgers coach C. Vivian Stringer, whose Scarlet Knights, unlike the Irish, advanced to the Final Four, "but they didn't believe it themselves. Everybody else knew it, though."

A light snow falls on campus as McGraw strides past the usher. Meanwhile in Satellite Beach, Florida, Marsha Lake is trolling the parking lot of a WalMart in search of loose change. This is her steady habit. When she finds change on the ground before a big game, the Huskies win. That the Huskies always win anyway is a moot point with Marsha.

Lake is worried. For the past week she has been walking five miles daily without finding so much as a penny on the ground. So this morning she decides that the parking lot of America's largest retailer may be harboring wayward coins. "I have to at least try," she says.

Today's game is being broadcast nationally on ESPN. If there is one tradition indigenous to women's college basketball that has caught fire with the general public, it is ESPN's Martin Luther King, Jr., Day afternoon telecast. This afternoon's game marks the seventh edition of the holiday game, which has always pitted UConn against another school ranked in the top five. This afternoon is no exception.

It was all Carol Stiff's idea. In the spring of 1994 Stiff was put in charge of programming women's basketball at ESPN. She attempted to schedule a game for MLK Day 1995, pitting then up-and-coming UConn versus a perennial power.

"So I phoned Pat Summitt to ask her if she'd be interested," says Stiff. "There was a long pause on the other end of the line and then she said, 'For the good of the game, I'll do it.'"

When UConn hosted Tennessee on January 16, 1995, they were ranked second and first in the nation, respectively. Two days earlier the Lady Vols had traveled to Auburn and won, 68-43. That evening they returned to Knoxville, and Summitt told her players to give her their sweaty road uniforms. She took them home and laundered them herself.

"I knew that I wasn't going to get much sleep anyway," Summitt says now. "I was going to be up all night watching film."

Summitt also knew that she was leading her tired team into an ambush. The Huskies revolved around the gentle grace of 6'4" Player of the Year candidate Rebecca Lobo. Her supporting cast—point guard Jennifer Rizzotti, off guard and roommate Pam Webber, power forward Jamelle Elliott and center Kara Wolters—understood that she was the star and took pride in their supporting roles. UConn was a program on the rise—the Huskies would lead the nation in attendance that season—and a hungry one at that, having never been ranked number one in the nation.

"It was our first big programming coup," says Stiff. "UConn won (77-66), and the crowd was just going nuts. I remember going back to the locker rooms to thank both coaches. I ran right into Pat.

"She shot me a frosty glare and held it for what seemed a lifetime," Stiff recalls. "Then she sorta smiled. All she said was 'For the good of the game.'"

After the win that day, some members of the women's team headed to Hartford to watch the UConn men play at the Civic

Center. Rebecca recalls the trip from Storrs to Hartford vividly. "Jen drove the two of us in her green Dodge Shadow—the only known Dodge Shadow to have a car alarm. She asked, 'If I speed to the game tonight and we get pulled over, do you think there's any way I'd get a ticket?' She asked the question like it was the most preposterous thought ever."

Geno was in his tenth season in Storrs when UConn beat Tennessee that day. To everyone outside Connecticut, however, January 16, 1995 is the day that UConn women's basketball was born. So it is that McGraw enters the JACC this morning under circumstances eerily similar to those of the '95 Huskies.

Like the '95 Huskies, the Irish have little bench depth. They are led by 6'5" Ruth Riley who, like Rebecca Lobo, is the first player in her program's history to be both a first-team Associated Press All-American and a first-team GTE/Academic All-American. The rest of the starting five are reliable role players. Junior forward Ericka Haney is a quick defensive specialist who can score along the baseline; senior point guard Niele Ivey is, after Sue Bird and Georgia's Kelly Miller, the best player at that position in the nation. Power forward Kelley Siemon complements her classmate, Riley. When Riley is double-teamed in the low post she finds Siemon, a Hitchcockian blonde, cutting to the basket from the opposite high post for an easy layup.

Riley is the soul of the Irish. Their most intriguing player may be shooting guard Alicia Ratay. The 5'11" sophomore is the best sharpshooter in college basketball, men's or women's. Currently she is leading all divisions and both sexes in three-point shooting at 62%. Adding to Ratay's aura is an expressionless face and a near-mute reticence that fuels her burgeoning legend as a silent assassin.

And then there's the questionnaire that all Notre Dame players are asked to fill out for the school's sports information department. Completing the statement "If I were president of the United States, the first thing I'd do would be," Ratay had written "Find out who killed JFK."

Jeff Goldberg, a reporter for *The Hartford Courant* who bought a copy of the Warren Report when he was ten, is fascinated by

Ratay. He is an avowed JFK-assassination conspiracy theorist and has said that his wish is to be at a press conference in which Alicia Ratay is seated in front of the microphone.

"When they let me ask my question," Goldberg says, "I'll just look at her and say, 'So, who do you think did it?'"

Half an hour before the 2 p.m. tip-off the players sit alone in the locker room, staring at an equation that one of them has written on the greaseboard: *sellout + big game + ESPN + undefeated + road test= crush job* the formula reads. This may be hubris, but it is well earned. On January 6, 1996, UConn walked into Tennessee's Thompson-Boling Arena and stopped the Lady Vols' NCAA-record 69-game homecourt win streak. Such feats are flavored with attitude. Ten minutes later the UConn coaching staff walks into the locker room. Geno, still looking somewhat ill, outlines the battle plan.

"Number one," he says, "Notre Dame's hit seventy-eight threes in sixteen games. We've hit seventy-six in thirteen games. So the question is, Do we let 'em shoot threes or twos? And the answer is, 'Twos.' If it's between double-teaming the post or getting to the three-point shooter, go out for the three."

Geno makes two more points, then asks, "How long will emotion carry them? My guess is five minutes. Maybe ten. Then it comes down to who has more talent and who executes better. They'll be intense, we'll be more intense. Let's show them how to win big games."

Outside, the arena is hopping. Because Notre Dame students are admitted free with their student IDs, the announced sellout of 11,148 is probably at least a few hundred low. The upper bowl of the JACC, all of it bleacher seating, overflows, giving the arena a madhouse effect.

Geno approaches McGraw at halfcourt. "You know," Geno tells McGraw, acknowledging The House that Ruth Filled, "this reminds me a lot of our game with Tennessee in Ninety-five. The best thing that could happen today is if Notre Dame won. Great for the Big East, great for ND, great for the game."

If this is to be Notre Dame's coming-out party, McGraw has dressed for it in style. Her black, high-slit miniskirt is the talk of press row. "She reminds me," says the *Courant*'s Jeff Jacobs, "of the librarian with the good wheels."

UConn wins the tip and, just as with the Georgetown and Providence games, Shea Ralph streaks behind the defense and the player who grabbed the tip (Sveta Abrosimova) finds her for an easy layup.

Or so it would appear. From nowhere, though, Notre Dame's Ericka Haney sprints determinedly after Shea and blocks her shot. Shea is stunned, insulted almost. Niele Ivey hits a short basket on the other end, and the Irish lead, 2-0. Two of the next three times downcourt, the Irish find Riley, who has the best low-post footwork in the nation, for easy buckets. When Riley is double-covered, she finds Siemon cutting from the free-throw line, or Ivey or Ratay perched beyond the three-point arc. With 11:22 remaining in the first half the Huskies trail, 23-12, their first double-digit deficit of the season.

UConn counterpunches with a 9-0 run. Svetlana's 12 first-half points keep the game within reach, 40-31. The four other starters—Shea, Sue Bird, Swin Cash and Schuey—shoot only 4 of 14, however. More important, the Irish are executing in the halfcourt offense, which neutralizes the Huskies' transition game. At the half UConn has only one fastbreak basket and one point off a turnover.

Most crucially, Ruth Riley has no fouls. Although the 6'5" center is the two-time reigning Big East Defensive Player of the Year, she fouled out of six games last season. Four of those disqualifications overlapped with Notre Dame's five losses. It's simple: Put Riley on the bench, beat Notre Dame. Riley, like UConn's Christine Rigby, enjoys blocking shots (putting the Ruth on 'em) but whenever she leaves her feet, whistles blow.

When Notre Dame played at UConn last season, Riley spent the entire game in foul trouble in an 18-point loss. She scored only four points. Notre Dame lost its composure that afternoon, including McGraw, who had a tear rolling down her cheek in the postgame press conference. Thus far today the Irish and Riley are grounded in every sense.

During halftime Sarah Darras places a call from her home in Connecticut to Marsha Lake in Satellite Beach, Florida. "Marsha," she says, "tell me you've found some change."

"I haven't found a thing," Lake sighs.

"Oh, damn."

To open the second half Sue and Sveta each hit three-pointers, cutting the Irish lead to 40-37. Then Ruth Riley turns up the poise. No single Husky defender can hang with her. Double-teams only invite Riley to feed open teammates.

Riley is unstoppable—she will score 19 second-half points—and still without a foul. With more than nine minutes remaining and UConn trailing, 63-50, Matt Eagan says, "Maybe it's time Geno puts in Rig to defend Riley." A minute later, with the Irish up 18, Rig trots to the scorer's table.

"I was kidding," says Eagan. "For the record, I was kidding."

The final score is 92-76. It is the Huskies' worst defeat in seven years, an ambush. Sveta has her best game in weeks, with team-highs in points (20) and rebounds (14). Sue, playing an inspired second half (she has lost just one game since her junior year in high school), finishes with 17 points and six assists. Shea and Schuey, however, each score only two points. Diana fouls out with six.

The story is Riley. She finishes with 29 points on 8-of-11 shooting from the field and makes all 13 of her free-throw attempts. "She was," affirms her coach, "the best player in the country today."

Geno, Sue, and Sveta enter the press room after McGraw and Riley leave. Sveta is morose, laconic. Sue is simply disgusted. "I'm embarrassed, personally," she says. "A lot of people on our team played hard, but collectively, no way."

Geno is a gentleman in defeat, dissecting the game objectively, as if he is unaware that UConn's 30-game win streak just ended. "I thought from the opening tip Notre Dame was better," he says. "In every aspect, they were better. In all of the areas where we needed to play the game, I thought they outplayed us.

"I know I'm gonna sound bad saying this, but I think our team doesn't like it when the other team shows up and plays well," he adds. "That's how immature some of the players on our team are. They'd rather phone ahead and say, 'We want the score to be fifty-two to thirty-eight.'"

The writers chuckle. He talks about the locker room of crying players that he has just left.

"You know, Diana Taurasi was broken up in the locker room, and she should be. That's the third time she's fouled out. Maybe it'll teach her to stop committing stupid fouls."

Geno still feels ill. He just wants to be home, but this imperfect day will not end easily. It is snowing hard now. The Huskies' bus gets lost enroute to the Michiana Regional Airport in South Bend. It is midnight by the time Geno and Kathy finally walk through the door—three hours late—that leads to their kitchen in Manchester. Michael and Meghan Pattyson, who has watched the kids the last two days, are waiting for them.

"Tough loss," says Meg.

"Yeah," Geno agrees. "Tough loss."

"Tough weekend for the Auriemmas all around," says Michael, referring to his PAL team's loss on Saturday. "Two undefeated teams went down."

Two hours later Geno is sitting all alone. He chuckles to himself. "Tough weekend for the Auriemmas all around," he says "You gotta love that."

Thursday, January 18 . . . What is it like to play UConn after they lose? "I think one of my assistants put it best," says Old Dominion coach Wendy Larry after tonight's 80-51 pasting by the Huskies at Gampel Pavilion. "It's kinda like kicking a hornet's nest naked."

Seven full seasons have passed since the Huskies lost two games in a row. Yet Geno's e-mail has been flooded in the last few days by upset fans. Fans who want to know how the greatest team ever could lose by 16. One even scolded him for wearing a cheap-looking watch on the sideline. It was a watch he'd received for winning the Big East championship, something the

Huskies have done for seven consecutive seasons, both in the regular season and in the conference tournament. But that was yesteryear.

"Save the day," says Geno with the proper note of sarcasm after tonight's win. "Our program lives to play another day."

Before the Notre Dame game the Huskies had won 30 straight and had been ranked number one in the nation for 30 consecutive weeks. Tonight's victory was UConn's 66th straight home win against Big East competition and its 43rd consecutive sellout at Gampel. Since Monday, however, Geno has heard and read nothing but doom and gloom.

"The reaction after Notre Dame, it's hard to understand," he says. "We're 50-2 [in the last two seasons] and if the reaction is going to be like that after every time we play poorly, then if I was a kid [on this team] I would say, 'What's the point?' We've created such an amazing standard that we can't live up to it and I think that's kinda sad."

Even Randy Smith chastised him—in print. That afternoon in South Bend Geno had referred to the Notre Dame loss as a "learning experience", and R. Smith wrote that UConn was far beyond that point in its evolution. "When I die," he wrote in *The Manchester Journal-Inquirer*, "on my gravestone it will say, Here lies R. Smith/It was a learning experience."

Geno enters the interview room at Gampel coughing and clearing his throat. His usual caffeinated energy is missing, his complexion sallow. He is beginning to accept that even his motor runs down, that last year's title run followed by the southern-hemisphere summer is finally exacting its price. His team looks tired, too, even with a 29-point win.

"It's a long season and some of us have been going for a long, long time," Geno says. "Me, too, I'm struggling, too. The gas tank is on 'E.'"

Only Svetlana Abrosimova has globe-trotted as much as Geno in the last year. She is still waking up in the middle of the night to dab her scratched cornea with medicine, but once again she plays brilliantly. Arguably, this is her best game since the opener versus Georgia, as she leads the Huskies in scoring (19), rebounds (13), and assists (seven). She must have a reserve tank.

Diana Taurasi also seems to be coming into her own, and has established her as the first player off the bench. The on-court telepathy between her and Sveta is blossoming. In the first half Diana had the ball on the left wing and zinged a no-look pass to Sveta, who had cut from the right baseline to the low left block. Easy layup.

Diana's thick brunette hair reaches down to her waist, as does her mother's. "Her freshman year she had the ponytail," says Webster, "and she'd whack people in the face with it as if it were a dinosaur's tail. Then she went to the bun."

Diana still wears the bun, a perfect brown sphere perched at the crown of her skull. Diana has textbook basketball morphology, with long arms that allow her to play even taller than her 6'0" height. That wingspan has always allowed her to cheat on defense. Whereas coaches stress that you play defense with your feet, *i.e.*, you slide your feet to establish position, Diana has been able, against high school competition, to block shots and make steals with her long arms.

"I hate to say a freshman is the key [to the season]," says WTIC radio's Scott Gray during a timeout, "but a freshman is the key. He's just got to let her go."

Geno realizes as much, but he still tugs on the reins. With 4:40 remaining in the game and the Huskies cruising, 70-41, Diana attempts a no-look pass in which she flings the ball behind her right shoulder. The pass is stolen and, before Old Dominion even attempts a shot, Geno sends Sveta to the scorer's table to sub for Diana.

She is rambunctious. The other night at The Qual she, Sue Bird, and Kathryn Fieseler were playing Pictionary against Morgan Valley, Stacy Hansmeyer, and a younger team manager. "We were kicking their butts," says Morgan, "but then Diana's team came back and won. Diana's prancing around the room, tossing stuff, and Stacy accuses her of cheating. She did cheat."

Diana got up in Stacy's face and started talking smack. Stacy grabbed Diana by the throat. Diana did not flinch. "What are you gonna do, Stacy?" she said to the assistant coach. "Hit me?"

Stacy's ire soon passed. That is part of Diana's gift. She can drive you crazy, but she's just too irrepressibly upbeat a person to harbor a grudge against. And in the clutch there's no one else you'd rather have on your team.

Saturday, January 20 . . . It is becoming increasingly evident that something is not right with Shea Ralph. Today in blizzard-riddled Pittsburgh, she scores two points, shooting 1 of 5 from the field in an ugly 83-43 victory. In the past two weeks Shea has broken or tied her career scoring low three times.

No one outside the team knows about her food-poisoning bout nor a cold that she has been unable to shake since December. Everyone wonders what's wrong, though. Even Ruth Riley. As she was waiting to be interviewed by UConn commentator Bob Picosi after the Notre Dame win, she asked him, "Do you know why Shea was on the bench?"

When Shea was a freshman, subsisting on Diet Cokes, No-Doz, and the aroma of academic and athletic achievement, she would get very worn down. "I had this friend on the soccer team," says Shea, "who introduced me to the idea of a 'personal day'. Sometimes you've just got to shut the world off. Just blow off everything you're supposed to do and do something for yourself. Go to the movies. Go to a tanning salon. You know, a personal day."

No one has seen Shea take one, at least not this season. Kelly Schumacher, however, plays with a zeal not seen since last April's NCAA championship game. Schuey scores 20 points and blocks a season-high four shots. She becomes the eighth different player to lead the Huskies in scoring this season, remarkable considering that this is their 16th game.

After the game Swin Cash, who celebrated her Iron City homecoming with a typically solid 14 points and eight rebounds, is besieged by autograph seekers. Dozens of young girls surround her but she is in no rush. The storm outside is so bad that the Huskies' flight will be delayed six hours. They kill most of the night at Dave & Buster's, a popular arcade-restaurant, before attempting the harrowing trek to Pittsburgh International Airport.

The plane sits on the tarmac for quite some time being de-iced as the snow falls heavily. Commercial flights are not taking off, but UConn's charter flight will. Seven days from now ten members of the Oklahoma State University men's basketball team traveling entourage will perish when their much smaller Beechcraft King Air 200, a turboprop aircraft, crashes in a field shortly after takeoff outside Denver.

Tonight's weather is abominable. The interstate to the airport was strewn with the carcasses of abandoned vehicles that had skidded off the road. Still, the plane takes off and the players, either inured to the hazards of flying or simply empowered by a youthful sense of invulnerability, do not give it a second thought. Everyone just wants to return home.

When the plane lands in Hartford, the only cause of distress is from Diana Taurasi. She won a Woody the Woodpecker stuffed animal at Dave & Buster's and, as she napped during the trip, someone absconded with it.

"Where's Woody?" she yawns, searching the overhead compartment. "Where's Woody?"

Svetlana Abrosimova stands up across the aisle from Diana. "Items overhead tend to shift during flight," she says with a grin.

Sunday, January 21 . . . The game of basketball, which was born in Springfield, Massachusetts, turned 109 years old yesterday. For Rebecca Lobo, who was raised 12 miles west of Springfield in Southwick, Mass., yesterday was an independence day from basketball. She flew from Connecticut to Phoenix to begin a driving tour of the western United States with no particular plans or purpose.

"I've been rehabbing my knee for the past eighteen months and doing everything that I'm supposed to," she says. "I just want to get away for awhile. Get away from basketball."

Rebecca returned home to the United States nine days ago. Her experience in the Canary Islands quickly turned into a nightmare. When her coach realized that Rebecca was not the same player who averaged roughly 12 points and seven rebounds per game in her first two WNBA seasons, before the pair of ACL injuries, he stopped playing her.

"We lost a game before Christmas in which I had three shots and three offensive rebounds," says Rebecca, who played two games. "You do the math on that."

The team cut Rebecca after just two games. The player who, as Randy Smith likes to describe her, "had sunlight in her eyes"as a collegian, has lost her joy for the game. She will land in Phoenix and from there drive to Los Angeles, where she will meet Doug Walker, a friend who is organizing a motorcycle ride for a charity foundation known as Head First, which raises helmet-safety awareness. The pair will map out next summer's ride, driving to the Grand Canyon and then to Denver, the Grand Tetons of Wyoming, Jackson Hole, Banff, Alberta, Vancouver and, eventually, Seattle.

Rebecca Lobo is taking a personal day, albeit an extended one. The most celebrated player in UConn history is disappearing into the wilderness, a place far from publicists and endorsement obligations and rehab and basketball itself.

"I've never done anything like this," she says. "I'm looking forward to being out of touch for awhile."

Monday, January 22 . . . Shortly after 11:00 a.m, some 90 minutes after practice has begun on this sunny day, Geno gathers the players around him under the northeast basket of Gampel. He speaks to them in hushed tones for nearly 15 minutes. Then he walks off the floor, his two All-American captains, Shea Ralph and Svetlana Abrosimova, silently trailing him.

They disappear for five minutes. Ten minutes. Twenty. Forty minutes elapse, and the three of them have still not returned. Chris Dailey runs practice, but the players' minds are with their teammates. What is he saying to them? What is he doing?

"When he pulled them off," Marci Czel will later say, "we were thinking, They must be getting killed right now."

Nearly 50 minutes later Geno returns. Shea and Sveta are not with him. He walks on the court and calls the team over to him. Then, all of them disappear.

When the Huskies enter their locker room, they find Shea and Sveta still wiping tears from their eyes. Whatever he said to them stung deeply. Now, however, he simply wants to talk to all of them about fear.

"What is your greatest fear in connection with this team?" Geno asks them. "What are you afraid of?"

He invites them to take out the notebooks they keep and to write down their fears. They comply. Players are asked to share what they have written. One by one they share their fears, which merge into one: that they have lost the magic. "The way we felt after the Georgia game," Morgan Valley will later say, "we're afraid that we will not feel that way again."

Geno collects their slips of fears. He tells them that right now, today, this is a turning point. Then Geno tosses the papers into a wastepaper basket, symbolically discarding their fears.

But the fears cannot be tossed aside as easily as refuse. Nor will wins against sub-standard opponents, no matter what the score, exorcise the demons. The fears will only erode when the Huskies play another worthy foe and prove to themselves that their arsenal is still lethal. A foe such as the team from Knoxville, whom the Huskies will visit in 10 days. Until then, Geno will do everything he knows to return them to early-season form.

Shortly after 1:00 p.m. Geno emerges from the locker room to speak with the Herde, who are gathered in the hallway outside. They ask about Shea and Sveta.

"They're both really frustrated right now because of their bodies," Geno says without elaborating on their specific maladies. "What bothers me right now is not that they're hurt, what bothers me is that they're frustrated. They have the highest highs and the lowest lows of anybody on the team.

"I'd love nothing better," he says, "than to sit both of them for tomorrow night's game."

Ten yards away Shea and Sveta are answering questions. Both look despondent. Sveta's rheumy eyes betray an earlier display of tears. She speaks barely above a whisper, and the reporters, in empathy, leave her alone. Shea, however, is up to the chore.

"I didn't think my role would be the same," she says, when asked about how this year differs from last. "It turns out that my role is a lot different. Just because I'm Shea Ralph doesn't mean that everyone's got to respect me.

"There's something that I've got to fix," she says. "Something that I don't really want people to know. But it's right here."

She points to her heart.

"It's a marathon," Geno says as Sveta and Shea exit the hallway, walking past him in silence. "You know, it's a long race. When someone crosses the finish line in a marathon, she's not smiling. Everything hurts."

Later this evening Geno phones Keirsten Walters. He asks her to drive Svetlana, who does not have a driver's license, over to his house. He wants to apologize.

"I did not want to go over," Sveta says later. "I was really mad at him. The things he said really hurt. But I went. He felt bad about what he said. I could see that."

Tuesday, January 23 . . . Marsha Lake is back. Turning the concept of snowbirding on its ear, Shea Ralph's mom has made her third journey from Florida to cold and miserable New England in the last month. She arrived earlier today—finding loose change at Bradley International Airport—and announced, "Mama Bear is here."

Lake's big-hearted folksiness is exactly what Shea and the team need right now. She strolls into the basketball office and peeks in on Geno.

"What watch are you going to wear tonight?" she says with a grin, referring to the critical e-mail he received after the Notre Dame loss.

Geno smiles at her—there's another wiseass in town— and says, "Son of a bitch."

Geno loves moms. He adores his own, Nona, as much as a son can. He speaks with her via cellphone during his morning commute to Storrs. He spoke to her on the morning after the Notre Dame loss, looking for guidance. "You need to go and find out what's wrong," she said.

Geno bought his mother a home in Phoenixville, Pennsylvania, after her husband Donato passed away from lung cancer in 1997. She stays with Geno's family in Manchester, though, for weeks at a time, eagerly attending to household chores. He will tease her, saying things such as, "Can't you make yourself useful around here?", and she will just beam with pride.

For all the All-Americans that Geno has coached and coached against, Marsiella Auriemma, Nona, is the most amazing woman that he has ever known. She was a young girl, her father already deceased, when World War II interrupted her family's placid rural life in Montella, Italy, south of Naples.

The family had a fat pig upon whose sale their livelihood depended. Such a beast made an inviting target for hungry German soldiers. Nona's mother sent her and her siblings into the mountains for two weeks, away from the looting soldiers and the bombs to safety, while she remained at the house and looked after the pig.

"My mother stayed all by herself," Nona, now 69, told Jeff Jacobs for a story he wrote last year. "If the Germans find her, they shoot her."

Nona wept much of the fortnight she spent in the mountains. When she returned home to find her mother still alive, she wept some more.

"I tell this story to Geno," she says. "He does not forget."

Jeff Jacobs had gone to visit Nona for the above story a few days before last April's championship game against Tennessee. For all the bitterness that Geno had felt toward Jacobs regarding the Nykesha Sales/Soupy Sales line in 1998, he respects Jacobs, or "Jake", as he's known. The only two newspaper stories that are framed and hanging in Geno's office were written by Jacobs.

So it was that Geno's younger brother, Ferruccio, agreed to serve as Jake's tour guide and quasi-interpreter when he descended upon Geno's Norristown roots to conduct an interview with their mom last March.

"Where did you come from?" Jacobs began.

"New York," Mrs. Auriemma answered.

"No, no," he said. "Before you arrived in New York where did you come from? Naples?"

"Napoli," Nona corrected.

With an understanding smile on his face, Ferruccio intervened. "How's the interview going so far, Jeff?"

Geno loves moms. Foreign-born moms especially. "My mom and Geno write letters to each other," says Svetlana Abrosimova. "It all started when she sent him a birthday card [March 23]. Now they write [in English] all the time."

The Italian-born coach and the Russian-born mother have never met in person, but Ludmila Abrosimova enjoys the contact with her daughter's unofficial guardian. For years Ludmila was Sveta's unofficial coach, setting up a basket in the family's three-room apartment when Sveta was eight years old.

"Sveta's passes were sometimes too quick," Mrs. Abrosimova had told Bob Sudyk in a ten-page cover story in *Northeast*, which ran two years ago. "We broke a mirror once, then a chandelier hanging from the ceiling. Then we broke a telephone on the wall."

Every day Sveta and her mom jogged along the Neva River, passing such historic buildings as the Winter Palace, where the Russian czars had lived for 300 years before Lenin and the Bolsheviks overthrew them. Ludmila, though she knew almost nothing about basketball, realized that it was her daughter's ticket out of this hard life. Just as Nona and Donato, though they knew little about the United States, understood that it would offer their children a better life. Geno sees this quality in so many of the mothers of his players. He cannot honor it enough.

"I remember going in for Swin Cash's home visit," he says, "and I talked to her mom for five minutes, and I thought to myself, 'We're going to get this kid.' What Cynthia [Swin's mom] wanted to hear, what she stands for, is exactly what we're all about."

Cynthia Cash is another formidable mom. When she was a junior in high school, she was a dominant player who seemed headed for a college scholarship. Then she became pregnant with Swin, who was born on September 22, 1979, during

Cynthia's senior year. She played that final season, often bringing her infant daughter to games and practices.

She certainly had not planned to have a child before she had finished high school, but Cynthia Cash could not turn back time. She lived with her parents while working two jobs and attending community college.

"You look at Swin," says Geno, "and you're seeing a direct reflection of her mother."

Some of the saddest days of Geno's time at UConn have involved mothers. In 1990 Kerry Bascom's mother, Eleanor, succumbed to multiple sclerosis after a decade-long battle with the disease. Geno canceled practice on the day of the funeral, and the entire team traveled to New Hampshire to attend.

"I remember sitting at the wake and turning around," says Kerry, who was a junior in the midst of a Big East Player of the Year season. "Geno, Chris, and the entire team were standing there. They had driven up and surprised me. I just lost it."

Geno attended Mrs. Bascom's wake. He paid for Jamelle Elliott's mother's funeral. Charlotte Elliott, like Eleanor Bascom, suffered from multiple sclerosis and was confined to a wheelchair. On Friday, March 26, 1999, the UConn coaching staff were in San Jose, California, attending the Women's Final Four. The Huskies had been eliminated in the round of sixteen, but the coaches were there for the Women's Basketball Coaches Association (WBCA) convention, and Geno was throwing his party as well.

No single day better illustrates the dichotomy of UConn's family atmosphere than that one. Geno hired a limo driver to take himself, Kathy, Georgetown coach Pat Knapp, and Meghan Pattyson on a tour of the vineyards of Napa Valley. They stopped for lunch in a town called Rutherford, and Geno went to check his phone messages. There was a voicemail from Jamelle's father, James, asking Geno to phone. James Elliott had never called Geno before.

"When Geno returned to the table," Meghan remembers, "he had this weird look on his face. He knew something was wrong."

Charlotte Elliott, 47, had died in a fire that broke out in the family's Washington, DC, apartment. No one else had been home. Firemen were unable to break through the windows, which were barred to prevent burglars from entering. By the time Geno's party returned to the hotel in San Jose, where Jamelle was, Meghan says, "It was the most tragic thing I've ever witnessed."

Geno and Chris Dailey took care of everything. He sent her to accompany Jamelle on a transcontinental flight to DC that evening. He paid for all of the funeral arrangements.

"People always say how generous Geno is," says Meghan, "but unless you hear specifics, it doesn't mean much."

Marsha Lake is not the only UConn mom in attendance at this evening's game against Miami. In Gampel Pavilion there are hundreds of, if not a few thousand foster moms. With six minutes remaining in a sluggish first half and UConn leading by just six, 23-17, Shea is whistled for a reach-in foul. There is silence in Gampel Pavilion, which is finally punctured when an anonymous female voice yells out, "Shea doesn't foul!"

The call ignites the Huskies, though, as they proceed to score the next 14 points. At halftime they lead, 41-20, on their way to an 81-45 victory. Yet the Huskies are still slumping. Shea, her confidence shaken, only attempts three shots and finishes with two points. Sveta gets only eight.

The lone bright spot, again, is Swin Cash. She scores a team-high 13 points and ties Tamika Williams for the most rebounds, with nine. Again Swin's rugged game performance belies her prima donna reputation in practice. A few days ago Stacy Hansmeyer took a Sharpie to the life-size poster of Swin that blankets Rosemary Ragle's training room door and penned in the words, "Rosemary, can I have an Aleve?", mocking Swin's neediness and hypochondriac traits. But maybe Swin has something there. Maybe a few other Huskies would benefit from a dose of pain reliever.

Thursday, January 25 . . . Pat Meiser-McKnett sits in her office at the University of Hartford on this frigid January morning, recalling Geno's salad days in Storrs. Meiser-McKnett was an associate athletic director at UConn in 1985. She remembers meeting with the women's basketball team in Storrs in the spring of that year, after then-coach Jean Balthaser had been dismissed. "I said to the team, 'We would like to hire a woman,'" says Meiser-McKnett, now the athletic director at the University of Hartford. "They said, 'We don't care if it's a woman, we just want the best coach.'"

Pat Meiser-McKnett always thought that UConn basketball, men's and women's, was a sleeping giant. "I was of the opinion that we should charge people to attend women's games," says Meiser-McKnett, who proposed as much to Lew Perkins in 1990. "He thought that the fans would never go for it, but give him credit, they allowed me to try it. That first year we generated fifty-three thousand dollars in revenue."

Meiser-McKnett picked a good season to affix costs to Husky fandom, as that was also the first season UConn advanced to the Women's Final Four. "It spread like wildfire after that," she says. "The year I left, 1993, we sold all the tickets at Gampel before October first. We sold out for the season before we'd even started our ad campaign in *The Hartford Courant*."

The program's fiscal growth is as remarkable a story as the Huskies' on-court success. "The first four or five seasons," says Chris Dailey, "part of my duties was to do the budget. I did everything, called all the hotels, figured out the little tricks to save money."

CD no longer does the budget. "Now the budget just doesn't get done," she says. Who needs a budget when your women's basketball team nets $2 million a year?

Accounting was not CD's only ancillary duty in those early days. She also had to teach a physical education class. "My class was jogging," she says, "which is a total joke because I don't like to run."

Nor did many of her students. She had to give a final exam, but she never expected anyone to fail it. She gave a true-false test, thinking, It's harder to fail a true-false jogging test than it is to pass it. Yet one student, a pre-med, defied her expectations. When he handed in his test, it was clear to CD that he was about to fail the most sure-fire "A" course on campus.

"If I were you," CD said, handing the exam back to him, "I'd check question 10 again."

"No," he replied, "I think it's okay."

"No, really, I think you should check it."

"I think it's fine."

When she returned to the basketball offices, flabbergasted, Geno and Howie Dickenman howled at the tale. "You can't flunk someone in jogging," Geno said.

"He's obviously a moron," CD replied. "He doesn't deserve to get into medical school."

Against her will, Shea Ralph is taking a personal day. Geno had ordered her not to practice with the team today. She is run-down and everyone, even Mama Bear, knows it. He had wanted her to stay away from Gampel altogether, but she begged him to allow her to watch. She wears a red top, indicating a player that is not permitted to participate in any live drills, and stands on the sidelines looking forlorn.

Half an hour into practice Geno has Tom Tedesco install a fiberglass bubble atop one of the rims. The device is a popular tool for rebounding drills, since it prevents shots from going through the basket. In this 5-on-5 drill, a defensive rebound will be worth one point and an offensive rebound worth two.

"We want all five guys to block out," Geno tells them. "I don't think there's going to be anything more important that we gotta do the next two months than block out."

Alas, when you put a lid on top of a basket, players unconsciously cease putting as much care into the shots they take.

Tom, who has been inserted as a sixth offensive player, then takes two straight long-range shots that graze the bottom of the rim and fall meekly out of bounds. "Tom," Geno chides, "hit the top of the rim. Geez, you can't even miss right."

It is that kind of afternoon. Diana Taurasi, who'd been working with the blue (first) unit in Shea's stead, throws away no-look passes on consecutive fast breaks. "You still don't get it, D,"

Geno says. "You just refuse to see it. I'm not going to put up with that nonsense."

This letdown is inevitable. Since October 14 the Huskies have been chasing history, each game another brushstroke in a masterpiece. But that dream died in South Bend. Every game mattered when an undefeated season was on the line.

Now the Huskies cannot go undefeated and, unless the Fighting Irish lose a conference game (unlikely since they do not play UConn again), UConn's seven-year streak of Big East regular-season titles has also been snapped. All that matters now is repeating as national champions. But that prize is a long way off. What will motivate them between now and then?

Friday, January 26 . . . When Morgan Valley was ten years old, her dad was pulling the family car into the driveway when he hit a patch of ice. The car skidded into the basketball hoop support, toppling the pole and basket. Morgan wept as if the family dog had just been run over.

"I know it sounds silly," says Morgan, "but that's how much I love basketball."

She is a no-frills New England kid who is happily stuck in a time warp where the earth is flat and does not extend beyond either baseline. Geno admires her dedication to the game. He often uses Moe, as he does in today's pre-practice talk, to illustrate the point that he wouldn't mind having a few more austere throwbacks in his program.

"Morgan," he asks her in front of her teammates, "do you have a cellphone?'

"No."

"Are you on the internet? In a chat room?"

"No."

"Why not? You are so behind the times."

Geno is frustrated that players who have more athletic gifts than Morgan lack her work ethic. Kennitra Johnson, for example. KJ is a shy, sloe-eyed sweetheart from New Albany, Indiana, whose raw talent Geno has yet to polish. He is renowned for this, for getting more out of players than they realize that they can give, Rebecca Lobo being Exhibit A.

Thus far he has failed with KJ. She is the quickest defender on the team and a superior three-point shooter, at least as good as Sue Bird. But KJ is a point guard who does not lead, and Sue Bird does. KJ is the only sophomore on the team and the quietest player as well, so she is oft-forgotten. She is the Huskies' classic middle child.

"Let's go, KJ, let's go," Geno implores enthusiastically at today's practice, which Sue is missing. "Be good today, you gotta take Sue's spot. Be good today."

Geno is a cheerleader this afternoon. "Gotta be in shape, guys, gotta be in shape," he tells them. "Stretch run starts February first. February one, we got sixty days. That's when you make a name for yourselves. Nobody's gonna remember what you did in December."

The Huskies host Syracuse tomorrow, and then do not play again until next Thursday in Knoxville. Most of today's preparation focuses on the latter opponent and, as was the case yesterday, defensive rebounding is the priority. Not long into the drills, Diana neglects to box out KJ, whom she is guarding. KJ, the shortest player on the court, grabs the board.

"Goddamnit!" Geno says. "Hey, D, what did you do after that shot?"

"Nothing," Diana says. He is standing against the basket stanchion. She is bent over, hands on knees, staring at the far court. Staring away from him.

"Nothing," he says. "That's your favorite pastime. You're not interested in winning. How you gonna win if you don't do that? Goddamn, that's so bad."

Shea, who has been here five years, knows that the best way to curtail a diatribe is to start the next play as soon as possible. She signals to Diana, who is running the point.

"Let's go, D," she orders. "It's all right."

"No, it's not all right, Shea," he corrects. "It's not all right. If it were all right I wouldn't get pissed off."

Shea takes the criticism well. To use a horse racing analogy, Geno knows that with Shea—and he is finding out, Diana—he can go to the whip more often. They can take it.

"A lot of people that coach this sport approach it like it's women's basketball," he has said. "I don't. I approach it like it's basketball."

So does Shea. She may favor stuffed animals, but Shea is not soft. And she never makes excuses. He loves that about her.

When she was a freshman and he did not play her in the first half against Providence, she did not complain. Not even to her mother. Her mother, however, had checked the boxscore of the game on the internet the next morning and phoned Shea at 7:30 a.m.

"What happened?" Lake asked.

"Everybody played in the first half but me," Shea replied.

Later that afternoon Geno called Shea into his office. He knows that Lake is no ordinary stage mother. How many moms have their retired jerseys hanging in the rafters of the same arena in which Michael Jordan played his college ball?

"Have you talked to your mother today?" Geno asked Shea.

"Yes," she responded.

"You called her, didn't you?"

"No, she called me."

"Well, what did she say?"

"She said, 'Play harder.'"

Geno is going to miss Shea. He already knows that in spades.

The Herde was allowed to sit in on the last half of today's practice, and afterward Geno takes his customary seat in the first row of the stands to chat with them. His face still looks puffy. The shine in his eyes is missing.

"What's up, guys?" he asks them. "How are the girls?"

"You tell us," Carl Adamec says.

"You talk to 'em more than I do."

"We actually like them."

"That's because you only see 'em once or twice a week."

Saturday, January 27 . . . The matinee at the Hartford Civic Center against Syracuse would seem to have all the ingredients for a blowout. The Orangewomen surprised the Huskies 18 days earlier, keeping the first half close, but UConn (16-1) is not a fool-me-twice program. Or are they?

The Huskies, who appeared unbeatable when the month began, find themselves tied at 34 at halftime. They commit 17 first-half turnovers against the Orangewomen. There is a list-lessness to the defensive pressure, a dearth of rhythm in the halfcourt offense. Then, too, the shooting is awful, as the Huskies go 1-8 from three-point range. During one timeout Geno, beyond the point of aggravation, simply pleads, "Could you guys at least look as if you've been coached?"

The Huskies recover in the second half, starting it with a 16-4 burst. Svetlana Abrosimova steals the show. First she thieves a pass and plays catch with Sue during a two-on-one fastbreak that culminates with Sveta making a layup. She buries a three-pointer, then, anticipating a cross-court pass near midcourt, steps between the two Orangewomen players for a steal and an uncontested layup. She is bending the game to her will, finishing with a season-high—for her or any Husky—25 points, as UConn wins going away, 84-60.

"Svet has that ability," Sue Bird, who had 12 points, tells the media afterward. "I think she can play like that every night if she wanted to."

Her last four words, that conditional "if she wanted to", do not pass unnoticed. "Was that a little shot there?" asks Mike DiMauro.

"No," says Sue. "It's true."

Geno sides with Sue. "I hope they're putting the heat on Svet," he says. "'Svet, we wouldn't mind if you pulled one of these out of your hat every night.' We need her to take it personally more often. I think that'll do wonders for her. Me, too.

"If you ask them who's the best player in the country," he continues, "they'd say 'Svet.' I mean, they're not stupid. I asked Svet when she was in my office the other day, I asked her if she follows much opera. I wanted to know, Does she know about 'prima donna'?"

It is a schizophrenic day in Hartford. The Huskies commit 17 turnovers in the first half and force 17 turnovers in the second. They play to a tie in the first half and almost double the Orangewomen's output (50-26) in the second.

"You know, this team needs a psychiatrist," Geno tells the Herde, clearly enjoying himself. "Someone more qualified than me. They don't like my therapy."

Monday, January 29 . . . Geno might have known better than to schedule a doctor's appointment in mid-season at 8:00 a.m.

As thousands of fans in Connecticut watched the second half of the January 15 Notre Dame game and wondered, Why isn't Geno calling a timeout?, one Hartford allergist had a different notion. Dr. Michael Krall took one look at Geno's face on his television screen and said, "He looks like shit. His sinus cavities are all blocked up."

As for Geno not calling timeouts late in the Notre Dame game, he has a simple explanation. "I called timeouts early in the second half and told my players what to do," he says, "and they didn't listen. After a while I thought, What's the point?"

Dr. Krall, who is Meghan Pattyson's allergist, implored her to have Geno come in for a checkup. A CAT-scan confirmed his diagnosis: all five sinus cavities are blocked, which explains the puffiness in Geno's face as well as the fatigue he has been feeling of late.

"Well, I have been feeling very tired," Geno told Dr. Krall.

"How long have you been waking up tired?" the allergist asked.

"About eight years."

"Eight years? What is your routine?"

"Well, Doc, I go to bed about three-thirty and then I wake up at six to help get the kids off to school."

"Something's gotta change."

"Well, I guess I *could* sleep in," Geno replied.

Dr. Krall scheduled sinus surgery for February 9. This morning he was to visit Krall for another check-up, but he has a sports banquet to attend in Philadelphia tonight. He sleeps in and then heads directly to the airport.

Practice is informal, anyway. Players are simply shooting around, having fun. Except Morgan Valley. She plays Diana Taurasi in a game of one-on-one which, over the course of the season, has become her Sisyphean pursuit.

"They have a sheet posted in Diana's locker," says Svetlana Abrosimova, "that keeps score of who has won how many games of one-on-one versus the other."

There are only marks on one side of the ledger. "Diana wins every game," says Morgan, "and I don't take losing very well. The last time she said, 'I'm not going to play you if you're going to get mad.'"

Morgan will lose a game, or miss two free throws in a row, and suddenly her right foot is sending the basketball on a trajectory unnatural for this sport. Some of her frustration punts are so majestic that players stop what they are doing and just "ooh" and "ah".

"I saw her kick one into the upper deck," says Maria Conlon. "Morgan has a cannon."

Today Diana has won five straight games. By the end of the fifth she and Moe are bickering back and forth like sisters. On another basket Sveta is practicing post moves against assistant coach Tonya Cardoza, but after a while Sveta looks for somebody else to play. She calls Diana over.

They play a modified game, as each uses only post moves against the other, but they still keep score. Other players on the court begin to nudge one another and point. Sveta versus Diana. They have never seen this before. The reigning queen against her successor.

"The guards started gathering around us," Sveta later recalls. "Everyone was cheering."

They were witnessing something special, and they knew it. Diana is the future, but Sveta has a steady hold on her throne. Jessica Moore, for example, has become a shot-blocking fiend—

Kelly Schumacher refers to Jess as "White Team [*i.e.*, scout team] All-American"—and keeps track of all the Huskies whose shots she has rejected in practice. The only name not on her list is Svetlana Abrosimova. "One of these days, though," Jessica promises.

Diana and Sveta are deadlocked. Next basket wins. Their teammates are whooping it up. Sveta has the ball. She spins, shoots, and scores. She walks off the court with a triumphant smile as her teammates cheer.

Inside the locker room Sveta finds a pen. On the greaseboard she creates a Svet/Diana tally similar to the one Diana has in her locker for Morgan. Under her name Sveta strokes a single mark. Long live the queen.

FEBRUARY

Thursday, February 1 . . . Knoxville. Unless you wear orange and know the chorus to "Rocky Top" (*Rocky Top, you'll always be/Home sweet home to meeee!/ Good ol' Rocky Top (whoo!)/ Rocky Top Tennessee*); unless you love driving on Pat Summitt Street on the University of Tennessee campus, or are overjoyed that the Women's Basketball Hall of Fame is less than one mile east; unless all of those things, then the University of Tennessee is the Death Star of women's college basketball.

Knoxville is the other pole of the womens' basketball empire, home to both the Women's Hall of Fame and the Lady Vols, the most famous women's basketball program in NCAA history. Its epicenter, Thompson-Boling Arena, is the place where teams come to die.

Since 1974, when Pat Summitt, then 22, launched her coaching career, the Lady Vols are 337-33 (.911) on their home courts (Stokely Athletics Center from 1974-87 and Thompson-Boling Arena from 1987-present). Only one school that has played in Knoxville more than once has a winning record here: UConn.

When the Huskies first visited Knoxville in January of 1996, the Lady Vols were in the midst of an NCAA-record 69-game home win streak and a national championship season. Tennessee, which lost twice to UConn the season before, was primed for vengeance.

"Early in that Ninety-six game," says Carl Adamec, "Rita Williams had the ball and was shoved out of bounds by a Tennessee player right in front of me. It was pretty blatant. The referee called traveling on Rita."

Adamec and Mike DiMauro thought the call was so ridiculous that they started laughing. Right on press row. "The UConn bench is directly across the court from us," Adamec recalls, "and Geno sees us cracking up. He yells across the court, 'Now you know why they've won sixty-nine in a row.'"

The Huskies proved that they were not going away that day, winning 59-53. Two years later UConn returned and, playing before the largest live audience in women's basketball history (24,597), lost 89-64. The next game out the Huskies demolished Providence 126-48, the most lopsided win in UConn history.

The rivalry has its lighter side, too. Last summer at the U.S. Junior National Team tryout in Colorado Springs, Geno, Chris Dailey, Pat Summitt and her associate head coach, Mikki DeMoss, were seated near each other watching a scrimmage. All four were mesmerized by the play of Alana Beard, a freshman-to-be at Duke who somehow had never appeared on UConn or Tennessee's talent radar. Manning that radar is Dailey and DeMoss's primary responsibility at their respective schools.

Exhilarated—exasperated—by Beard's precocious play, Geno turned to Summitt. He pointed at CD and DeMoss. "Those two," he said, "should be fired."

Summitt nodded her head in agreement.

It is 10:30 a.m. Inside the cavernous Thompson-Boling Arena, the Huskies' white team runs through Tennessee's offensive plays. Maria Conlon, who at last is playing as if she belongs, drives past Svetlana Abrosimova, who lunges to block her shot. There is contact, a foul.

"Why'd you do that?" Geno asks Sveta irritably. "You're either being stupid on purpose or just plain dumb. That's the same thing you did the first play of the last Tennessee game."

Geno leans into Sveta hard for this infraction. "See, that's the difference," he says. "Dumb people do not learn from their mistakes. They just do the same dumb thing over and over. Smart people learn from their mistakes. That's how they get the label 'smart'."

Geno needs Sveta to pull the sled tonight. He had said as much in a conference call with the media two days ago. "The way it works best is when our best player is leading the charge," he said. "We haven't been the same since Christmas, you know, because our major-domo has not been there."

UConn runs its offense. A few plays into this exercise, Kennitra Johnson attempts a skip pass that a white team defender intercepts. "It's very simple," Geno says casually to CD. "We used to have a team where I said, 'Pass it from here to here' and they'd do it. And we used to win. Now they're all smarter than me."

Tonight's game will be televised on ESPN. Approximately 330 miles due east, the top-ranked Duke men's team will host neighborly rival North Carolina in a game that will be televised on ESPN2. Duke-North Carolina is the best rivalry in all of college basketball. This may be the second-best.

"Every person who badmouths women's basketball," says Randy Smith, "should be made to attend a Tennessee-UConn game."

He's got that right. Shortly after 6:00 p.m., a soft sun sets along the Tennessee River as fans begin streaming into Thompson-Boling Arena. The streets of the University of Tennessee—such as Summitt's eponymous roadway and Chamique Holdsclaw Drive— are gridlocked. The first time the Lady Vols sold out a game, in 1987 versus the University of Texas, traffic was so snarled that Summitt, who lives across the river, abandoned her car on a bridge and walked the final mile to the arena. She has since learned to arrive earlier for the big games.

The arena is fully amped. Noisy and overflowing and hostile. Tonight's bout needs no hype. In fact, those on press row who witness it in person will, to a man and woman, say that the first six minutes of play are the most breathless basketball they have ever seen.

UConn wins the tap, and Sveta hits a three-pointer in the corner.

3-0.

Kara Lawson, the Lady Vol point guard and a former fullback on a junior high boys football team, drives and nails a 12-footer.

3-2, Huskies.

Sveta rebounds a UConn miss and puts it in. The Lady Vols' Semeka Randall buries a 17-footer. Sveta hits a 15-footer from the free throw line. It continues this way for more than five minutes. The referees swallow their whistles—no foul is called, nor violation—and no ball sails out of bounds. No subs can enter the game, since there has been no stoppage of play. It's just pure, unfettered, up-and-down the court, playground ball. The pace is enervating, awe-inspiring.

Sue Bird dribbles the ball to the top of the key and attempts a pass to Shea Ralph on the right wing, but Randall has anticipated it. She steps between Sue and Shea and steals the ball, her motor in high gear as she heads upcourt. Sue, the fittest of the Huskies (she wins every suicide drill), drops her head in exhaustion, too winded to give chase.

Thirty-nine more seconds pass before a referee whistles UConn for a three-second violation, the game's first stoppage. Ten gasping and grateful players head to their respective benches as an announced crowd of 21,350 take their first breaths in six minutes. UConn leads, 17-16.

"I've never seen anything like it," says Jeff Jacobs. "Six minutes. That was terrific."

The rest of the half is a spirited skirmish between two great teams. Sveta, inspired by Geno's morning rebuke, scores 14 points. The output of Tennessee's Lawson, the erstwhile football player, should be measured in yards per carry. She is dragging the Huskies up and down the floor, scoring 15 points mostly in transition. On the final play of the half she stampedes upcourt and, just below the free-throw line, crashes into Shea, a collision of the sport's two most physical players. Shea careens backward as Lawson's shot misses. No foul is called as the buzzer signals halftime. Geno lets referee June Courteau know that that was a bad non-call, then heads into the locker room, his team trailing 45-44.

Early in the second half the Lady Vols take a 56-52 lead, when Lady Vol guard April McDivitt drives right by Sveta, a replay of what Maria did at this morning's shootaround. Sveta foolishly reaches over her opponent's shoulder to block the shot. Whistle plus the basket. *Smart people learn from their mistakes.*

"Unbelievable!" Geno cries, staring straight at Sveta. She looks away.

The Lady Vols keep UConn at arm's length. They lead 63-56 when the Huskies rebound their own miss and kick it out to Diana Taurasi. An orange map of Tennessee adorns the court with the center of the state corresponding to midcourt. When Diana catches the pass, her feet are on the orange map, at least 30 feet from the hoop. She buries the shot. "That," Jeff Jacobs exclaims, "was from Bristol [Tennessee]."

After a timeout Diana hits a 17-footer and Sveta drains a three to give UConn a 64-63 lead. With just over ten minutes left Diana attempts another three-pointer. Sveta, who is standing above and slightly to the left of the free throw line, anticipates the miss and scrambles into the lane to get the rebound. As she does, a Lady Vol defender steps into her path. Sveta bunny-hops to bypass her but, in so doing, lands awkwardly on her left foot. She crashes to the floor face-first along the baseline, her features twisted in a grimace.

There is no cry of pain. Sveta hobbles to the bench. At worst, it appears, she has suffered an ankle sprain. Tennessee has played all night without their Player of the Year candidate, Tamika Catchings, who suffered a season-ending ACL tear two weeks earlier. Now the sides are even.

UConn still leads 64-63 when a pass finds Diana in the left corner, right in front of the UConn bench. As Geno yells, "Stick it!", Diana shoots and buries the three. Running upcourt after the basket, she extends her right hand and musses Geno's hair.

Sveta checks back into the game briefly, but she is in too much pain. Meanwhile Tennessee, led by sophomore forward Gwen Jackson, an unlikely heroine who will finish with 28 points, regains the lead. Diana hits two more threes—she will finish with a career-high six of them along with 24 points—but UConn trails 83-79 with just over a minute left, and Diana has four fouls.

Now Lawson has the ball again, steamrolling forward on a fastbreak. Again, as at the end of the first half, Shea stakes her position and prepares for a charge. Lawson barrels into Shea and flips the ball to center Michelle Snow on her right, who is mauled by Diana to prevent an easy layup. The whistle blows.

Is it an offensive foul on Lawson? A block on Shea? Or a foul on Diana?

The call goes against Diana. She has fouled out. The arena erupts in cheers. On the far sideline, Geno steps toward mid-court, fuming. In the second half the Huskies have been called for twice as many fouls as have the Lady Vols. This call is the *coup de grace*. He puts both hands to his throat, indicating the choke sign.

Another whistle blows. Technical foul, UConn bench. At the end of that bench, Sveta sits with tears in her eyes, an ice pack wrapped around her bare left foot. The game is lost. Maybe more.

Tennessee wins 92-88, before the fifth-largest crowd to ever watch a women's game. Former Lady Vol Chamique Holdsclaw, whose "23" jersey was retired at halftime, is the first person presented in a packed interview room. "I've been to a lot of women's basketball games," says Holdsclaw, who last year was voted the Naismith Women's College Player of the Century, "but this is definitely the most exciting game I've ever been to."

Everyone in the room seems to agree. The questions asked have a superlative degree to them, as do the responses. When the three Lady Vols—Jackson, Lawson, and Randall— are asked to comment on Diana, two of them, Jackson and Randall, simply meet eyes in amazement. They exhale loudly in disbelief. No words necessary.

When Geno later takes the stage, with Diana seated next to him, he agrees. "She's a unique player," he says. "She makes spectacular plays and drives you crazy at the same time. She's the most fearless player we've ever had."

Geno spots Sally Jenkins, who pummeled Diana in print last October for her ego. "And," he adds, "she's managed to keep her ego in check all year, which is really good. She came with a reputation of having a huge ego."

Diana beams. She wishes that she had said it herself. Later Svetlana emerges from the locker room on crutches, a thousand-yard stare in her eyes. Her left foot is still wrapped in ice. Before hurting her foot she had 18 points, eight rebounds, and zero turnovers in 25 minutes. She was well on her way to her best game of the year. Who knows what the outcome of the game would have been if she had been healthy?

A man approaches Svetlana to wish her well but uncharacteristically she does not acknowledge him. She keeps hobbling out toward the team bus, wearing an expression that no one here has ever seen on her before. She wears fear.

Saturday, February 3 . . . At 10:00 a.m. Geno gathers the team around him at midcourt at Gampel. The words flow easily today. Normally Geno addresses them at a volume only they can hear, but today his words echo into the seats.

"The two Tennessee games and the Notre Dame game, the three biggest games we've played this year," he says, "what have you done to show people that you are better than last April second?"

He looks at Schuey. At Shea. At Swin. At Asjha. "What have you four done?" he asks. "Schuey, you haven't had one block in any of those three games. Nine blocks in the national championship, people were talking about you as a Naismith candidate. You act like a freshman. How many compliments do you need?

"Shea, when's the last time you hit a jump shot in a game? Do you remember?"

He continues. Svetlana Abrosimova is not present, but those who are stare right back at him as he speaks.

"If it ain't that important to you guys, why the freak should it be so important to us?" he wonders. "'Cuz it's our livelihood, 'cuz it's how we've chosen to make a living. And it's a goddamn thing when your livelihood, your ability to make a living, depends on twenty-year-old kids.

"Our success as coaches is defined by how well the players we are coaching respond to what we are telling them," he says. "A professor who fails his class either has stupid students or is a bad teacher. So what are we?"

Nobody thinks his students are stupid. He knows that. Not with three former National High School Players of the Year on the roster. He identifies a prize pupil. "Morgan's out here all the time working on her game," he says. "What do people call her? 'Obsessive'? I used to have three or four guys like that every year."

He cites his overachieving starting five from 1991: Debbie Baer, Kerry Bascom, Wendy Davis, Laura Lishness, and Meghan Pattyson. None of them was rated among the top 100 high school recruits nationally, yet they came within six points of beating Virginia in the Women's Final Four. "We had five white guys who couldn't walk and talk and chew gum," he tells them, "but they didn't turn the ball over. Greatest class we ever had."

The Huskies go through their customary early-practice drills before moving into a three-player offensive drill. As they do, Svetlana enters the gym. She is wearing blue team sweats and a yellow Nike top. Her left foot, wrapped in an Ace bandage, is covered by an oversize tube sock. Her face looks haggard, as if she has not slept.

For a solid 25 minutes, the Huskies run the offense smoothly. Geno gradually adds elements—from three players to four to five; an extra pass here, another screen there— layering the lesson deftly. When Shea Ralph buries a three-pointer, all is right.

"Nice job, Shea," Geno says. "That's pretty good."

Then Diana Taurasi makes her second errant pass of the morning. From the right wing she tries to throw a skip pass to the left wing but instead tosses it out of bounds. "Let me tell you guys something right now," he says, exasperated. "The next guy who throws a pass more than fifteen feet, just go in the goddamn shower, because I'm not putting up with that shit. I don't know where you guys learned that, but it doesn't go here."

They break for water, then return to the court to work on defense. "Notre Dame and Tennessee kicked our asses because we couldn't guard them," Geno says. "Not because we couldn't score. Three biggest games this year, we played lousy on 'D'. We used to be a great defensive team."

Geno works only with the guards, setting up a three-on-three situation with one guard on the point and the other two on the wings. "Rule number one," he tells the defenders, "we don't switch on screens. Rule number two, we force the ball out of the middle. Rule number three, we don't let 'em dribble by us."

Emphasizing the final point, Geno says, "Do not let anybody dribble inside the three-point line."

On the very first play Maria Conlon, one of the slowest guards, dribbles right past Kennitra Johnson, the quickest. KJ could sooner have sung "Rocky Top" and shocked him less. In the background someone says, "Nice try, KJ."

Salt in the wound, that. Geno halts practice, calls everyone in. "You know what the most overused and worst statement is?"

he asks. "'Nice try.' That's a girl statement. As if the object was trying. No such thing as a nice try. Good players measure themselves by what they get done. I don't ever want to hear you say, 'Nice try' to a teammate. Say, 'Good job', 'cuz they got it done or be pissed off at 'em.

"Did you see the movie *The Rock*?" he continues. "Did you see it? Sean Connery tells Nicholas Cage what he has to get done. And Nicholas Cage says, 'I'll try.' And what does Sean Connery say?"

The line from the film is profane, so Geno checks himself. "I'll give you half of it. 'Losers say, "I'll try". Winners get it done and go home . . .'"

"'And,'" Shea interjects, "'get with the prom queen.'"

Shea and Diana laugh. Geno, off-guard, throws them a smile. Sue Bird, who is the team's designated cinephile, cracks her first grin of the day.

"How come Sue was smiling?" asks Geno. "Because she knows the whole scene by heart."

Sue blushes. There are times, such as now, when Geno reminds you of no one so much as he does of Tom Hanks's baseball manager, Jimmy Dugan, in *A League of Their Own*: cantankerous, chauvinistic, politically incorrect, and funny.

"It's supposed to be hard," Jimmy Dugan once told his star catcher, Dottie Hinson (Geena Davis). "If it wasn't hard, everyone would do it. The hard is what makes it great."

Geno is saying as much to them now. *Don't expect me to coddle you.*

The Herde begins to filter into Gampel. They usually are permitted to observe the last 30 minutes of practice and so have missed most of the morning's theatrics. Most, not all. Asjha Jones, who receives less vocal rebuke than anyone on the team, makes a great post move on one play but then follows it up with a terribly timid move on the very next play.

"You've only been doing post moves five months," Geno yells at her. "That's what you've learned?"

He kicks over a table in frustration. Carl Adamec, sitting halfway up the lower level of seats, chuckles. "He did that before the 1991 East Regional final in Philadelphia," says Adamec. "He kicked the bleachers during the shootaround, but they were like cement. He started hopping around he was in so much pain.

"And Kerry Bascom," Adamec says in a low whisper, "asked, 'What's a matter, coach, you need a toe truck?'"

The offense picks it up. Morgan Valley, playing with the blue, or first, team, hits three consecutive long-range jumpers. Then Diana throws a pass that is stolen. "You are . . .," he says, clearly flabbergasted, "I don't want to say it."

Geno takes a seat in the first row of seats and crosses his legs. Shea takes over. "Run it, D," she commands.

Diana, at the point, starts the next play. The passing is flaw-less, efficient and the ball finds its way again to Morgan, who is open from 20 feet. She passes the ball to Diana.

"Whoa, whoa, whoa," Geno interrupts, looking straight at Morgan. "What was that? You make the last three shots, and now you're not allowed to shoot anymore? This ain't the fishing show, where you catch your limit and gotta throw it back."

Sue and Shea, both standing on the sidelines, bury their faces in their jerseys, trying not to giggle. How can one person be such a bastard and such a comedian? they wonder.

"We had a practice today that was one of the best practices we've had all year," Geno tells the Herde afterward. "We showed them a mirror of everything that they don't want to see."

It was certainly his best practice of the season. He knows that folks in Connecticut believe that the sky is falling, but he has more faith in himself and his team than that. So do the Herde. Jim Fuller, a dry-witted writer from *The New Haven Register*, asks, "Did Lew [athletic director Lew Perkins] give you a vote of confidence?"

Geno smiles. He loves when they catch him off-guard. "It's worse than that," he tells Fuller. "I haven't spoken to him since I got back from Knoxville."

Sunday, February 4 . . . "I can't make any predictions right now," Geno tells the media after this afternoon's 75-39 defeat of Villanova at Gampel Pavilion. "The only prediction I can make is that we're going to be unpredictable."

After a morning shootaround in which he blistered the frontcourt players for their dispassionate play, Geno started four guards—Diana Taurasi, KJ, Shea Ralph and Sue Bird—along with Tamika Williams. Villanova starts three guards normally so Geno's lineup was an educated gambit.

"This starting five couldn't beat Notre Dame or Tennessee in a million years," Randy Smith groused from his press-row perch.

"This [Villanova] isn't them," answered T.C. Karmel.

"But isn't that the point?" he replied.

Not today. The point today was intensity. Play the five players who look the hungriest. Shea quieted the critics early, driving to the basket aggressively for a layup and knocking down a three-pointer in the Huskies' game-opening 11-0 run. She finished 5-5 (3-3 from three-point range) and had a game-high 14 points.

A dichotomy of emotions accompany this afternoon. Anxiety at the sight of Sveta entering the arena on crutches, dressed in street clothes for the first time in her career. Relief in seeing Shea rediscover her confidence and her outside shot.

In the postgame press conference Shea's return to form is the hot topic. Are her knees feeling better? she is asked. Her patience is brittle on this line of questioning. She is thinking ahead three months to the WNBA draft and worries, with good reason, that every word a prospective team reads about her knees will lower her stock. It is beginning to look as if, like tech stocks, Shea's value will never return to what it was a year ago. The Herde's preoccupation with her knees only aggravates the situation.

Shea gives an uncharacteristically terse response. Mike DiMauro is not satisfied with it. "What," he asks, "is four-four-three-two-eight-two?"

Shea looks at DiMauro quizzically. What is he talking about?

"Those are your point totals in the previous six games before today," he says.

DiMauro has kicked the hornet's nest. Naked. Tamika Williams, seated next to Shea, comes to her defense. "You guys have no idea all of the things that Shea does for us," she scolds as Shea eyes her gratefully. "I understand [the questions], but there are so many more things that she brings to my game, to our game, that we don't even think about the points because we know when we need that, she'll do that, too.

"You know what Sue always says?" Tamika says. "Sue always says, 'What are we going to do next year when Shea's not here?'"

It is a rare, almost unheard of, adversarial scene. It passes quickly as a summer shower, but the point is made. Leave Shea alone. You don't know what is bothering her, and we are not about to tell you.

By the time Geno enters the room, the awkwardness has passed. He is asked about Diana, whose circus pass assist on a fastbreak was the game's standout play in an otherwise, for her, mundane performance.

"The other night D looked like Jerry West," Geno says. "Today she looked like Mae West. But she did make a pass today that nobody else can make. That looked like a one-timer Lemieux to Jagr. Man, that was fantastic. If I were sitting in the stands, I'd bitch at me for taking her out, too."

Monday, February 5 . . . The storm is coming. Elementary schools in central Connecticut are closed this morning in anticipation of a winter storm that is sweeping the Atlantic Coast. By noon winter storm Crystal will hit, a unique blizzard that with sudden and beautiful ferocity will dump two feet of snow in the greater Hartford area.

"It exploded," one local weatherman will later say of Crystal. "It's what we call an East Coast bomb."

This is no day to drive but Svetlana Abrosimova must keep an appointment to have her foot examined. Coincidently Tamika Catchings of Tennessee, the reigning Naismith Player of the Year, is having surgery on her torn ACL today in Knoxville. Catchings, who like Sveta is a senior, is done with her college career.

Sveta does not expect a similar fate. "I'll be back for Senior Night," she said on Saturday. "I'm going to play."

Around 11:00 a.m. Sveta, Keirsten Walters and Rosemary Ragle pile into Rosemary's white Chrysler Cirrus to drive approximately 33 miles west to the UConn Health Center's John Dempsey Hospital in Farmington. The storm is just beginning when the three young women arrive. The X-rays yield a terrible revelation, a ligament tear at the top of Sveta's left foot. Surgery is scheduled for Wednesday. Her season is finished, the doctors inform her, as is her college career. Her parents, who are scheduled to come in two weeks for Senior Night, will never see her play in a UConn uniform.

When Sveta, Keirsten, and Rosemary emerge some 90 minutes later, the ground is already covered with snow. How swiftly the landscape changes. In the backseat of Rosie's car, Sveta stares out the window as they head back to Storrs along Interstate 84. The earth is a sea of white, of nothingness. All except for I-84, which is a veritable parking lot.

Travel is hazardous and it is slow. Keirsten, Rosemary, and Sveta will spend the next four hours in the car, alternately laughing and crying and wondering aloud about food.

As they inch eastward on the interstate, the sky is too dark and occluded with snowflakes for them to notice the billboard on their left. Stationed just beyond Exit 46 is an ad for UConn's Medical Center and, ironically, an unintentional personal note to Sveta. IF YOU LIKE OUR WOMEN'S BASKETBALL TEAM, YOU SHOULD SEE OUR HEALTH CENTER.

Tuesday, February 6 . . . When Svetlana Abrosimova enters the arena at 11:30 a.m., she is upbeat. "Let's go watch the big guys," she says, meaning the post players. "I never get a chance to see them play."

She is resilient. Whatever grieving Sveta has done in the past 24 hours, she displays none of it here. Ashley Battle walks over and sits next to Sveta. "I bet Jess [Moore] was mad when I get hurt," Sveta says.

"She was," says Ashley. "She was walking around the lockerroom saying, 'Not Sveta. She's the only one whose shot I haven't blocked.'"

Ashley and Sveta are not the only wounded in action today. KJ is also missing practice, suffering from back spasms. "I know what that feels like," says Sveta. "God, I know what all these injuries feel like."

On the court the Huskies are doing 4-on-4 halfcourt defense. Schuey, Shea Ralph, Sue Bird and Swin Cash are on the blue first team. Nykesha Sales is on the white team. Normally, Sveta would guard Keesh but now Schuey, who is too slow to cover her, guards the former All-American. Nykesha dribbles right past her for an easy layup.

"Shea," Sveta calls in a low voice, not wanting Geno to hear, "tell Schuey to guard Marci Czel. Put Swin on Kesha."

"Swin, get Keesha," Shea orders. "Schu, take Marci."

They do as Shea tells them. This is what Geno, a military history buff, would recognize as chain-of-command. Sveta to Shea, both five-star generals, delegate to the rest of the team. The question becomes, Where does Sue Bird fit in? With Sveta out of commission, she must become more of a presence.

"Tonya," Geno asks assistant Tonya Cardoza, who coaches the guards, "who has more steals, Sue Bird or Shea?"

"Sue, I think," Tonya replies.

"But you're not sure?" he asks. "It's not clear-cut?"

"I know Sveta was leading."

Sue Bird is the best point guard in the nation . . . when she wants to be. In Knoxville Sue scored seven of her 14 points in the final minute, once both Diana Taurasi and Sveta were gone from the game. In last season's game against Notre Dame she scored nine of her 14 points in the final three minutes. Why does she wait until then to impose her will on the game?

"Somebody needs to explain to me," Geno will say, "why a player like Sue Bird will pass up open shots."

Among educated Husky followers Sue Bird is the sleeper pick to settle many a debate. Deadlocked over whether Shea or Sveta is the team's most valuable player? Say Sue Bird. Is Diana or Sveta the Huskies' most deadly three-point shooter? Sue Bird. Who is the most comely—yes, such matters do inspire debate here— Sveta or Swin? Sue Bird.

Geno has the utmost faith in her oncourt maturity. "Sue Bird's the first player I've had in a while," he'll say, "where I've said to her, 'Everything that happens on this team that I don't like is your fault. As long as you understand that nothing you do will be right, you'll be pretty good.'"

Sue listened. She accepted the challenge. She buys the company line.

In many ways this is Sue's fifth season of college basketball. She was raised in suburban Syosset, New York, on Long Island. After her sophomore year of high school it was evident that Sue had major-college talent. She wanted to play year-round with some of her teammates from AAU ball, who attended Christ the King High School in Queens.

"In order for Sue to be eligible to play without sitting out a year," recalls her mother, Nancy, "we had to establish residence in that district."

Sue's parents rented an apartment on the corner of Metropolitan Avenue and 74th Street. One parent, either Nancy, a school nurse, or Sue's father, Herschel, was always at the apartment with Sue.

"She didn't miss anything," Mrs. Bird says. "She was happy."

Christ the King is a college program disguised in plaid skirts. The team travels nationally and in Sue's two seasons only lost one game, to Oregon City (Oregon) High School.

"I remember Sue telling us that they had game-day shootarounds at Christ the King," Tamika Williams once said. "Can you believe that?"

Back at practice, Diana is wide open at the elbow beyond the three-point arc, but she attempts a pass back to the top of the key. Nykesha steals the pass and goes in for an uncontested layup. Geno tears into Sue even though she was sitting out that play. She was standing on the sideline.

"I haven't heard you say a word all day," he tells her. "Not one word. Matter of fact, if I didn't know better, I wouldn't be able to tell the difference between you and Morgan."

Mostly, though, Geno is upbeat. They are down today, with the news of Sveta. They need a hand, not a lashing. He understands.

"When you get the ball right there," he pleads with Diana, motioning to the three-point elbow area, "and you're wide open, please do me a favor: Shoot the ball. You don't know what I know. 'Cuz when you pass the ball inside, at best it's 50-50. If we're going to win, you need to shoot the ball."

After Five Spots, he pulls them in close for a huddle. Tonight the Huskies travel to Blacksburg, Virginia, where tomorrow they will play Virginia Tech. UConn has never played there (this is Tech's first season in the Big East), and the challenge is daunting. The Hokies are 9-1 at home this season, their only loss coming to Notre Dame.

"Can we win the game with our best player on the shelf?" Geno asks them. "What's going to happen tomorrow night when you get down by ten? And you will get down by ten. What happened at Notre Dame? You just fell apart.

"I keep asking you the same question that you don't want me to ask," he says. "'What are you better at today than you were last April second?' You don't want me to ask that. 'Cuz it forces you to think, 'cuz it forces you to accept responsibility."

Wednesday, February 7 . . . Svetlana Abrosimova reclines on a bed in the recovery room of John Dempsey Hospital in Farmington. The sun shone brightly yesterday, allowing for the roads to be cleared quite well. Keirsten Walters and Sveta embarked from campus shortly after 5:00 a.m. for this morning's 7:00 a.m. surgery, and they arrived in plenty of time.

Sveta is wearing a white T-shirt that says "Russian Olympic Committee" and gray UConn sweatpants. She gazes at her left foot, in which orthopedic surgeon Kevin Shea inserted a metal plate during this morning's one-hour surgery. "I had the option of having screws inserted, which is the traditional route," says Sveta, "or a plate. The disadvantage of the screws is the chance of arthritis later in life, since they go directly into the joint. So I went with the plate."

Sveta explains the procedure blithely, as if she had been selecting the color of a new automobile. Keirsten, meanwhile, is fired up. She had asked to observe the surgery of her roommate, and everyone obliged. "It was really cool," Keirsten tells Sveta. "You won't believe how tiny that plate is."

"This is actually good luck," says Sveta. "Today is the seventh day of the month, the operation began at seven o'clock, and they did it in operating room number seven. Those are good signs."

She hasn't yet fully absorbed her injury and its cruel ramifications—for the Huskies, for Senior Night, etc. Yesterday it was front-page news in papers statewide, inspiring elegies such as the following from *The Hartford Courant* columnist Jeff Jacobs:

> *There is something very sad and hauntingly unfulfilling about this news delivered in a driving snowstorm, something very Russian. It harkens to one of the final scenes of Doctor Zhivago when an aging Zhivago thought he*

saw his Lara on the street after many years and began to walk after her. The walk became a run and just when he thinks he'll catch her, a sharp stab in his heart. It was the end for Zhivago.

"How long will the recovery take?" Sveta asks Dr. Shea.

"You keep asking me that," he says, "and I keep giving you an answer that does not satisfy you."

At Covenant Village, an upscale retirement community approximately fifteen miles south of Hartford, a UConn game broadcast is a rallying point. A few dozen residents who refer to themselves as "Chris's Kids", after Chris Dailey (who is young enough to be their kid), assemble in front of the TV in the community room.

"We used to call ourselves 'Geno's Bambinos'," says Dave Peterson, the group's unofficial president. "But then coach Dailey paid us a visit in person, and we changed to 'Dailey's Dribblers'. Now it's 'Chris's Kids'."

In retirement villages and and assisted-living centers statewide, similar pockets of Husky fandom exist. The Connecticut caucus of the Greatest Generation adores Geno's team in great numbers. Maybe it has to do with their wholesome image. As Peterson says, "The boys have so many tattoos on their arms."

In fact, half a dozen Huskies have tattoos that, except for Kennitra Johnson's, are cloaked by their uniform or, in Shea's case, by a strategically-placed lower calf wrap.

"There's another difference between the men and women," says UConn alumnus Alden Carlson, 68, who watches the game with his wife of 45 years, Arlene. "There's only about six good women's teams. The men are much more competitive.

"These people here," he says *sotto voce*, "want to see a blowout."

They do. In Blacksburg, playing before a season-high Virginia Tech crowd of 7,402, the Huskies explode for a 41-15 lead at the half. Sue Bird is up to Geno's challenge, and she will score a season-high 17 points to lead the Huskies.

At Covenant Village the residents listen to play-by-play announcer Bob Picosi and color analyst Meghan Pattyson do the CPTV broadcast. "Svetlana is in the infirmary on campus tonight," Meghan informs viewers late in the second half. "She is watching the game with Rita Williams and Kathy Auriemma. They had Kathy's homemade lasagna for dinner."

"I'm not sure we should be talking about lasagna during the game," says Picosi.

"When the score is eighty-two-thirty-three," says Meghan, "what else do you talk about?"

"We could talk about UConn's school-record fourteen three-pointers."

"I'd rather talk about food."

Picosi mentions Villanova men's basketball player Gary Buchanan, who earlier this evening broke the NCAA record for consecutive free throws made with 65.

"What's the most free throws you ever made in a row?" Picosi asks.

"Not sixty-five," Meghan replies. "I don't know of anything I've done sixty-five times in a row."

"Our director wants to know," says Picosi, responding to the voice in his ear, "if Meghan ever made sixty-five classes in a row."

She cackles. "No comment . . . Meals! I think I've made sixty-five meals in a row."

The Huskies win 90-38, in some respects their most impressive win all season. Back at Covenant Village, resident Cynthia Mankowski leads Chris's Kids in their traditional closing antiphon. "Do you have a favorite CD?" she asks.

"Yes!"

"Is it a CD-ROM?"

"No!"

"Is it a compact disc?"

"No!"

"Is it a certificate of deposit?"

"No!

"Is it Chris Dailey?"

"Yes!"

Friday, February 9 . . . "The biggest thing we are going to miss about Sveta," Geno tells the Herde this afternoon after practice, "is, you know, I tell the kids, basketball isn't a game of how-to, it's a game of when-to."

The prima donna had a flair for the dramatic. In her sophomore year in a game at Rutgers, playing in front of the largest crowd ever to see a women's basketball game in New Jersey, Svetlana Abrosimova stole the ball, grabbed an offensive rebound, and scored the winning basket all in the final minute of a 56-55 win. Afterward she explained, "Coach called a time-out and said we needed a steal."

Geno put the ball in her hands in the final seconds of the team's only loss last season. Tennessee, playing at Gampel Pavilion, had just gone up by one point on an amazing shot by Semeka Randall with 4.4 seconds remaining. UConn called timeout, and Geno looked at Sveta and said, "Score!"

Sveta got the inbounds pass and dribbled upcourt to just below the top of the key, with enough time to launch a shot. Two Lady Vol defenders converged on her. She saw Tamika Williams cutting to her left, nearer to the basket. She passed the ball. Tamika seemed surprised to receive it, and her layup attempt glanced off the bottom of the backboard. It was one of the few times that Sveta had voluntarily surrendered the spotlight, and UConn paid with its only loss of the season.

Save for that lone exception—albeit a major one—Sveta was the apotheosis of a crunch-time player. In contrast, Morgan Valley is discovering that all of her hard work and preparation does not directly translate to success in games. She played poorly in Blacksburg, her dearth of quickness exposed by quicker Virginia Tech players.

Before this season Morgan had known nothing but success. When she was in the fifth grade, her parents read about a state championship CYO squad from nearby Essex, Vermont, which was looking for a team to scrimmage. Her mother, Margie, rounded up Morgan and her sister, Ashley, and a few other kids from the neighborhood, and arranged a game. Mrs. Valley acted as coach. Morgan and Ashley's team won the two games by the scores of 89-2 and 91-0.

"That's when we realized that our daughters had something special," Mrs. Valley says.

Morgan's Rice Memorial High School team did not lose a game in her final two seasons. She started all four years there, setting school records for points (1,363), assists (477), and steals (385), and hours spent in the gym. Thus far, though, her court quickness is inadequate and, it would seem, in the last few weeks, that she is suffering from stage fright.

During a drill this afternoon in which four defensive players guard seven offensive players, a crucible of defensive quickness, Morgan starts out on the blue (first) team but is swiftly demoted. "Morgan, go white," Geno says. "You play too scared on blue. Guys who have slow feet have to learn to talk and to anticipate on defense. You don't do either of those things. Not yet, anyway."

Geno has spent much of the past month praising her work ethic in public, hoping the shot of confidence would relax her. Now he is going the other route, trying tough love. She has size, a terrific shot, and court intelligence. All things that Sveta had. She could be a huge boon to the team during a title run. If she would only relax.

During a free-throw session, Morgan and her partner, Maria Conlon, make 5 of 8. Both report that they made 7 of 10. The team fails to make 84%, so they must run. As they line up on the baseline, Geno asks, "Who got only seven?"

Morgan alone raises her hand.

"You got seven? Seven? You're in here thirteen hours a day, and you got seven?"

Morgan fumes quietly. Honesty, or pseudo-honesty, does not pay. If only, she thinks, he knew how many free throws the others missed. But he does. He does.

Sveta, sitting in the first row, just grins. "It's a lot different," she says, "when you see things from here."

It is amazing. Sveta, the polished senior, and Morgan, the raw freshman. When in reality Morgan is only nine months younger than Sveta. After practice the Herde, who have not had a chance to speak with Sveta since before the severity—and finality—of her injury was diagnosed, descend upon her as she sits in a first-row seat in Gampel.

"Wait," Sveta says, glibly preempting their interrogation, "I think I know all the questions."

She proceeds to list them.

"How do you feel?"

"Are your parents still coming?"

"Are you disappointed about Senior Night?"

"What about your WNBA future?"

"What do you think of the fans sending you all the stuff you're not supposed to get?"

"What about your career here? It's come a long way . . ."

"So," says Rachel McLoughlin of *The Connecticut Post*, "how *do* you feel?"

"I'm trying to stay positive," Sveta answers. "Everything happens for a reason. Too bad I can't find one yet."

Thirty feet away Geno expounds on Sveta's condition. "I don't think it's hit her yet," he says. "I think there's going to come a point in time when it's going to hit her pretty hard."

Already this week stuffed animals, cards (many with cash enclosed), baked goods, and other paraphernalia have flooded UConn's basketball offices, all addressed to Sveta. The athletic department issued a press release yesterday reiterating that, career-ending injury or not, Sveta is not entitled to receive any extra benefits.

"I think Svet transcends the game," says Geno. "She's not a basketball player anymore. She went from an unknown to a basketball player to a cult figure. People who know nothing about UConn basketball know about that Russian kid. She's like Jackie O or Princess Di."

Sunday, February 11 . . . The NBA All-Star Game is being staged today in the nation's capital and televised nationally to a republic that relates to its denizens less and less each day. The league's image problems are manifold. College basketball is experiencing an epidemic deforestation of talent, as the best players either head directly from high school to the NBA (*e.g.*, Kobe Bryant) or attend for one or two years, tops. In men's college hoops, the two-time All-American has gone the way of the Victrola.

The college men's game gets strip-mined, and the pro game gets a cruder brand of gem. The result is a league MVP, Los Angeles Laker center Shaquille O'Neal, whose free-throw percentage in his MVP season was 52.4. That's worse than any player on UConn or Tennessee's women's teams.

Thus as the league convenes in Washington, DC, today, *The Washington Post* offers a trenchant commentary decrying the state of the men's game and offering a modest proposal. It is written by staff writer Sally Jenkins and entitled "An Oasis in the Middle of a Hoops Wasteland." It begins thusly:

> *If you want to see basketball as it was intended to be played, if you appreciate a pleasing collaboration as opposed to the sullen, swaggering acts of isolation performed by certain members of the NBA, then you needn't watch the All-Star Game. A far more superior product is being played, and it's called women's collegiate basketball, and if you don't agree with me, I'll sleep tonight because I can name someone who does: John Wooden.*

Nearly 500 miles northeast of Washington, DC, a caravan of 66 buses has made its way from various parts of Connecticut to the Conte Forum on the campus of Boston College. The Huskies play the Eagles at noon, and at least two-thirds of the 8,606 fans in the arena are for UConn.

In the passageway between the locker rooms and the court, the Eagles huddle to say a pregame prayer. They begin singing "Amen" but are drowned out by a din of noise. From the court cheers of "U-C-O-N-N! UConn! UConn! UConn!" burst through the alcove like an oven blast. Boston College forward Becky Gottstein gathers her teammates closer. "I don't care how many fans they have or how loud it gets," Gottstein says. "This is still our house!"

> *I used to hate women's basketball,* Jenkins writes. *I'd go to a Final Four and I'd see heavy, doughy babes who couldn't jump, you could barely slip a credit card under their sneakers, and they shot air balls. They made me cringe for my gender. Now I cringe for the opposite sex —
and so does Wooden, who is no great fan of the NBA.*

Doug Flutie, the 1984 Heisman Trophy-winning quarterback from Boston College, has a front-row seat for today's game. Flutie, 37, still plays in the NFL. One of the things he does to stay in shape during the offseason is practice with the Eagles' women's basketball team.

"Doug is here a lot," says a Boston College official. "He's a big fan of women's basketball. He likes the way that they play."

The score is tied 17-17 score at the 9:26 mark of the first half. Compounding matters Sue Bird is once again being too altruistic with the basketball. "Sue Bird!" Geno barks in frustration after she passes up an open ten-footer. "Shoot the goddamn ball!"

UConn goes on a 10-0 run in two and a half minutes, and BC never gets close again. With four and a half minutes remaining, the Huskies lead 66-43. Diana Taurasi, whose high school jersey (23) was retired two nights earlier back in Chino, has the ball in the low post. She is out of position but, like an enthusiastic understudy who knows all of the characters' lines, relishes the opportunity to display her repertoire.

Using her left forearm to hold off her defender, Diana throws a soft hook shot off the backboard and into the basket. There are not 20 college centers who could make that shot so effortlessly. Diana looks at the Boston College defender and says with a swagger, "That's my hook shot."

On the bench Geno turns to Tonya Cardoza. "What did she say?" he asks.

"She said, 'That's my hook shot,'" Tonya replies.

"That's what I thought she said."

> "I'm a purist and I think the men have gone to show-manship too much," Wooden said in a phone interview from his home in California. "I don't know much about promotions, maybe that's what draws people, but the showmanship is too much . . . It's more like wrestling. If I want showmanship I'll go see the Globetrotters."

The Huskies win 78-53. After the game Diana's shot—and her punctuation of it— is a hot topic. The game is still innocent, and an act such as Diana's, so commonplace in the men's game that they are churlish, is not so much ominous as it is endearing.

The whispers have already started with Diana. She may be the first female college basketball player to jump to the WNBA early. Is she the missing link? Will she open the Pandora's Box of women's college basketball with her prodigious talent and, for better and for worse, make women's basketball that much more analogous to men's?

"Diana can go oh for eleven and I'll tell you what," Geno says, "she'll make the next five. She's got something different running through her veins."

Monday, February 12 . . . Svetlana Abrosimova sits courtside at this afternoon's practice, happy to be escaping the doldrums of February workouts. Next month she will miss all of this. But right now she is enjoying the novelty.

"Now I am on the bottom bunk, and Keirsten is on the top," she says, a switch made to accommodate her immobility. "I like the bottom bunk."

Around her neck is a gold crucifix. "My best friend in Russia gave this to me before I came to America," Sveta says. "Then when I arrived here, my friend called me on the phone hysterical. She said, 'I had a dream where you died.'

"'That's okay' I told her," Sveta says. "'If you die in someone else's dream it means that you'll be okay.'"

Since landing on the bottom bunk Sveta has been having lots of dreams. Or at least recalling them with greater clarity. "I'm always playing basketball in my dreams," Sveta says, "and you know what? I'm really playing well in them."

If Sveta plays the star in her dreams, her teammates today are playing like a nightmare. Less than an hour into practice, Geno has seen enough. "Five Spots," he tells them. "That's it. That's it. I gotta get outta here. This is a waste of time."

They ran "Spread", their basic offensive set, as if it made less sense to them than "Jabberwocky". Kelly Schumacher was the source of three consecutive turnovers. Then Kennitra Johnson drove, got airborne along the baseline, and only then realized that nobody was open. She made an acrobatic pass to Nykesha Sales, who was playing defense.

"That's as bad as anything I've ever seen," Geno tells them in an even voice as they huddle. "That's where we miss Svet. You know what would happen if this happened in a game? Svet would get a three. Svet would drive in for a layup and make something happen."

Sveta listens in at the edge of the huddle, leaning on her crutches, smiling inwardly. "If you decided to play as bad as you wanted," he tells them, "you couldn't play as bad as this. You couldn't. You couldn't. There wasn't one guy stepping up to get the job done. You know what happens if that happens in a game? Notre Dame all over again."

With an hour of their lives unexpectedly returned to them via the shortened practice, many of the Huskies hang out in the lounge. Some of them watch MTV's *Total Request Live*, which is the music channel's successful attempt to create the world's coolest after-school hangout. Popular videos are played, and hip artists stop by to chat with Carson Daly, the show's blandly popular host. Today's guest is white rap artist Jon B., whose presence incites a debate among the Huskies' connoisseurs of hip-hop.

"I don't like him," says Sue Bird. "I like Eminem better."

"Why?" asks Tamika.

"'Cuz he's a wigga," says Diana Taurasi ("wigga" is a street term, a contraction of "white nigga", i.e. a white person who appropriates urban African-American slang, fashion, etc.)

"At least Eminem keeps it real," says Sue.

Tamika Williams bursts into laughter. Now who' the wigga? she seems to be saying.

Tamika's parents, George and Josephine, live in Dayton, Ohio, and are probably traveling to or from a basketball tournament as you read this. Tamika's older brother played college basketball at the University of Miami of Ohio. Then there was Tamika, who was the USA Today National High School Player of the Year. Now Tamika's younger sister, Tiffany, is a high school freshman and, at 6'3", is already taller than Tamika. She is also rapidly becoming more famous.

Tiffany is one of the stars of a documentary series in the midst of a 13-week run on The Disney Channel. *Totally Hoops* chronicles the on-and off-court endeavors of the Dayton Lady HoopStars AAU team. Every Sunday night at 8 p.m. Tamika and various Huskies find a television set to watch the program, which follows the team from February through August of last year.

"Tiffany gets recognized everywhere she goes now," says her mother. "Kids want her autograph. Now Tamika gets 'Are you Tiffany's sister?'"

As the 23-person *Totally Hoops* documentary crew got acquainted with the players' families, George and Jo Williams became strong supporting characters in the series. People refer to them as the Cosbys, an homage to their being paragons of the well-adjusted, upper middle-class black American family.

The Williams are a portrait, African-American Gothic. Both grew up in Mobile, Alabama. Mr. Williams received five scholarship offers to play football, all from black colleges. He was raised in a single-parent home, however. His father had nine children by two women and sent very little money to help them. College was not an option, so George enlisted in the Air Force and, in April 1965, found himself in Vietnam.

Two months later the Vietcong attacked Bien Hoa Air Base, 20 miles south of Saigon. Williams, a staff sergeant, was part of a group that was deployed at the perimeter of the base to ward off the attackers.

"The Vietcong were sending black-pajama guys with explosives strapped to 'em," he says, "so if you hit 'em, they'd explode. There were four of us in a bunker and we'd been there twenty-five to thirty minutes when the area we were in got illuminated by flares.

"Then I got hit," Williams says. "It hurt. H-U-R-T. Hurt real bad. I got hit in the side, it came out the back."

There is no sorrow or pain in his voice. No bitterness about the wound that nearly killed him. "That's just the way it was," says Williams, whose face houses a perpetual grin. "You can't let the past slow you down. Find the brightness."

While George was in Vietnam, Jo was attending Alabama State University in Montgomery and taking part in civil rights marches, such as the one in Selma. Eventually, George returned from Vietnam and married Jo. Both of them not only graduated from college but earned master's degrees in education.

There have been days this season when Tamika wonders about her place at UConn. Here she is, a former high school National Player of the Year who is not starting in her junior year. Before one game she sat in front of the locker room muttering discontentedly.

But Tamika keeps this mostly to herself. If there is one player whom Geno never has to bark at, it is Tamika. Every day, no matter what she may be feeling inside, she lives the lesson of her parents. She finds the brightness.

Tuesday, February 13 . . . Half an hour before practice begins, Geno lies on the burgundy leather couch in his office, watching game tapes of tomorrow's opponent, Rutgers.

Ann Marie Person raps on the door. The Big East Banquet is just three weeks away, and the conference is soliciting nominations from its coaches for its season awards. "Is there anyone you'd like to nominate for the Big East awards?" she asks hopefully.

"For Defensive Player, I'd nominate Tamika," Geno says, "and for Most Improved, I'd nominate Marci Czel."

"Marci Czel?"

"Can you think of anyone who since last April second has improved more?"

Ann Marie shrugs and writes the names down. When practice starts at 2:30 p.m., Geno uses awards as his theme. He reminds them that no one from UConn has been named Big East Player of the Week or Big East Rookie of the Week yet this season.

"This stuff should piss you off," he tells them. "See, I live in a constant state of being pissed off, but you're just not like that."

Who is to blame? Geno is, and he knows it. First, he does not play his starters enough to allow them to put up gaudy offensive numbers. Second, UConn's offense is the least discriminating in the conference. That's how the Huskies have managed to have eight different high scorers in 22 games. Geno calls it, "the Connecticut Deli", as in "you never know what number you're going to get".

Besides, who needs weekly honors when you monopolize the annual ones? Since 1994 the Huskies have had exclusivity on the conference's Player of the Year award and Big East Tournament Most Valuable Player honor.

Of course, every silver lining has a cloud. In those same seven seasons Geno has only won the Big East Coach of the Year award three times. In all three of those seasons, 1995, '97, and '00, his teams were undefeated in the conference and won the Big East tournament. In the other four years the Huskies won the Big East Conference regular-season championship and tournament but did not go undefeated—and someone else was named Big East Coach of the Year.

"Coach of the Year?" Carl Adamec asks Geno when the topic is broached after practice. "You've been mathematically eliminated."

"Yeah," Geno agrees. "I lost a game."

The discussion turns to tomorrow's foe, Rutgers. The Scarlet Knights are coached by C. Vivian Stringer ("C. Viv," as the Herde call her), who in 28-plus seasons has 638 victories, third all-time behind Jody Conradt of the University of Texas and Pat Summitt of Tennessee. Last year C. Viv took the Scarlet Knights to the Women's Final Four, where they lost to Tennessee. This season they are once again solid, their 17-5 record earning them a No. 11 national ranking.

Rutgers is an obstinate, albeit oft-repelled foe. C. Viv may be only 1-10 versus Geno since arriving at Rutgers six years ago, but Rutgers always plays UConn tough, especially at home. Besides, nobody else in the Big East has done any better. When, in 1998, Rutgers beat the Huskies for the first time, 74-70, Stringer's squad carried her off the court.

"You know, for the last six years," Geno said then, "it seems that anyone who has beaten us has treated it like it was for the national championship."

In 1998, the season that Rutgers beat the Huskies, UConn was 34-3 overall and 17-1 in the Big East. Rutgers finished 22-10 overall and 14-4 in the conference. Stringer was named Big East Coach of the Year.

At the end of practice Geno learns that Diana Taurasi has been named Big East co-Rookie of the Week. She shares the title with Providence freshman Kristin Quinn. Adamec, the best straight man on the beat, asks, "Are you honored that Diana is Big East co-Rookie of the Week?"

"Honored?" says Geno. "I'm shocked."

Wednesday, February 14 . . . Valentine's Day. In the stands at Gampel are signs made by both the broken-hearted ("FEEL BETTA SVETA") and the lonely hearts ("SUE, WILL YOU BE MY VALENTINE?"). On the sideline Geno is modeling a pink shirt and Rutgers black uniforms.

The colors pink and black mesh about as well as the thought of UConn and Rutgers having a date on Valentine's Day. Between the schools there is little love lost.

"The most talkative team I've ever played against in my whole career," former Husky Nykesha Sales has said. "Their whole starting five had something to say to us. Unbelievable."

There is animus between the two programs, which plays out in subtle and intriguing fashion. Tonight, for example, Geno starts Asjha Jones. While Asjha is certainly one of the Huskies' five top players, especially in the absence of Svetlana Abrosimova, she is also a native of Piscataway, New Jersey. Asjha grew up no more than ten minutes from the Rutgers campus and, while it was not exactly preordained that she would become a Scarlet Knight, the odds seemed good.

Asjha is African-American, as is Stringer, and comes from a single-parent home in an urban area. For years blue-chip players such as Asjha headed to Knoxville or Iowa (where Stringer had coached before coming to Rutgers) but not to Storrs. "You want to play with slow white girls?" a white coach once asked Tamika Williams when she named UConn as a school that she was considering.

"There were black coaches who did it, too," Tamika has said. "They called UConn a white school."

Credit Jamelle Elliott with dissolving the color barrier. While UConn had African-American players before her, Jamelle was the first such Husky who left a mark on the program. She was—and still is—a tough SOB from inner city Washington, DC.

Members of the Herde tell a favorite story about Jamelle in practice during her playing days. The Huskies were doing 4-on-4 defensive drills and Jamelle, a senior, was less than pleased with the execution of teammate Carla Berube, a junior. Carla was no limp scrub: She had been the sixth man on the 35-0 team as a sophomore. But on this day, in this drill, she was not measuring up to Jamelle's standards.

According to the Herde, Jamelle yelled to Geno, "Get her the f___ off the court!"

What is amazing is not that Geno complied with Jamelle's request. What is amazing is that as Carla sulked off the court, she said to Geno, "Tell Jamelle I'm sorry."

Though her name does not resound on a national level as does that of Rebecca Lobo or Nykesha Sales, Jamelle's credentials are outstanding. "There are only two players in the history of Connecticut basketball who have at least a thousand points and a thousand rebounds," says Chris Dailey. "Rebecca Lobo and Jamelle Elliott. How many other six-foot power forwards do you see in college basketball?"

Jamelle had come to Storrs, laying the tracks for an underground railroad of African-American talent to UConn. In her wake came Nykesha Sales and then Rita Williams. Then in 1998 came the bonanza year in which Swin Cash, Asjha Jones and Tamika Williams, high school power forwards 1, 1-A and 1-AA in no particular order, signed with UConn.

Asjha's choice of UConn was seen as nothing less than apostasy in central New Jersey. When the Huskies played at Rutgers her freshman year, she was booed during introductions and heckled throughout the game. And so one is left to wonder if Asjha starts this evening as a dig at Rutgers or simply because she has earned it?

Doesn't matter.

The Huskies start tonight's game with a 10-0 run. Rutgers rides out the storm, maintaining its trademark deliberate offensive pace. At the 7:21 mark of the first half, UConn only leads 13-11. The Huskies are playing Rutgers' game.

Rutgers has talent. Point guard Tasha Pointer and center Tammy Sutton-Brown, both seniors, are legitimate first-round WNBA picks. The Scarlet Knights often seem to execute their offense, though, the way a teenager grinds gears when learning to drive a stick-shift. There is little fluidity. In the second half, UConn begins to pull away.

With 8:32 remaining UConn leads, 54-36. Diana Taurasi, who has missed eight consecutive three-point attempts while jawing with Pointer much of the game, at last connects from beyond the arc. As she turns to head upcourt, she releases some frustration by clapping in Pointer's face. Whistle. Technical foul on D. Geno pulls her from the game, which UConn will win, 70-45.

He is less than enchanted with Diana's antics. She is not the first UConn player to receive a technical foul. Sue Bird, whose oncourt composure is normally beyond reproach, got a technical foul in her first college road game, two years ago at UCLA.

"In the first half I had two fouls and no points," Sue recalled a few weeks ago, "So early in the second half I get another foul called on me. I'm angry at myself, and I utter a profanity. The ref saw me say it. In fact, it was on camera. And you know, in college a technical foul counts as a foul, so I had four fouls and no points. That was pretty much the end of my day."

Sue did learn a lesson, though, and shared it with the team. "Now we talk into our shirts when we're mad," she said. "I'll lift up my jersey as if I'm going to wipe off some sweat, and sometimes I am. But more often I'm letting off steam. And the camera can't read your lips."

Diana will learn these things. For tonight, though, Geno simply warns the squad that the next player to cross the line will sit out one game. "There's only room for one dumbass on this team," he explains, "and that's me."

Friday, February 16 . . . "Geno used to come to me like I was John Wooden," says Buddy Gardler, Geno's high school coach at Bishop Kenrick in Norristown. "Now he talks to me like he's John Wooden."

Buddy Gardler is a lifer in the Philadelphia Catholic League. For the past two decades Gardler, 54, has been the boys coach at Cardinal O'Hara High School. Before that he coached at Kenrick, another Catholic League school, for 11 years.

Gardler is Geno's mentor. "Just about everything you see Geno do in practice or in a game," says Jack Eisenmann, who played with Geno at Kenrick, "he learned from Buddy."

If Gardler had not noticed Geno playing pick-up basketball after his freshman year, if he had not mentioned to Jack Eisenmann that Geno should try out for the team, Geno would probably never have gone into coaching.

"You have to understand," says Jack's younger brother, Phil, who also played for Gardler, "that Buddy was like a god to us. He walked on water as far as we were concerned."

Gardler, who played collegiately at St. Joseph's University in Philadelphia, and his former point guard still talk all the time. "I probably argue with him more than anyone," Gardler says on this rainy afternoon in Philadelphia. "But every summer we go down to the Jersey shore and spend a lot of time together. Just playing cards and hanging out."

Gardler gets asked about Geno all the time and does a poor job of pretending that it annoys him. "Everyone asks me why he's so successful," Gardler says. "My wife may have said it best. She says, 'Geno's a good-looking guy with a great personality.' What more do you need?"

Saturday, February 17 . . . Philly. Geno has so much history in this city. So does the modern version of women's college basketball.

"The history of women's basketball," says Tom DeCamillo, the sports information director at West Chester (Pa.) University, 20 miles west of Philadelphia, "begins in that gym right outside my office. Hollinger Fieldhouse."

West Chester, a Division II (D-II) school, is integral to the story of women's college basketball. Hollinger Fieldhouse was the site for the inaugural Women's National Invitational Tournament (WNIT) in 1969, which West Chester won, a 65-39 defeat of Western Carolina.

West Chester is also Geno's alma mater. But Geno is not the most important women's basketball coach to have graduated from West Chester. Not from a historical perspective. That would be Cathy Rush.

Like Geno, Rush never played basketball at West Chester. Very quickly, though, the game began to consume her. "I graduated from West Chester on a Sunday in May of nineteen sixty-eight," she says, "and married Ed Rush six days later. I was twenty-one."

In 1966 Ed Rush had become, at age 24, the youngest referee in the history of the NBA. In 1970 Cathy applied for the head coaching job at Immaculata College in plush, residential Broomall, Pennsylvania, about ten miles northeast of West Chester.

"It was four hundred fifty dollars a year and Ed was traveling a lot," says Rush. "I thought it would be fun."

Immaculata was a tiny, 450-student, female-only commuter school run by the Sisters of the Immaculate Heart. That first season Rush, who never recruited, welcomed a freshman post player named Theresa Schank, whose matriculation there was purely accidental. "I had no idea who Cathy was," says the former

Schank, now better known as Theresa Grentz. "She had no idea who we were."

Providence brought them together. Grentz had an academic scholarship to Mount St. Mary's College in Emmittsburg, Maryland. However, on March 15, 1970, her family's rowhouse in Glenolden, Pennsylvania, burnt down from causes unknown.

"I was the last one out of the house," says Grentz, who is 6'3". "All I had left was the pair of yellow pajamas on my back. How could I leave my family? Everyone was devastated. I made the decision to go to Immaculata. It's not what I wanted to do but what I needed to do."

Without realizing it, the nuns at Immaculata had laid the foundation for a women's basketball dynasty. The Mighty Macs, as they were known, started 10-0 in that 1970-71 season. Then Grentz broke her collarbone in a car accident, and they lost their final two games.

The following season saw the arrival of freshmen Rene Muth (now Rene Portland, the coach at Penn State), a post player, and Marianne Stanley (now Marianne Crawford, an assistant coach in the WNBA), a point guard. The Mighty Macs had no gym (it too had burnt down, so they practiced at a nearby novitiate) and no travel budget. All they had was talent.

In 1972, the Association of Interscholastic Athletics for Women (AIAW) staged women's college basketball's first truly national championship, in Normal, Illinois. "We couldn't afford to bring the entire team," says Rush, who was pregnant with her first child. "We sold toothbrushes door-to-door to raise money and even then we didn't have enough. So I cut the squad to eight players and myself. No assistants, no trainer, no manager, nothing. Myself and eight players at the national tournament."

The Mighty Macs flew standby from Philadelphia to Chicago. They played four games in 48 hours, washing their uniforms (tunics, actually) in the hotel sinks between games. Immaculata's opponent in the final? West Chester. The Mighty Macs won, 52-48, with Grentz scoring exactly half of the Mighty Macs' points.

"We flew home first-class," recalls Portland, "and West Chester was on the same flight with us. There was a big crowd waiting for us at the gate, so the pilot asked the rest of the flight to get off the plane first."

Imagine that. The West Chester players marched down the plane's aisle, past the team that defeated them, and then deplaned directly into the Mighty Macs' sea of fans.

"It was the school president's idea to fly us home first-class," recalls Portland. "The nuns got rid of him after that."

A phenomenon was born, its parents a glamour couple named Ed and Cathy Rush. "We were the richest people we knew," says Cathy of their newlywed days. "I mean, we were in our twenties, we bought a house, we had two Mustangs. We were featured in *People* magazine."

Summers were spent in Puerto Rico, where Ed refereed in an amateur league. "The games were so violent and the fans so crazy," recalls Cathy, "that the Puerto Rican refs didn't want to work the games because people knew their names and how to find them."

"So here I am in my early twenties," says the blonde Rush, who at 53 is still a head-turner, "living in a two-bedroom condo on the beach and hanging out all day at the pool with the American coaches they'd brought down there, like Jimmy Lynam and Paul Westhead. I picked up a lot of basketball and had a lot of fun."

Cathy Rush was both a pioneer and a revolutionary. "Twenty-five years ago," says Portland, "she'd walk into practice with index cards that showed practice schedules: 'At three o'clock we're doing press-break, at three-oh-five out-of-bounds plays.'"

"I was a chemistry major," says Grentz, "but for some reason I'd write down everything we'd done in practice. I would go back and copy the notes."

An improbable and wonderful alchemy took hold. Ed Rush, who appreciated the magnitude of what was brewing before his eyes, would catch red-eye flights home from his NBA games in order to attend his wife's. Armed with a walkie-talkie, he would sit high up in the stands, calling out plays or defenses for Cathy to use. Cathy, in the interest of spousal harmony, would hand her walkie-talkie to a manager at the start of the game, literally tuning her husband out.

"I don't think she ever listened to him," says Portland, "but Ed took those games as seriously as we did. I'd see him emerging from the pressbox with his wristwatch broken."

Meanwhile, Portland's father, who owned a hardware store, formed an impromptu cheering section called the Bucket Brigade. In Grentz's sophomore year Immaculata built a new gym but did not install bleachers. Thus, Mr. Muth brought galvanized steel buckets to serve as rump rests. Before long, however, he realized that with dowels serving as drumsticks, the buckets made outstanding percussion instruments.

"It was chaos," says Portland. "Visiting teams would come into our gym and see a bunch of nuns either standing or sitting in folding chairs. Then there was my family, banging on their buckets."

And then there was Grentz.

"Theresa scared the living daylights out of *us*," says Portland, whose own stare can wilt a flower. "She used to warn (point guard) Marianne Stanley not to dribble into the lane and then dish off a pass to her because it clogged the lane.

"So one day at practice Marianne dribbled down the lane and Theresa clotheslined her," says Portland. "Knocked her flat on her back and just walked away. I looked down at Marianne and I said, 'She warned you.'"

Immaculata would win the first three AIAW national championships and the hearts of hoops fans. Headlines hailed them as "Girlsterous" and "The UCLA of Women's Basketball". Among those breathless converts was Dick Weiss, then a garrulous young beat reporter for *The Philadelphia Daily News*.

"Cathy Rush was the perfect poster child for the sport at the time," says Weiss, who fell in love with Immaculata at first sight. "I saw them scrimmage Temple in McGonigle Hall, and I couldn't believe this team's skills. Theresa was the outstanding player of her era. Marianne, she would use one hand to hike up her skirt as she dribbled between her legs."

The Mighty Macs played in the first nationally televised women's basketball game, at the University of Maryland in 1975. They also played in the first women's basketball game to be staged at Madison Square Garden, in front of 12,000 people, also in 1975. "They played Helen Reddy's 'I Am Woman' as an intro for us to run out onto the floor," says Portland, who went 85-5 as a player at Immaculata. "Someone said, 'I'm not walking out to that'. We were very conscious of not looking like PE majors."

In fact, Grentz and Portland were bridesmaids at one another's weddings. As Rush's two best players were settling into married life, Rush's marriage was coming undone. "It was sad because we loved him [Ed], too," Portland says, "but she was struggling. We just knew that it was falling apart."

By 1975 Rush had two small sons and intercollegiate athletics, thanks to Title IX, (which guarantees female students equal access to athletic facilities and scholarships), was starting to catch up to the Mighty Macs. Rush vented her frustration in the press.

"Beggars is what we are," she said then. "Maybe someday the school administration will take a keener look at what we are doing at Immaculata. Maybe they will realize what basketball can mean."

"Oh, I got into a world of trouble over that," says Rush now. "But I felt that we weren't being appreciated."

Someone who did appreciate Immaculata and women's hoops was a young nebbish-like copy clerk at *The Philadelphia Daily News* named Mel Greenberg. He had been a manager for the Temple men's basketball team in the late Sixties, where he'd befriended Weiss, then a student there as well and covering the Owls for the school paper. Weiss took Greenberg to his first women's game, Immaculata versus West Chester.

"Mel probably thought of it as nothing more than an anomaly at the time," laughs Weiss. "Who knew?"

In 1976 Jay Searcy, the sports editor at *The Philadelphia Daily News*, asked Greenberg to create and oversee a weekly national women's college basketball poll. This was tantamount to President Jefferson asking Lewis and Clark if they'd like to take a little trip.

"You have to remember," says Greenberg, "this is before the fax machine, before call-waiting, before the internet, before *USA Today*. It was a nightmare."

For the next 18 years of his life, Greenberg became singularly devoted to his distaff basketball poll. On Sundays he would place two phone calls to each coach that voted. First he would call and give them the scores from the past week's relevant games, and later he would call to get their rankings, which he would then painstakingly compile. The poll would run in Wednesday's editions of his newspaper.

To appreciate Greenberg's daunting task, first you must appreciate him. He is a friendly, frumpy, lifetime bachelor who has lived in the same Philadelphia home for all but two of his 54 years. Mel mumbles and speaks in a stream of consciousness that has more tributaries than the Amazon, which can make a conversation with him, as affable as he is, an arduous experience.

"God, I hated Sunday nights," groans Grentz good-naturedly. "You can't just spend five minutes on the phone with Mel. By the time my older son was old enough, he'd be the one taking the phone calls."

Greenberg, who eventually ceded his poll to the Associated Press in 1994, genially tortured the premier women's college hoops coaches each Sunday night for the better part of two decades. "The thing about Mel," says Tennessee coach Pat Summitt, "is that it's not like you're going to get right to the voting. I enjoyed Mel, really, once I learned to understand him."

"He would talk and talk and talk," moans Rush. "I would finally just tell him, 'I gotta go.'"

By 1977 Rush had the same sense about her coaching career. Unable to compete with Division I schools that were offering scholarships, she bowed out after seven seasons, with a 149-15 record. In Rush's final season Portland, who by then was the coach at St. Joe's, beat her mentor by one point. "That," Portland recalls, "was one of the hardest nights of my life."

It was over, Rush knew. She had won three national championships and taken her Mighty Macs to two others. It was time to be a full-time mother. Besides, by then she had created a niche for herself that would cast an equally indelible imprint on the future of the sport.

Six years earlier, in the summer of 1971, Cathy and Ed had launched the Cathy Rush Basketball Camp, a hoops camp exclusively for females. The camp opened doors for a lot of young coaches. To read a partial roll call of former counselors at Rush's camps is to see a formidable number of today's most influential women's college basketball coaches: Geno Auriemma (UConn), Charlene Curtis (Wake Forest), Jim Foster (Vanderbilt), Theresa Grentz (Illinois), Pat Knapp (Georgetown), Muffet McGraw (Notre Dame), Dianne Nolan (Fairfield), June Olkowski (Northwestern), Harry Perretta (Villanova), Rene Portland

(Penn State) and Debbie Ryan (Virginia). Portland and Phil Martelli, now the men's coach at St. Joe's, were the camp directors. As with most summer camps, the counselors had far more fun than the campers.

"Oh, it was wild," says Nolan, the Fairfield coach. "You did basketball all day then lost years off your life at night, killing brain cells."

"Every morning Ed Rush would stand on the front porch of his cabin and fire us," says Portland, "and then Cathy would hire all of us back."

Rush has had hundreds—no, thousands—of counselors work for her over the years. "It's funny," she says, "I get so many letters from people who say, 'I worked at your camp. Can I use you as a reference?' and I'm like, Who was that person?"

But she remembers Geno. "Oh sure," Rush says.

Why?

"Well, probably because he was so good-looking," Rush replies. "He'd wear what we call the Italian T-shirt which nobody liked except on him. He'd be outside all summer, the hair getting blond streaks in it, this gorgeous tan, and the blue eyes and, you know, no one forgot him.

"Plus, he's just a personality," she adds. "He's a funny, funny guy."

It was a time for women's college basketball coaches to get in on the ground floor. Title IX was creating a slew of jobs and there were not enough people to fill them. "I'd always dreamt of returning to coach at Immaculata," says Portland, "but then Colorado phoned in nineteen seventy-eight and offered me twenty-three thousand a year and I was like, Whoa!"

Portland left St. Joe's, and Jim Foster took her place, taking Geno with him as his assistant. The two had met when both played at Montgomery County Community College. "I earned three thousand a year," recalls Foster, "and Geno earned a thousand a year."

One year later Geno, eager to coach boys and given an opportunity to work at his old high school, Bishop Kenrick, became Martelli's assistant coach there. When, in the summer of 1981, Debbie Ryan offered Martelli an assistant's job at the University of Virginia, he declined. But he did suggest Geno in his place. Ryan liked the idea. So did Geno.

Soon after, Geno and Kathy packed their life into a Honda Civic and a U-Haul trailer. They were headed to Charlottesville, a $13,000 a year job and, he knew, the biggest opportunity that life had ever given him.

Cathy and Ed Rush divorced in the late Seventies. Today he is the NBA Supervisor of Officials. She still runs her summer camps, now known as Future Stars, which each summer have an enrollment of some 10,000 campers.

When the Women's Basketball Hall of Fame opened in Knoxville in 1998, Cathy Rush was not elected on the first ballot. Rene Portland, who to this day addresses her former coach as "Mrs. Rush", was so incensed at the slight that she refuses to step inside the facility . . . Theresa Grentz incorporates the notes that she copied after each Immaculata practice in her own coaching career. At Rutgers she would post a schedule of each day's practice on a bulletin board in the locker room, and each night they would be missing. Chris Dailey took them. She still has them . . . Grentz and Portland rank seventh and eighth in victories, respectively, all-time in women's college basketball . . . Leon Barmore is listed as the winningest coach in terms of percentage (.871) in men's or women's college basketball history, but Cathy Rush, who coached too few games to merit inclusion, has a .915 career percentage. In her final game Immaculata lost in the 1977 AIAW national semi-finals to a University of Tennessee squad coached by Pat Head, now known as Pat Summitt . . . Today Mel Greenberg is known by all in the sport as "Mr. Women's College Basketball" . . . Immaculata College still plays women's basketball, but the school and its aura no longer strike fear into the hearts of foes. At last year's Women's Final Four in Philadelphia, Penn State played UConn in one semifinal. Rene Portland, hoping to intimidate her former camp colleague, got tickets for 23 nuns from Immaculata to sit directly across the court from the Huskies bench. UConn won 89-67 . . . The West Chester Daily News, the only paper that covered the original Women's NIT in 1969, sent in a request for a media credential to that game and the national championship game. The request was denied.

Sunday, February 18 . . . Harry Perretta is a lifer. Perretta, 43, has spent more than half his life as the Villanova Wildcat basketball coach. He has been around this long: In 1982 Perretta, then in his fourth season, took the Wildcats to the AIAW national semifinals, where they lost to a Rutgers team that had a center named Chris Dailey.

He is lanky, dark-haired, and balding. Full of nervous energy and self-effacing wit. Now in his 22nd season at Villanova, Perretta is the dean of Big East coaches, though he behaves more like a nutty professor. Yesterday he had joked about how many free baskets Villanova would have to give Svetlana Abrosimova, who is fifth on the Huskies' all-time scoring list (1,865 points), in order for her to break Nykesha's record.

"She's only, what, three hundred or so points shy," he'd said. "We'll have to exchange a lot of baskets."

Perretta has seen it all. The best player he ever coached, Shelley Pennefather, is now a cloistered nun. Villanova's career scoring and rebounding leader, Pennefather won the 1987 Wade Trophy, which is given to the nation's top collegiate female player. She was a three-time Big East Player of the Year. Today she lives in an abbey in Alexandria, Virginia.

In 1991 Pennefather, now known as Sister Rose Marie, entered the order of the Poor Clare nuns, taking vows of chastity, poverty, obedience, and enclosure. She has virtually no contact with the secular world. Once a year she is permitted to have visitors but can only talk to them from across a screened partition.

The first time Perretta visited Sister Rose Marie, in 1991, the Wildcats were in the midst of an exasperating 11-17 season. Cloistered life was looking good to him. "I'm coming over the wall!" he cried.

"Maybe," said Sister Rose Marie, who may also have taken a vow of sarcasm, "God meant for you to be a mediocre basketball coach."

This year, however, the Wildcats are far from mediocre. They are 18-6 and peering at their first NCAA berth in 12 seasons. Last month they beat Rutgers, a monumental win that Perretta missed. He was with his wife, Helen, a former player of his, who was giving birth to their second child. "Notice how well Villanova does," Geno had joked, "when Harry isn't there?"

Half an hour before the noon tip-off, a record-crowd of 6,229 files in to Villanova's Pavilion. Rapper Mystikal's "Shake Ya Ass" blares from the speakers. On the UConn bench Sveta sits hers, her left leg resting across three seats. Behind her a procession of well-wishers, at least three dozen people, forms as if waiting in a wedding reception line.

Inside the Villanova locker room, Perretta is in full comedic rant. "I'm sick of college sports," he tells his players and coaches. "I told you when I'm ready to leave how I'm going to do it. When the last game's over, I'm just going to walk down Lancaster Avenue talking to myself, saying, 'It's over, it's over.'"

"You'll be seventy-five then," says assistant coach Joe Mullaney.

Minutes earlier Perretta had been sequestered in the men's locker room with Geno. The two friends had stolen a few moments alone to discuss an incident that Perretta witnessed at last night's Villanova men's game. The Wildcat fans had started a "Lappas Must Go" chant, a reference to the men's coach who had only averaged 19 wins per season over the last nine years. Thus Perretta's expression of disgust with college sports, which was equal parts facetious and sincere.

"Greatest day of the year," Perretta continues, "is the day after our last game because it's the longest time between our last game and our next game. On that day, I wake up at six and go to bed at midnight just to make it last longer."

Mullaney tries to lift Perretta's spirits by informing him of the record crowd in attendance. "I don't want any fans," says Perretta. "I told everybody the game starts at two o'clock."

The Wildcats say a Hail Mary and then alight from the room brimming with energy as if they have taken Mystikal's lyrics to heart. Perretta trails them, looking like a man with a colonoscopy in his near future. "I'll be the happiest man in the city at two o'clock," he says.

The Huskies start the game sluggishly. Diana Taurasi commits a turnover on the first possession. She redeems herself, in her inimitable fashion, a few plays later. Standing at the right elbow, she leaps in the air to catch a high pass from Shea Ralph, who is on the left wing. Before her feet hit the ground, Diana has already flung a pass—no-look, of course—to KJ in the right corner, who hits the three-pointer.

Diana is not scoring. Nor is Sue Bird. They're not even shooting. The backcourt duo have combined for five shots and zero points, as Sue dribbles upcourt with just seconds remaining until halftime and the Huskies clinging to a one-point lead. Geno is at a loss to explain how Sue can vacillate so easily between emphatic and phlegmatic. "The only one who can guard Sue is Sue," he has said. "She stops shooting the ball. I don't know why."

Years ago Perretta had had the same difficulty with Pennefather, whose oncourt supremacy was often in conflict with her piety. "I'm not shooting the ball too much, am I?" she would ask Perretta.

"I'll tell you when you're shooting the ball too much," he would answer."

On this play, with just seconds left, Sue takes over. She uses a screen from Kelly Schumacher at the top of the key and drives in for a layup before the buzzer. She erases the doughnut next to her name, but the Huskies' 29 points is their lowest first-half output of the season.

The second half opens with UConn scoring seven straight points. The first two buckets are pull-up jumpers by Sue, who must have received an earful of Geno at halftime. The Huskies begin to pull away, thanks mostly to their defense and 'nova's horrid shooting. The Wildcats go nine minutes in one stretch without a field goal.

With 14:30 remaining in the game, UConn gets a terrible scare. Villanova freshman Courtney Mix, dribbling the ball upcourt, gets her legs entangled with Diana, who is guarding her. Diana crashes to the floor, tears in her eyes.

Geno rushes straight from the bench to Diana's side. Have they lost Diana, too?

A few minutes pass before Diana is assisted to the bench. Only Tamika Williams stands to clap for her as the crowd is doing. The rest of the team remains seated as if in shock. Losing Sveta was bad enough. Without Diana, well, no one wants to consider that.

UConn plays methodically the rest of the way, winning 61-43. In the press conference everyone wants to know about Diana's status. "Fortunately, it doesn't look too serious," says

Geno. "She's walking around in the locker room. Then again, I thought Svet would be out two weeks. What do I know?"

Monday, February 19 . . . From 1874 until 1891 author and humorist Mark Twain lived with his family in a 19-room mansion in Hartford. There he wrote classics such as *The Adventures of Tom Sawyer* and *The Adventures of Huckleberry Finn*. Twain was the most quotable person in Nutmeg State history until Geno Auriemma arrived. The author is reputed to have once said, "The coldest winter I ever saw was the summer I spent in San Francisco."

Twain massaged the truth. If he spent 17 winters in central Connecticut, one of those was his coldest. Connecticut has not yet experienced a thaw, which is defined as a 24-hour period of temperatures above freezing, this year. "The most serious charge which can be brought against New England," another author, Joseph Krutch, once said, "is not Puritanism, but February."

Is it any wonder that the region's most renowned poet was a man named Robert Frost? Or that in 1978 the roof of the Hartford Civic Center caved in under the weight of accumulated snow? The "brrr"-ometer has been holding steady all winter long. And on that rare occasion when a Husky sees a chance to light a spark, to create a little heat, well . . .

"I went into Foot Locker to check out a pair of tennis shoes this morning," says Shea Ralph, as she shoots around before practice with Morgan Valley, "and I see this totally hot guy. And I'm wearing all my UConn gear. So I'm hoping he'll talk to me. After a bit he approaches me, and we're talking. I'm feeling good. Then he says, 'Can I get your autograph for my girl-friend's mother?'"

The beauty of Shea, though, is that off the court she takes herself none too seriously. For example, she and Stacy Hansmeyer frequently visit a salon, Forever Tan, on the edge of campus. Her repeated forays there give her skin an other-worldly, orange-ish tint. Directing her eyes upward to her flaxen mane, she says, "There are a lot of colors on me that aren't natural."

Shea fashions herself a "Southern girl" and hates Storrs's version of winter. This is her fifth. Why did she return this season when she could have applied for the WNBA draft last spring? Because college sports are laden with passion, and she is all about that.

"She has always worked hard," Chris Dailey says, "but in the last two years she has taken it upon herself to push the other players. Players with Shea's intensity don't always get their teammates to come up to her level. But she has."

Another reason Shea returned: Diana Taurasi. Shea hung out with Diana on the eve of last season's championship game, so anxious was she to welcome Diana into the fold. Shea wanted a year to play with the prodigy from Chino. The feeling was mutual. "Diana has tremendous respect for Shea," says Randy Smith. "She'd rather have Geno yell at her than have Shea do it."

As the season plays out Shea has bonded with all of the freshmen. Her leadership is all primary colors, bold and simple. Freshmen are drawn to that. So it is that Morgan Valley and Shea meet each weekday at Gampel at 11:00 a.m. to shoot around. Just the two of them. Shea meets with Maria Conlon at night to practice three-point shots at the Fieldhouse.

"They shoot threes until both of them get a blister on their index fingers," says Marsha Lake. "If you look closely, Shea has started wearing a band-aid on her index finger."

Indeed she has. After practice today Shea stays late to speak with Carl Adamec and T.C. Karmel. They are the two beat writers who have been here the longest, analogues to Shea in that sense.

"Believe it or not, I'm leaving," Shea says as the three of them sit alone in Gampel. "It's going to be tough, especially with the freshmen. I feel like I've really bonded with them."

The reporters tell her that it's time for her to move on. She amiably agrees.

"But there's still a lot left to do here before I go," says Shea. "We've got three more regular season games, then the Big East and then the NCAAs. I'm really excited about the next month of my life."

As she says this, Stacy enters the gym. Shea finishes with Carl and T.C. and walks off the court arm-in-arm with Stacy. They have a date with some ultraviolet rays.

Tuesday, February 20 . . . In the wake of Svetlana Abrosimova's injury, UConn's offense has been a model of caprice. There are games such as Virginia Tech and Boston College, when the Huskies established a record for made three-pointers (14). Then there's one such as Sunday's, when Villanova held them to 29 first-half points.

The defense, though, has been outstanding. In the five games since UConn lost to Tennessee, the Huskies have held opponents to a combined 28.2% (73-258) from the field. The bad guys on *Magnum, P.I.* used to shoot more accurately. Only one opponent, Boston College, scored at least 18 points in each half. Virginia Tech shot an abominable 0-15 from three-point range.

"There's never a night where you should have a bad night on defense," Shea Ralph explained yesterday. "It's all effort."

Tonight UConn hosts the University of West Virginia at the Hartford Civic Center. This is their first game without both Diana Taurasi and Sveta. They are UConn's best offensive players but, if you listen to teammates' whispers, the worst defensive players.

Midway through tonight's first half, then, it is not altogether shocking that the Huskies are pitching a shutout. They lead 19-0 before the Mountaineers' Zsofia Horvath finally makes a layup. The rest of the half serves as the coming-out party of Maria Conlon. Geno sends her in the game with six minutes remaining, and she promptly buries a three-pointer. Then another. And another. The 16,294 fans here, almost all of whom know of her high school exploits in making a state-record amount of threes, cheer wildly. At halftime the Huskies lead 50-18 and Maria, with 11 points, is their leading scorer.

The Connecticut Deli is open. In the second half Swin Cash plays as if she'd been mainlining ginseng during the intermission. On one particular play she rebounds Asjha Jones's miss, misses the putback, gets that rebound, misses another putback, grabs that board, and then finally makes the shot and is fouled. She hits the free throw, thus cashing in with three rebounds and three points in one offensive possession. She will finish the evening with 20 points and 20 rebounds.

"Swin got twenty rebounds?" Shea asks in the aftermath of UConn's 97-34 win. "Really? Ten of them were her own [misses]."

Swin enters a few minutes later. She did not hear Shea's comment but still, the first words out of her mouth are, "Okay, for the record, I wasn't padding my stats."

Geno, too, is grinning. The Huskies held the Mountaineers to 19.2% shooting from the field. Only one Mountaineer, Russian native Darya Kudryavtseva, scored in double figures. A spunky guard, Kudryavtseva scored 16 points and played with a fearlessness that her teammates lacked. When she got her first break of the game with three minutes remaining, the HCC crowd gave her a thunderous ovation, a rarity for a visiting player. One wag suggests to Geno that the fans were acknowledging her courageous performance.

"I don't know," says Geno. "I think they just like cheering Russians."

Thursday, February 22 . . . Ludmila and Oleg Abrosimova's flight from St. Petersburg arrives at John F. Kennedy Airport tonight, an event that in certain quadrants of Connecticut is considered the biggest invasion JFK has hosted since the Beatles.

John, Paul, George, Ringo, Ludmila and Oleg.

The Russians are coming. Ever since Sveta's season, and hence collegiate career, was pronounced dead more than two weeks ago, the UConn athletic department has been in siege mentality. Bins of mail, all addressed to Sveta, inexorably grow in the corner of Jamelle Elliott's office.

Colleen Webb, who answers the phones in the women's basketball offices, patiently provides Sveta's address to the 30 or so callers daily who request it. But even Colleen's tolerance has its limits.

"People call and ask, 'How's Sveta's foot?', all day long," she says. "I tell them, 'We had to amputate it.'"

Photographers drive three hours to JFK just to snap a photo of Oleg and Ludmila reuniting with their crutch-wielding daughter. Would you expect anything less from a populace that, when Sveta grew her hair out last summer, was divided between those who favored her old pixie look and those who liked her longer locks? *The Hartford Courant* even ran a story about the debate with the headline, "Hair Peace".

Geno has concerns about Senior Night and the inordinate amount of attention Sveta is receiving. "Because of what happened with Svet, events have conspired to make this a Svet memorial, and that's not fair," he says. "If you're asking me what will be the most telling moment tomorrow night, it's that Shea Ralph is still doing things five years after she got here."

The other reason for Geno's heightened sensitivity is more personal. As the immigrant son of two parents whose English was either absent or extremely limited, he does not want to see Oleg and Ludmila endure a media circus. Sure, it's a great story—so is his, and that's why the media used to seek out his parents, Donato and Marsiella. But his father never understood the attention that his son received. When Geno was first hired at UConn in 1985 and told his dad that they were going to pay him to coach basketball, Donato innocently asked, "What happens when there are no games?"

It's that type of guileless charm that the Herde, understandably, craves. But the Abrosimovas have traveled all this way to see their daughter, not to be quoted.

Diana Taurasi is not at practice, but her teammates are stepping up in her absence. They make dumb, errant passes that confound their coach's sensibilities.

"I don't want to see anyone else try a difficult pass," Geno warns. "Anyone tries a difficult pass, I'm gonna be pissed."

Minutes later Swin Cash makes a great steal but then tosses a lead pass to KJ out of bounds. That and a few other incidents coerce Geno into abruptly ending practice an hour early.

"Five Spots," he calls.

"No! No!" a few of the upperclassmen plead.

"You think I got time for this?" Geno tells them. "When we lost to ND, we didn't get to play 'em again the next day. You don't always get a second chance."

They jog to the corners to run Five Spots. "Finish strong!" Shea shouts. "Nobody miss. Make all our layups."

Usually this is a given, but today Jessica Moore misses her layup halfway through, so the team must start again from the beginning. Sue Bird, under her breath, says, "I'm sick of this, man."

The drill finished, Geno calls them in. What he saw in the last hour has put him in a dark mood. There are no West

Virginias where the Huskies are going next month. "You know, we played with Sveta against Georgia, it was great," he says. "We couldn't have played any better. I was thinking this morning, We've lost Sveta, but we can still get back to that.

"Now I'm thinking, No way," Geno says. "No way. Two weeks or so, when we go to Pittsburgh or wherever to play in the [NCAA] regionals, that'll be it. The season will be over. You can all make spring break plans because that's as far as we're going. Then you'll be wishing that you'd pushed yourselves harder on days like this."

Friday, February 23 . . . Connecticut Public Television (CPTV) is not only televising tonight's Senior Night, co-starring lowly St. John's (8-17), but later this weekend CPTV will re-air the game. "It's going to be the only fifty-five point win in history to be rebroadcast," quips Matt Eagan.

Actually, it's going to be the only 74-point win in history to be rebroadcast. Yet tickets are being scalped on e-Bay for $400. "We're just glad we could witness this in person," says fan Shirley King, who sits with her husband, Gary, in the top row of Gampel Pavilion. These Kings do not have the royal box. "We don't care where we sit."

This is all about love. Not so much from the Huskies' fellow classmates on campus as from the scores of middle-age and senior fans who have adopted these players as their daughters. They haven't come to see basketball. They've come to see Svetlana Abrosimova limp on crutches out to midcourt accompanied by her real parents. As a sign in the student section reads, "OUR MOMS [heart] SVETA . . . MORE THAN US."

The pregame ceremony is scripted. Christine Rigby is introduced first, then Marci Czel, then Kelly Schumacher. Then comes Sveta's intro:

> "Accompanied by her parents, Ludmila and Oleg, from St. Petersburg, Russia, number twenty-five, SVETLANA ABROSIMOVA!"

As Sveta hobbles to midcourt, clad in her uniform for the first time since the Tennessee game, tears form in limpid pools around her eyes. It is bittersweet to see her on crutches, which prevent her from holding her parents' hands as they stride besides her. She gives Geno a long hug. He whispers something in her ear and then hands her a number 25 UConn jersey, framed.

Shea Ralph follows.

> *"Accompanied by her mother Marsha Lake and husband Roy Lake and by her father Bob, from Fayetteville, North Carolina, number thirty-three, SHEA RALPH!"*

Shea, accompanied by her posse of parents—Roy, Marsha, Bob Ralph and his wife—all march to midcourt. Geno hugs Shea, then Marsha, who is clad in a striking "Notice Me!" red dress. Earlier today she brought Geno the ugliest watch that she could find, a jab at the fan who'd criticized the one he wore at Notre Dame, for him to wear this evening.

Sveta is introduced as one of the Huskies starting five. The PA announcer's words "Starting for the one hundred fifteenth and final time . . .", are buried in cheers. Yet Shea is still announced last. "That's the way it would have been had Svet not gotten hurt," Geno will later say. "We didn't need to make this bigger than it was. It was already big."

Other gestures have pragmatic value. Sveta's parents, for example, are seated in the middle of a row, to protect them from well-wishers, *et al.* In the breast pocket of Oleg's olive suit, someone has stuck a "Do Not Disturb" placard.

The pregame ceremony was scripted. The game might as well be. Marci Czel, getting her first start in four years, takes the Huskies first shot, a three-pointer, and buries it. As the crowd erupts, Randy Smith pushes out his chair on press row and stands to leave. "There's too much love here for me tonight," R. Smith says. "I'm going home to compose."

R. Smith is likely being more literal ("compose myself") than cynical. Not a few of the Herde have been both anticipating this evening and dreading it. "I don't know if I'm going to be able to keep from crying," Mike DiMauro said earlier. Earlier, in December.

The Huskies, every last one, are unstoppable. In one stretch UConn outscores the Red Storm 46-2. Christine Rigby, given 21 minutes of playing time, scores a team-high 21 points. "Don't worry," Geno later tells her, "you only shot when you had the ball."

"Could I have scripted it any better?" Geno says at the press conference, repeating a question posed to him. "Without getting in any trouble? No."

"We came out ready to have a great time," says Shea, who scored 19 points and had seven assists, "and that was our only goal of the game. It was the best night of my life."

"The first thing my parents said was, 'We can't believe we're seeing people, not pictures,'" says Sveta. "To them it was a dream."

When she is asked about her regrets, about not being able to play in front of her folks, Sveta says, "There is nothing to be sad about. Nobody died."

On the court later, the stars of the evening are the last ones to filter out. Shea, Sveta, Geno, and their respective families take turns posing for photos with one another. Nona Auriemma, who speaks Italian, and Ludmila Abrosimova, who doesn't, stand by each other and somehow communicate. They are both transfixed by the smile on their favorite player's face.

"My mother has a life-size poster of Sveta on the door leading into her garage," Geno wisecracks as he, Kathy, Oleg, and Ludmila pose for a photo with Sveta. "I always ask her how come she doesn't have any of me."

"My mother already knows two English phrases," says Sveta. "'America is beautiful' and 'Svetlana is the best'."

One guess who taught her those.

Sunday, February 25 . . . Two days earlier Geno was discussing Diana Taurasi. He was standing in the hallway outside the women's lockerroom with a few members of the Herde, who lingered in the hopes of grazing more quotes. Geno stood in his customary spot, his back against the wall, one leg bent backward so that the sole of his foot was flush with the wall as well.

"That kid, I don't know where her head is," Geno said. "Last week we gave her about a dozen forms to fill out. You know, housing application, grant-in-aid stuff, *et cetera* for school as well as a USA Basketball bio factsheet for the [Junior National] team she'll play on this summer. She filled the factsheet out and returned it to us in fifteen minutes. We haven't seen any of the other forms yet."

He shook his head the way a dad does when discussing his teenage son's third speeding ticket. "That kid has a one-track mind," Geno said as he started toward his office. Then his expression changed, a broad grin crossing his face. "And I love it."

Diana Taurasi lives for hoops. So does Jackie Stiles. Stiles is a 5'8" senior guard for Southwest Missouri State University in Springfield, who has become the talk of women's basketball this season. She needs only 20 points to break the all-time women's collegiate scoring record (3,122) held by Patricia Hoskins of Mississippi Valley State.

But Jackie Stiles is more than a hotshot. She is a hardwood vestige of the American way. Though a tad undersize, Jackie Stiles has a lean, sinewy figure, dishwater blonde hair, and sparkly, blue-eyed pearls of wonder. Jackie Stiles looks as if she belongs in a Chevy truck commercial.

Stiles was born and raised in Claflin, Kansas, exactly 100 miles due south of the geographic center of the continental United States in a town of 630 people and no traffic light. At Claflin High School Stiles started a routine in which she had to make 1,000 shots daily before she would let herself go home.

"Then after I go away to college," says Stiles, Kansas's all-time prep scoring leader with 3,603 points, "my mom decides to put up a basket in front of our house."

Geno and Chris Dailey visited that green, two-story home to recruit Jackie Stiles. And Jackie Stiles signed a letter-of-intent to attend UConn. She just never sent it. "I wanted my family and friends to be able to see me play," she says.

Stiles chose Southwest Missouri State, 237 miles southeast of Claflin. Had she chosen UConn, she would most surely have earned one national championship but would be nowhere near the scoring record that she is on the verge of surpassing this week.

"Jackie Stiles is a terrific shooter," says Geno after practice today, "but I'm not sure if, in our offense, she would have averaged more than fifteen points per game."

Which, of course, is no knock on Jackie Stiles. Players choose UConn at the expense of individual glory. Big fish, small pond or small fish, big pond?

"If you're making home movies in the garage," Geno asks, "are you a star? If you've got one minute in a Mel Gibson film, maybe that's better."

Tuesday, February 27 . . . For Catholics, Mardi Gras, which is tonight, represents a rowdy farewell to good times as they prepare for Ash Wednesday, the beginning of Lent.

What will the Huskies give up for Lent? Will Diana Taurasi give up no-look passes? Will Shea Ralph stop visiting Forever Tan? Will Morgan Valley *take up* something, such as dessert?

Tonight's opponent, Seton Hall, is all that stands in the way of UConn tying Notre Dame for the Big East regular-season championship, which the Huskies have won seven straight years. Notre Dame lost at Rutgers nine days earlier, opening the door for UConn to tie them. Though they cannot win it outright, sharing is better than not having.

"I had resigned myself to the fact that Notre Dame's going to win it, and good for them," Geno said on Sunday. "Now we're back in it. Do we like tying? No. But we'll take it."

"We felt," says Shea, "like we were given a second opportunity this year."

A 15-0 run midway through the first half puts UConn comfortably ahead 42-11. Still, Geno is upset at halftime because the Huskies have 12 turnovers, and the Pirates are not even pressing on defense. "If this were tennis," he tells his players, "there'd be a lot of unforced errors on us."

If this were tennis, Diana would lead the team in double-faults. With 14:34 remaining and the Huskies leading 53-28, Diana pulls up for a jump shot at the right elbow. As she goes airborne, Swin Cash positions herself under the boards to grab an offensive rebound. That's when Diana decides to pass the ball to Swin. The ball zooms past Swin, nearly bopping her on the head, and out of bounds.

On the sideline, Geno turns to Chris Dailey and says, "I'm not even talking to her any more" as he sends a sub in for Diana. Further down the bench Stacy Hansmeyer and Sveta Abrosimova are giggling.

The Huskies win 83-48 in perfunctory fashion before 2,406 people. Shea Ralph puts together the type of game (11 points, six assists and zero turnovers) indicative of someone who knows that her games are numbered. Shea, after five seasons, is appreciating her final lap.

"I bottomed out at Notre Dame," she says after the victory as Geno stands off to the side in the interview room, "but I've worked too hard, and people talked to me. They said I'd worked too hard to end my season that way."

"Who talked to you?" someone asks.

Shea says nothing. Instead, she directs her gaze toward her coach, who simply stares straight ahead. Staring into a new season.

MARCH

Sunday, March 4 . . . Marci Czel wears a zippered grin as she sees Shea Ralph enter the locker room before tonight's Big East tournament matchup against Boston College. "All right," says Marci Czel, "Tournament Shea is here."

Tournament Shea, like Malibu Barbie, is a blonde, bronzed, and enhanced model of an already proven brand. Tournament Shea is, in three seasons of Big East tournament experience, UConn's leading scorer (14.7 points per game), its defensive hellion and, most important, 9-0.

"Tournament Shea will not let us lose," Marci Czel says.

Shea Ralph and Geno Auriemma were both born in March (the 12th and 23rd, respectively) when, in college basketball, the spoils of war are claimed. They are both warriors come March, a month named for the Roman god of war. Better than any two people in the UConn program, Geno and Shea understand that March dictates their legacy.

Not all of the Huskies do. Geno's withering critiques, which have become more caustic of late, are upsetting some fragile psyches. Shea told him as much a few days ago. "Diana and I can take it," she said, "but some of the others can't."

"Hey, Shea," he replied, "go into that locker room and tell them they better not be so sensitive. I don't give two shits about their feelings, I'm just trying to win a championship for all of us."

Of all the manifold statistics used to prop up Geno's career in Storrs, none is quite so impressive as this: since 1995 UConn is 42-4 in March, with every one of those games a do-or-die affair, either in the Big East or NCAA tournament.

The Big East tournament, which will be played entirely at Gampel, is a dress rehearsal. Although a loss tonight to Boston College would eliminate the Huskies from the conference tourney—and end a run of seven straight conference tournament titles—it will not endanger their chances of making the NCAAs.

"This," Swin Cash said yesterday, "is where the fun begins."

The Eagles, borrowing a page from Rutgers's defensive playbook, use a matchup zone against the Huskies. UConn thwarts it with outside shooting, as Diana Taurasi calmly buries three threes in the first 11 minutes. The only factor seemingly not in UConn's favor early on is the foul situation. In the game's first seven minutes, the Huskies are whistled for five while BC receives only one.

Geno seethes as the Huskies build a lead in points while falling behind in fouls. This is reminiscent of last April's national title game when the Huskies found themselves ahead of Tennessee 21-6 while at the same time having been whistled for nine fouls to the Lady Vols' two. "It's twenty-one to six and nine to two," Geno reminded referee Sally Bell not so gently, banging his fist on the scorer's table for emphasis. "Twenty-one to six and nine to two!" When Asjha Jones is whistled for traveling, Geno erupts (it looked as if she had her shot blocked, and should either be a foul on BC or a jump ball) and is whistled for a technical foul.

Afterward—and this may just be coincidence—the next six foul calls go against the Eagles. Concurrently, the Huskies embark on a 16-0 run, taking a 40-15 lead. The remainder of the evening holds little drama. UConn wins easily, 96-53. Tournament Shea leads the Huskies in assists with five and is second in points (16) and rebounds (5).

"I've waited my whole life for this," says Shea, "so I'm going all out."

With Svetlana Abrosimova out, Shea now starts at forward. The backcourt is Sue Bird and Diana, the latter of whom scored a team-high 22 points this evening, making six of 12 three pointers.

Sue does not play in the second half. Her lower back is bothering her and, in fact, she spends much of the second half lying belly down on the court at the end of the UConn bench, a heating pad on her back.

"How you doin'?" Geno asks Sue after the game. He is relaxing in his office, reliving the evening with high school buddies Jack and Phil Eisenmann, who will be frequent companions the rest of the way.

"I felt it crack early in the game," says Sue. "It just didn't feel right."

"I know, I know," Geno says, blithely unconcerned. "You're not used to having to remain in your defensive stance for that long."

Sue's father, Dr. Herschel Bird, who is a board-certified internist but makes his living handicapping horses in Las Vegas (the Birds are divorced), pokes his head in the door. "Who does this team remind you of?" Geno asks him. "Secretariat or Zippy Chippy?"

Dr. Bird chuckles. Secretariat, the 1973 Triple Crown winner, is the greatest thoroughbred in the history of the sport. Zippy Chippy is his antipode, renowned for being winless in 89 career races. Zippy Chippy is so hapless that he once lost a race to a man.

"Let's hope Sue's back gets better," Geno says, "or else we may have all our money on Zippy Chippy."

Monday, March 5 . . . The headline on *The Hartford Courant* says it all in bold caps: "IT'S GOING TO GET UGLY."

Connecticut is bracing for a storm that, beginning this afternoon, is expected to drop between 18 and 24 inches of snow whipped around by 30-to-40 mph wind gusts. Last night Governor John Rowland warned that this could be the "Storm of the Century," though as one local wag put it, that warning is "not as ominous as it might if he were saying it, you know, ninety-nine years from now."

The governor, in the interest of traffic safety, is banning all tractor-trailers from driving on state highways as of 5:00 a.m. today. The only Rig likely to pull any duty today wears No. 44 for UConn. "Maybe we should move the tournament to the Hartford Civic Center," Geno remarked last night, noting the treacherous backroads that lead to Storrs, "or Miami."

And yet Gampel is awash in giddy anticipation. Tonight's semifinal doubleheader may be one big slumber party. Matt Eagan and Jeff Goldberg of *The Hartford Courant* bring pillows and blankets. Ann Marie Person plans to spend the night on the couch in Geno's office. Shea Ralph and Stacy Hansmeyer, who live six miles off campus, are sleeping over in the players' lounge.

Why go home? Everyone except the two teams that lose in tonight's semifinals will be back tomorrow. If the two favorites, Notre Dame and UConn, win this evening, the Big East championship game will pit the No. 1 and No. 2 teams in the nation. That would be UConn's third 1 vs. 2 matchup of the season. Let it snow, let it snow, let it snow.

The flurries begin shortly before 4:00 p.m. Notre Dame plays Virginia Tech at 6:00 p.m. The Irish use a 24-3 run early in the first half and put the Hokies away easily, 67-49.

UConn's semifinal game with Rutgers begins at 8:00 p.m. Outside, the snow is falling at a swirling, 45-degree angle. Inside a sign proudly proclaims "This is Husky Weather". Ruth Brechlin, who lives some 40 miles away in Middlefield, is typical of the 4,500 strange souls who have ventured out tonight. "We don't know where we're spending the night yet," she says of herself and three friends. "We're diehards."

Brechlin is 72 years old.

UConn is playing without Sue Bird, whose back spasms continue to bother her, and, of course, Svetlana Abrosimova. Nevertheless, the Huskies bury the Scarlet Knights under an avalanche, jumping out to a 26-3 lead. With just under four minutes remaining in the first half and the Huskies up 41-20, the storm makes its presence felt indoors. Scarlet Knight point guard Tasha Pointer, dribbling upcourt, is the first to notice a small puddle forming near midcourt. The roof is leaking.

The leak must be fixed or the game stopped. Geno is resigned to the idea that no more basketball will be played this evening. "It wasn't going to be like Wimbledon," he later says, "with guys stationed at midcourt running back and forth with towels."

The Huskies and Scarlet Knights return to their respective locker rooms. Gampel Pavilion building superintendent Bill Sehl, 44, is hoisted up, up, and away, 143 feet to the domed Gampel roof, in a skylift. As the crowd cranes their necks to watch this stunt, Sehl (pronounced "Sell"), carrying only duct tape and towels, looks every bit like the Wizard ascending from Oz.

A chant of "Bil-ly! Bil-ly!" gains momentum as Sehl ascends to put a new spin on the term, raise the roof. Crawling through a trapdoor suspended from the apex of the domed ceiling, Sehl disappears into a cupola. Fifteen minutes later he reemerges, having sealed the leak. Sehl's 286-foot roundtrip vertical journey allows the game to resume at 10:34 p.m. UConn eventually wins as midnight draws near, 94-66. The Huskies are now 27-2.

It is nearly midnight when C. Vivian Stringer enters the press room. "Connecticut is probably the finest team that I have seen in my life, and I think that Coach Auriemma is brilliant," she says. "He's a genius."

Her gracious words in defeat are soon drowned out by a philippic she unleashes on the media. "Is Chris Elsberry here?" she asks, mentioning the name of the sports columnist of *The Connecticut Post*. Elsberry, a gray-bearded man in his early forties, raises his hand.

Stringer took issue with a February 15 column he wrote about her team. Elsberry's column, penned in the wake of UConn's 70-45 win back on Valentine's Day, did seem a tad mean-spirited. He wrote:

> *When is Coach C. Vivian Stringer going to get that (Rutgers and UConn are not equals) into her team's head? All the tattoos, all the black uniforms and the headbands and the bravado you take to the court doesn't mean a thing when you don't have the talent, or the respect, to say that you can stand with the best. Even though they talk the talk, Rutgers does not walk the walk.*

Stringer has written a two-page letter of response and takes this opportunity to read it to the reporters. As the minutes tick past midnight and the writers become increasingly anxious about their deadlines, already taxed due to the roof leak, Elsberry attempts to take one for the team. "Coach," he asks, "I understand that you have a problem with what I wrote, but could we discuss this afterward? A lot of people in here have deadlines to make."

Stringer continues reading. Indeed, she has a point even if she has chosen a most inopportune time to make it. "We went twenty-six-and-eight last year and to the Final Four," she says. "Are we a bunch of bums? I don't think so."

"*Rutgers has never been able to (hang with the Huskies)*," Elsberry wrote in his column. "*That street style has never meshed well against the Huskies' poise and depth.*"

C. Vivian Stringer, who is African-American, as are her key players, took umbrage at the "street style" reference. The Scarlet Knight players with visible tattoos concealed them with oversize band-aids for tonight's game. It was a not-so-subtle poke at UConn's girls-next-door image, but, as is the case with this diatribe, exhibited a poor sense of timing.

"I believe in not judging a book but [*sic*] its cover," Stringer concludes her letter, inserting an ironic misquote. "I hope that you feel the same way."

When Geno steps up to the podium a few minutes later, it is clear that he overheard the exchange. He smiles at the Herde and says, "Be nice."

Talk turns to the evening's hero, Bill Sehl. Jeff Jacobs, who had spoken with Geno's brother, Ferruccio, during the delay, reports that Ferruccio said, "I was the one who had to go up to fix the leaks at our house [in Norristown] because Geno was afraid of heights."

Geno laughs at the revelation. "Ferruccio is full of it," he says. "My mother got up there and fixed that roof. I wasn't going to get on the roof, 'cuz I had a career to think about."

Outside, the storm has abated. The Herde wrestle with their keyboards, banging out stories that they hope will convey the unique, even legendary aspects of this evening.

Inside the subterranean players' lounge, Shea Ralph and Stacy Hansmeyer prepare to bunk down for the evening. Shea limps over to a couch, gingerly hoisting her legs onto it as if they are lumber. Tournament Shea led the Huskies in assists and rebounds (seven each) tonight, but now every motion seems pained, every joint rusty.

She looks over at Stacy. "Three games in three days," she sighs wearily. "I'm getting old."

Tuesday, March 6 . . . Kennitra Johnson enters the windowless tomb that is the players' lounge. Switching on the light, her jaw drops as she spots Shea Ralph and Stacy Hansmeyer sprawled on the sofas.

"What time is it?" Shea asks sleepily.

"Eleven-thirty," KJ responds. "We've got shootaround in half an hour."

"Is it still snowing outside?"

"Yep."

The Hartford Courant dubbed yesterday's arctic blast "THE IMPERFECT STORM" in its front-page banner headline. For all of the furious flurries, the actual accumulation of snow is half the 24 inches that had been predicted. Reports of its depth, it turns out, were greatly exaggerated.

Inside Gampel Pavilion the Huskies partake in the shootaround. All the surrealism of last night has made it easy to forget that in seven hours they play No. 1 Notre Dame. The rematch.

In the last 50 days there have been moments at practice when Geno has rattled off the stats from the January 15 game without even mentioning the opponent. He would say something like "eight for eleven, thirteen for thirteen from the line, twenty-nine points", citing Ruth Riley's numbers without mentioning her. Or he would cite the free throw disparity (13 attempts for UConn, 46 for the Irish), which, when you consider that both schools made 29 field goals, was as much the difference in the game as any. But he never explicitly said "Notre Dame".

The Huskies have lost much to Notre Dame this season. First, the Irish absconded with UConn's No. 1 ranking and dreams of a perfect season on that bleak day in South Bend. Then, at last Friday's Big East banquet the Irish claimed five of the six major postseason individual awards. Muffet McGraw was named Coach of the Year, while senior forward Kelley Siemon was named the conference's Most Improved Player. Center Ruth Riley, to no one's surprise, was named Big East Player of the Year, Defensive Player of the Year, and Scholar-Athlete of the Year. The committee, wisely, sat Riley as close to the podium as possible.

Friday night marked the first time in 15 seasons that the Huskies were completely shut out of the aforementioned awards (Georgetown's Rebekkah Brunson edged Diana Taurasi for Freshman of the Year). Further sowing the seeds of reprisal,

Hartford Courant staff writer Lori Riley, in her weekly Tuesday "Super 16" rankings, has UConn (26-2) at No. 3 today behind both Notre Dame (27-1) and Tennessee (29-2). Every national poll has the Huskies second.

"Can you believe that?" Geno says before the shootaround. "Then they have the nerve to call me up and ask what I think of the poll?"

The final insult? Because the Irish earned the tournament's top seed, UConn is technically the visitor in Gampel this evening. The Huskies will sit at the visitors bench and will wear their national-flag blue road uniforms. "That's just one more thing to give us incentive," says Shea.

During shootaround the Huskies engage in one of their favorite drills, "Eleven Spots". It is a fullcourt drill which, as described earlier, is hectic and harried and obliges the Huskies to score 35 points in five breathless minutes. Time is ticking down and the Huskies are stuck at 32 when Sue Bird gets the ball off a miss. Dribbling to halfcourt, she sees that the clock is ticking down, 3 . . . 2 . . . 1 . . .

Sue launches a halfcourt shot just before the buzzer sounds. The ball sails through the air, a guided missile, and swishes through the net. The Huskies clamor around Sue, whose back is obviously feeling better, as if it were a real game-winner.

The play reminds Svetlana Abrosimova of another basketball dream she once had. "After we lost to Tennessee last year," says Sveta, who in that game passed the ball to Tamika Williams instead of taking the last-second shot herself, "I had a dream about that play. I dreamt that we inbounded the ball to Sue instead of me. And you know what? Sue made the shot."

At 7:30 p.m. Gampel Pavilion does not have an empty seat. The storm outside has ceased; the storm inside is coming. There is a different vibe to the UConn fans, a bloodlust to exact revenge for January's ambush in South Bend. The Irish are oblivious to it, jumping out to a 6-0 lead.

"This is the next evolution for the Notre Dame Irish," ESPN2 color analyst Doris Burke tells a national audience. "Just as Connecticut had to [once] go down to Knoxville and prove they could win there, this is a Notre Dame team that must prove they can win here at Gampel Pavilion."

"And it's tough to do," agrees play-by-play partner Robin Roberts. "One hundred sixty-eight and fifteen, that's [UConn's] record here at Gampel."

UConn comes right back. Diana buries a three-pointer against the Notre Dame 2-3 zone to slice the lead in half. Asjha Jones makes two straight jumpers, and the Huskies have their first lead of the season against the Irish, 7-6. Gampel sounds like an airplane engine. "This," Meghan Pattyson tells Kathy Auriemma, with whom she is sitting, "is the loudest I've ever heard this place."

Both teams are finding the best within themselves. UConn, which battled malaise in January and Sveta's loss last month, is playing with a tenacity unseen since last April's national championship win. Notre Dame, which has never beaten UConn in this state, is playing with a poise that has eluded them in the past.

Back and forth both teams exchange blows, until UConn leads, 23-22. Then, suddenly, Tournament Shea takes over. She scores 11 of the Huskies' next 15 points, mostly on her patented drives, staking UConn to its biggest lead of the game, 39-32.

"When Abrosimova went down with the injury, Shea Ralph's numbers went up," says Burke. "She had been struggling at points, but here's what she's made a career on, dribble penetration into the heart of the lane."

Notre Dame calls timeout. After the timeout Siemon steals a Sue Bird pass but misses a gimme layup from the left side. Ruth Riley swats at the rebound as if it is a tetherball, and it skips out to the top of the three-point arc, where Shea is standing.

She grabs it and dribbles upcourt on the left-hand side. Shea invented the 70-foot drive to the basket, remember? No one's gonna stop her.

Nearing the basket and driving past Notre Dame's Jemeka Joyce, Shea plants both feet, readying for her layup and perhaps a foul.

A shrill cry pierces the night. The ball ricochets off the glass, falls shy of the rim. Shea, who reached for her left knee as soon as she'd planted that foot, lands awkwardly, sending a second, longer, heartbreaking wail into the void.

"Eeeyaaaaaaa. . ."

Gampel is silent. Shea punches the blue paint of the free-throw lane three times and then keels over on her right side. Swin Cash, hands on both knees, kneels over her.

"Shea Ralph, oh, goodness," Robin Roberts moans. "Oh, no."

Rosemary Ragle is the first person to Shea's side. Shea tugs at her gray skirt in delirious pain. Geno and Chris Dailey arrive. Geno lays his left hand on her right calf, his right hand pressed against his forehead in disbelief. *Not again. Not Shea.*

"There are women's college basketball fans around the country looking at this," says Burke, "absolutely shaking their heads at the number of times this happens to premier athletes."

Shea is helped up, her bandaged right finger (from the blisters she gets shooting threes with Maria Conlon) wiping the tears from her eyes. In the stands, Marsha Lake sits, her right hand covering her face. "When she pounded her fist on the court, I knew it was torn," Lake says later. "I had been waiting for this to happen again."

On the UConn bench Stacy Hansmeyer looks nauseous. On the Notre Dame sideline Siemon leads the Irish in a prayer. Pointguard Niele Ivey, who tore her ACL two years ago, is shaking.

For the second time in as many nights, the game comes to an abrupt halt late in the first half. Play resumes in front of a subdued arena, and soon UConn finds itself up 49-46 with 1.9 seconds remaining in the half.

After a Notre Dame turnover, UConn inbounds in the backcourt right in front of their bench. Kelly Schumacher lobs the pass over Ivey's head to Sue, who catches it one step in front of Siemon. Sue deftly sidesteps Siemon to the left before even dribbling. She dribbles twice with her left hand and, reaching midcourt, heaves the ball.

"It will not—"says Roberts. "Ohhh! Ohhh! It counts! Are you kidding me?"

Sue, always cool, signals the three-point-shot sign with her arms and trots down the court and into the arms of her teammates. Geno, walking toward the locker room, makes a quick detour to press row as Gampel is engulfed in noise. Leaning over, he tells me, "You saw us practice that today."

In the locker room, Marci Czel pulls the team into a huddle. Looking at Shea and pointing to her own heart, she says, "It's all about right here." As the Huskies shoot around before the second half, Shea walks on the court, her left leg in a soft cast. She walks gingerly to the sideline, approaching Sveta, who has tears in her eyes. "Don't cry," Shea tells her teammate, embracing her. "There's no reason to cry."

The second half lacks the first's furious pace and offensive potency. Even the fans appear spent. With 3:51 remaining the score is again tied, 73-73. Riley has four fouls as does Diana, who has collected two of them foolishly, by swatting at shots from behind. In UConn's previous losses this year, versus Notre Dame and then Tennessee, Diana fouled out.

With three minutes left Nancy Bird, Sue's mother, is overcome with anxiety. "I gotta pace," she tells her boyfriend, Dennis Burden. She walks up the steps to the main concourse. Secluding herself in a corner concession area, she spots an usher. "Don't worry," he tells her, "you're gonna win."

Nancy Bird returns to her seat with 1:15 remaining and no change in the score of the game. The Irish have the ball. Riley, with the ball on the baseline, finds Siemon streaking down the lane. Siemon catches the pass, takes one step toward the basket, and collides with Diana, who had ventured over from the weak side to assist. Referee Dennis DeMayo makes the call: blocking, number 3, UConn.

Diana, who fell backward on the play, flips her head back in disbelief. "Oh, my God!" she cries. She has fouled out with 14 points. Siemon, who made just three of 16 free throws against UConn in January, steps to the free-throw line. Her first shot hits the rim and bounces away. Her second shot is an air ball.

The score remains tied.

Sue hits a three-pointer with 49.2 seconds left. UConn's first points in more than five minutes give the Huskies a 76-73 lead. The clock originally reads 0:47.9 after Sue's shot, because the ball was inadvertently kicked out to midcourt, running an extra 1.3 seconds off the clock. The referees stop the game and restore the lost time.

"Every second, every tenth of a second," says Roberts, showing prescient skills, "is so precious in a game like this."

Notre Dame answers swiftly. Riley makes a pretty, reverse-spin move, faking toward the lane first and then going around Schuey along the baseline to close the gap to 76-75, UConn, with

0:38 remaining. Notre Dame calls timeout. When Schuey reaches the UConn sideline, Geno, a grim smile on his face, asks her, "Are you kidding me?"

UConn has the ball and a one-point lead. Notre Dame, for the first time tonight, switches to a man-to-man defense. Sue is guarded by Ivey, who swats at the ball right in front of the UConn bench. It falls away and out of bounds with 16.3 seconds left. Possession is given to Notre Dame.

"No!" says Sue, shocked, to referee Angie Lewis. "Oh, my God!"

"It went off of you," the referee replies.

The Irish run the same clear-out play to Riley on the low block. Riley again uses the spin move but misses. However, a foul is called on Schuey with 5.1 seconds left.

Sue immediately walks to the far end of the court to speak with Geno. "What do you want to do?" she asks.

"Just get it and go," he says.

Riley misses the first shot. Sue jogs down to the free-throw lane and approaches Swin. "Just give me the ball," she says.

Riley makes her second free throw, tying the score at 76. Perhaps the Irish expect UConn to call timeout and set up a play. Instead, Schuey grabs the ball and inbounds to Sue. As Sue takes the inbounds pass crossing the lane, Swin sets a pick on Ivey, who is chasing Sue. The screen springs Sue, the fastest player on either team. Ivey is helpless to catch her.

Siemon finally impedes Sue in the frontcourt, forcing her to go left just beyond the three-point arc. Sue takes one more dribble, then a herculean leap of a jump stop. She is ten feet from the basket when she launches a fall-away jumper just beyond the outstretched arms of the 6'5" Riley.

The buzzer sounds as Sue stumbles awkwardly toward the Husky bench, twisting as she keeps her eyes on the ball. It kisses the front of the rim with a dull clang, then climbs over and into the basket.

Sue's third buzzer-beater of the day.

Riley crumples to the floor in frustration and slaps both hands on the court. 78-76. The Huskies have done it again. Notre Dame is now 0-5 versus UConn in Big East championship games.

An hour later a small crew lingers outside the UConn locker room. Sveta sits against a wall, looking emotionally spent, as her parents stand nearby. Oleg and Ludmila will return to Russia tomorrow, where the weather is probably better. Geno hugs them both, saying, "Goodbye".

Shea remains in the players' lounge with her family. The fewer people that she sees tonight, the better. In the postgame press conference one of the UConn physicians had said, "the very probable prognosis at this time is that she tore the anterior cruciate ligaments in her left knee."

It is some time after 10:00 p.m., but nobody wants to retire for the evening yet. There are too many emotions to sort out. Giddiness at the memory of Sue's unforgettable open-field run to victory. Sadness at the realization that Shea's college basketball career is over. Tomorrow Geno and the Huskies—and the Connecticut citizenry, for that matter—must deal with the prospect of entering the NCAAs without both of their first team All-Americans. Tonight, however, he will hold a muted celebration at his home.

A dozen or so family and friends gather to watch the game on tape. Outside, Connecticut lies dormant under a blanket of snow. Inside the Auriemma house, the party continues as Nona, 71 years young, begins clearing plates and food from the family room. It is 5:00 a.m.

Sunday, March 11 . . . ESPN has brought a camera to Gampel Pavilion for today's Women's NCAA Tournament Selection Show. The 64-team field is to be announced and seeded in one of four regions: East, Mideast, Midwest and West. UConn, by virtue of its Big East tournament victory and probable reinstatement at number one when the polls come out tomorrow, will likely land the top seed in the East.

Geno, surrounded by his players, sits in a hospitality room in Gampel, waiting to see whom the Huskies will face in the first round. The broadcast crew at ESPN headquarters in Bristol, some 50 miles west of Storrs, will interview him during the show. Diana Taurasi sits next to Geno with a homemade sign that she plans to flash when the camera turns on. It reads, "BIG UP, CHINO."

"What does 'Big Up' mean?" asks Mike DiMauro.

"You know," she says, "it's like a shout out."

Oh, says DiMauro, who at 32 suddenly feels very old and unhip.

Diana, named Most Valuable Player of the Big East tournament on the strength of her 17.3 points per game, has begun to draw national media attention. Even *The New York Times* is profiling her, the theme of the piece being Diana's swift maturation.

"Maturity?" Diana bristles at the suggestion. "Let's not go that far."

She may not want to admit it, but Diana has traveled a Svetlanesque journey in the past six months. Though she did not have to deal with a language barrier (excepting such phrases as "Big Up" and "shout out"), Chino, California, is almost as many thousands of cultural miles from Storrs as is St. Petersburg, Russia.

Like Svetlana Abrosimova, she has one older sister and no other siblings. Like Sveta, Diana is uncommonly close with her mother. Her father, also like Sveta's, is a soft-spoken European who works with machinery. Geno believes that Diana has the talent as a freshman to hoist the Huskies atop her shoulders. Just like Sveta.

"Without sounding mean," Geno said last month after Sveta's surgery, "name me a skill that Sveta has that Diana doesn't have."

Diana can be irresponsible and reckless. Witness her eight consecutive three-point misfires the first time UConn played Rutgers. She kept firing.

"If you stop shooting then," she'd said, "you end up oh-for-eight."

Good point. Diana did make her last four threes that night. "I always think the next one's going in with her," says Geno, "and so does she. She throws the ball off the backboard to herself so she can score. And then she wants an assist, too."

Like Sveta, Diana's parents have never seen her score a basket for UConn in person. They have only seen her play once in person this season—at Pepperdine, where she did not score. Yet D never seems homesick. The SoCal transplant is loving her frigid and dairy farm-encircled digs. Never mind the backdrop; she is standing on the greatest stage in women's college hoops at the moment, and the spotlight finally found her.

How close she came to signing with UCLA. In November the Bruins lost an exhibition game to an AAU team, called Love and Basketball. When Diana heard the news, she phoned Lily. "Mommy," she said, "do you know how miserable I would be if I were there?"

Thursday, March 15 . . . Shea Ralph and Svetlana Abrosimova are shooting around at the same basket before practice. Sveta tucks her crutches under her armpits when she shoots. Shea, who will forgo surgery until after the season, has her left knee swaddled in a white bandage.

Even with a torn ACL in her left leg, Shea's set shot is as viable as ever. She makes five, six, seven 18-footers in a row. "Whaddaya think?" Shea asks. "Should they put me out there? And it's only been a week. Who knows how good it'll be next week?"

Shea ran on the treadmill in the UConn training room the day after she tore her ACL. Whereas Sveta has been the most patient of patients, stoically accepting the terminus of her college career, SheRa stubbornly lays claim to her superpowers.

"Obviously, if I can help, I want to do it," says Shea, who turned 23 on Monday. "I'm not in denial. I'm just different. I'm different than your average person."

When practice starts, Shea pulls a folding chair from the bench area and moves it closer to the sideline. Her feet are practically on the court as she sits, elbows resting on her thighs, exhorting her teammates as they scrimmage.

The Huskies move to a halfcourt offense, running their blue team against a 2-3 zone that looks eerily similar to Notre Dame's. On Sunday the NCAA Tournament selection committee put the Irish and the Huskies in the same half of the tournament draw. They could meet in the national semifinal. In other words, Notre Dame and UConn, who between them spent all but two weeks this season at number one in the national polls, have both been seeded lower overall than Tennessee.

"Hold up," Geno says, after Diana Taurasi has a crosscourt pass intercepted by Nykesha Sales. "D, why you wanna pass the ball? 'Cuz you missed the last two shots? We can rebound the miss.

247

"We never pass up open threes against the zone," Geno tells the entire squad. "Never. That's our rule."

Geno's mood is buoyant. His children are on spring break this week, and Kathy, Alysa, and Michael are all at practice. He glances back at D, a wry smile on his face. "I don't wanna see any of that California garbage," he says. "Pass the ball to the right person.

"And you, Einstein," he says, turning his gaze to Maria Conlon, who is positioned on a wing. "You gotta hit that shot. I can get Alysa to stand there and shoot airballs."

Of the four top seeds, the tournament selection committee has saddled the No. 1 ranked Huskies with the most pothole-filled road to St. Louis, site of the Final Four. After this weekend, when UConn should dispatch its first- and second-round opponents at Gampel with ease, the remaining four hurdles to a national title potentially include four of the nation's top six teams: in order, Georgia, Louisiana Tech, Notre Dame, and Tennessee.

"I said last year I thought the committee did a better job than anytime I could remember," Geno said on Sunday. "I said [that] was the best bracket I'd ever seen. Well, this year it's one of the worst."

In a conference call with the Herde on Sunday, Maryalyce Jeremiah, chairwoman of the selection committee, denied that Shea and Sveta's absence influenced the team's seeding. She told the Herde that the committee placed a premium on a team winning its regular-season conference title, as Tennessee and the Irish had.

"Notre Dame won the conference," said Jeremiah. "UConn won the conference tournament. If you're going to split that hair, you could say, week in and week out, [UConn] didn't win the conference."

"Actually," Lori Riley of *The Hartford Courant* said, "Notre Dame and UConn tied for the Big East regular season title."

On the other end of the phone line, there was silence. Jeremiah never responded.

Still, Geno is in a good mood, radiating confidence and encouraging freshmen like Maria Conlan and Morgan Valley, whom he will have to play more than he might like in the upcoming tourney. Maria has appeared more confident on the court since her 16-point performance versus West Virginia. Morgan is becoming more comfortable off the court. "I've noticed Morgan picking up the lexicon," Sue Bird says. "She was heading out after practice the other day and made the peace sign, and said, 'Deuces.'"

Before practice today Morgan set about making 50 consecutive free throws. She made 43 then missed. She hurled the ball but this time to parody herself.

"She's come so far," says Shea, who has shooting contests with Morgan daily. "If she wins, I can only drink milk or water the rest of the day. If I win, Morgan has to eat a Ding Dong. I've seen her do it."

Back at practice, Geno's cheerful disposition is being challenged by Diana's "dumbass passes" in the halfcourt offense. Even her teammates get on her case.

"Shoot the ball!"

"Shoot the damn ball!"

"C'mon, D, shoot the ball!"

She takes the ball at the point again. Play starts and, like nails on a blackboard, Diana throws away yet another no-look pass. Her eyes bore holes in the floor in front of her.

"You're acting like a goddamned baby," Geno tells her. "You expect us to feel sorry for you?"

"No," she says.

"Good," he says. "That's the first thing I've heard you say in fifteen minutes."

Friday, March 16 . . . Tony Bozzella is a man of many hats, all of them fedoras. "I have three of them," says Coach Bozzella, who is in his first season at Long Island University (LIU), UConn's first-round opponent in the NCAA tournament tomorrow night. "One for conference play, one for the NCAA tourney, and one for just walkin' around."

The opening round of the NCAA tournament at Gampel is traditionally devoid of suspense. There was the 71-point defenestration of Hampton last year. The 68-point evisceration of Lehigh in 1997. What makes the weekend memorable is not the games but colorful characters such as Bozzella, a fedora-donning Cinderella whose glass slipper is half-full.

"He's got his head screwed on straight," Geno says. "Somebody told me that when they went out to play at San Jose State, he didn't go to practice. He played Pebble Beach instead. That's a guy after my own heart. It's refreshing to see a guy come in here and not act like it's the Gulf War."

Bozzella, 35, is youthful, bespectacled, and lilliputian— "I'm five-five," he says, "but my wife says I'm five-four"— with a self-effacing humor that belies his ability. In this, his first season at LIU, he is taking the Blackbirds to their first NCAA tourney. Two years ago, before his arrival, the Blackbirds finished 2-24.

"I received over seventy phone calls," Bozzella says, referring to LIU making the NCAAs. "My ex-girlfriend, from middle school, called. She's got twins now, so I told my wife not to worry."

Bozzella, too, has no illusions about his squad's chances tomorrow. "It's like Alfalfa said to Spanky," he quotes from *The Little Rascals*. "The bigger they are, the harder we fall."

For Geno, Bozzella offers a sense of *deja vu*. He, too, was 35 the first time UConn made a trip to the NCAAs. The Huskies won their first Big East title that year, too. "I'll never forget that first time we won the conference," Geno says wistfully. "Going to the NCAAs. Feeling as if you've finally made it."

Jim Fuller of *The New Haven Register* raises his hand to ask a question. "When you won the conference in nineteen eighty-nine," Fuller deadpans, "was the committee chairman aware that you had won the conference?"

Geno laughs at the poke at Maryalyce Jeremiah. "Actually," he answers, "since *The Daily Campus* (UConn's student paper) was probably the only paper covering us back then, probably no. Their guy covering us was probably off having a beer at Ted's."

"He's probably right," Matt Eagan of *The Hartford Courant* whispers in my ear. "I was that guy."

Saturday, March 17 . . . "If we're within twenty at halftime," LIU coach Tony Bozzella said yesterday, "I would be ecstatic. The second half, we make a couple of threes, and maybe they get tight. Is that realistic?"

Six minutes into tonight's game, the Blackbirds are still within 20 points. The score is 18-0, UConn.

The Blackbirds, who have not played in front of a crowd larger than 621, appear starstruck and overwhelmed before Gampel's 10,027. But the Huskies are also bigger, faster, better and deeper.

"It was kind of frustrating," 5'9" Blackbird forward Tamika Dudley, who misses all but one of her 15 shots, says later. "I was just happy when my shots weren't coming back at me."

The Huskies win 101-29, setting NCAA tournament records aplenty: fewest points allowed (29), fewest points allowed in one half (10, in the second), and lowest field-goal percentage allowed (15.4). Sue Bird scores more points in the first half (11) than all of the Blackbirds do in the second (10).

Geno does all but play four at a time to mitigate the carnage. No Husky plays more than 22 minutes. No Husky scores more than 13 points.

During much of the game Bozzella sits on the court in front of his team's bench. He tucks his right leg beneath his rear, as if he's in the den watching TV. On the far end of the bench, an assistant coach snaps his point-and-shoot camera, capturing memories. "It would be a dream," says LIU sophomore guard Kim MacMillan, "to come here and play basketball for life."

After the press conferences are over, Geno retreats to his office with Kathy and most of the same friends who gathered at his home after the Big East final. Paul Ghiorzi, a restaurateur pal from New York City, has brought fresh mozzarella and pro-sciutto from Arthur Avenue in the Bronx.

On the television the second game of tonight's doubleheader at Gampel, Colorado State-Maryland, is airing. The winner plays UConn on Monday night. The Terrapins are a better open-court team but the Rams of CSU shoot the ball exceptionally well from outside, making threes at will against Maryland's zone. It would behoove the Terps to change to a man-to-man, to force the Rams to put the ball on the floor and drive past them.

"Why don't they get out of that zone?" asks Phil Eisenmann.

The threes keep piling up for CSU. Seven, eight, nine. Maryland never switches out of its zone. CSU finishes with an NCAA tournament-record 14 three-pointers and an 83-69 win.

"What do you think, Phil?" Geno asks, alluding to the Rams. "Can we beat them?"

"Oh, yeah, G, yeah," Phil says. "Just don't play zone all night."

Sunday, March 18 . . . Tom Collen, the coach at Colorado State University, is the poster boy for male coaches in women's college basketball. In four seasons in Fort Collins, Collen's record is 105-26. That's a fantastic winning percentage (.802) for any four-year interval of a coach's career, but for the first quadrennial, it portends greatness. And yet . . .

"If I want to get a job at a major school," claims Collen, 46, "no one's going to come looking for me. I've never gotten a call about a job opening. They always have a list of up-and-coming women's coaches, and all of them have one thing in common: never any males on those lists."

"He should talk to me," Geno later says. "When I got here I thought I'd use this as a stepping stone to a better job. Then I realized, there are no other jobs." After the Huskies went 35-0 and won the national championship in 1995, the head coaching position at Duke University, one of the premier institutions in the nation in terms of athletics complementing academics, became available. Geno expressed interest. Duke responded, "Send us a resume."

The job does have its perks, though. Collen is engaged to be married to Nicki Taggart, his former assistant coach. When Taggart, 27, moved to Fort Collins to accept the job, he rented her a room in his home. A relationship soon blossomed, one that Collen and Taggart never attempted to conceal. She stepped down as an assistant before this season, under administrative pressure, and now works part-time as a radio broadcaster for Ram games.

Love at UConn is much simpler. Coaches inquire about players' romantic lives on an informal basis, the degree of intrusion depending upon the individual. When you are attempting to win a national championship, romance is a variable that must be, if not harnessed, monitored. Kelly Schumacher, for example, had been moping after Valentine's Day, saddled with a case of the boyfriend blues. Just before the Big East tournament began, Geno sat her down in his office. "Yeah, I know, that's tough for a person of your age," he said compassionately. "Schuey, look at it this way. For the next four weeks, *I'm* your boyfriend."

Another Kelley, Kelley Hunt, used to complain to Geno that he didn't play her because he did not care for her boyfriend. Looking back on those days now, Hunt chuckles ruefully. "Geno told me that as a matter of fact I might be better off without him," says Hunt, "but that had nothing to do with me not playing. I should've listened to him."

When Hunt was a senior, her boyfriend was arrested on campus for voyeurism.

This year's dating scene has been relatively quiet. Swin Cash is the only Husky with a long-standing relationship. She dates a basketball player from Duquesne University whom she has been with since high school. Maybe—maybe not, who knows with these matters—that explains why Swin has been the team's most consistent performer this season.

Marci Czel had left a humorously irascible message on the greaseboard the other day. Four years ago, when she was a walk-on trying to make the team, she was too intimidated to dress or shower in the locker room. Now Marci Czel's locker is a sundries closet, well-stocked with shampoo, lotion, deodorant. Naturally, the other Huskies began pilfering their affable teammate's supplies. But Marci Czel is no longer awed by the company she keeps.

"You cheapskates," she wrote in mock anger, "keep your hands off my stuff!"

At the afternoon press conference, Collen has the podium. "If there's a downside to what happened last night," says Collen, "it's the fact that we hit fourteen threes in front of Geno and his players. Their goal is probably to not even let us have a three-point shot."

When Geno takes the podium, he as much agrees. "With all due respect to CSU or LIU or Maryland," he says, "if we play our A-game tomorrow night, then we're not going to lose, and there's nothing Colorado State can do about it."

If they want candor, he can give them that. An e-mail he received this morning has left Geno as uppity as Marci Czel. It came from an attorney on Long Island. The correspondence, if not relayed here verbatim, read: "I'm a lawyer in New York, and

I woke up this morning and saw that your team won 102-29 last night. I didn't see the game, but you should be ashamed of yourself for running up the score like that."

"Can you believe that?" Geno said before practice today. "He didn't even see the game, and he's criticizing me."

It's not easy being Geno. Lose, or win by less than 30 points, and you must answer myriad questions about what's wrong with your team. Win by what you're capable of and you get e-mail from clueless lawyers across Long Island Sound.

"So I wrote him back," said Geno. "I wrote, 'I've never seen you try a case, but you must be a crummy lawyer. How do you expect to win a case if you never look at the evidence?"

Monday, March 19 . . . In Greenwich Village Sally Jenkins is arranging her apartment so as to have a simultaneous NCAA tourney double-feature, using two screens. Colorado State plays UConn on ESPN beginning at 9:00 p.m. At the same time Southwest Missouri State plays Rutgers on ESPN2. She positions her bedroom and living room TVs so that it is little trouble to go from viewing one game to the next. This, she stresses, was not her idea.

"My dad phoned," Sally says, "and he was frustrated because both games are on at the same time, and he doesn't want to flip back and forth. He only has one TV in his apartment."

The nation is beginning to catch on to Jackie Stiles and the Southwest Missouri State Bears, who look and sound as if they all just emerged from a Tammy Wynette song. Stiles broke the NCAA career scoring record on March 1, and the humility that she has displayed all season long is refreshing. She and her teammates are charming a nation, Dan Jenkins included. He has studied the Bears' heartland faces, their down-home folksiness, their varying hues of hair color, which range from brownish-blonde to blondish-brown. It had bothered him for awhile, who these girls reminded him of. Where had he seen them before?

Then it came to Dan. "He told me," says Sally, "that they all look like waitresses. He calls them 'the Dinettes'. But he loves them. Loves Jackie Stiles."

Jackie Stiles and the Bears will win tonight, beating Rutgers on their hostile homecourt, 60-53. At Gampel, the Huskies use a 12-0 run midway through the first half to put the clamps on

Colorado State, 89-44. The Rams shoot 3 for 17 from beyond the three-point arc.

The Huskies, meanwhile, look potent. Geno had the analogy yesterday that, as a music fan, he's just putting a new band together. Tonight, they play a tight set. Asjha Jones scores 16 points, while Swin Cash is a monster again, scoring a game-high 18 points and grabbing 11 rebounds.

Diana Taurasi shoots a dreadful 2-14 from the field, including 0-7 from beyond the arc, but compensates with crowd-pleasing plays. Early in the game she swoops in for an offensive rebound and, realizing that she will be unable to grab it, taps the ball with one hand behind her blindly. The ball falls directly into Kelly Schumacher's hands as the audience buzzes.

As the final minutes wind down, the realization begins to hit the seniors. This is their final game at Gampel. Marci Czel, who all season long has had a penchant for burying crowd-pleasing, three-point exclamation marks at the end of home games, launches her last one with 30.5 seconds left. It swishes through, UConn's final points of the season on this court. On the bench Sue Bird, Marci Czel's closest friend on the team, prances down the bench, dispensing high-fives to each teammate. That's usually Marci Czel's job.

At the postgame press conference, Randy Holtz, a reporter for Denver's *Rocky Mountain News*, makes an observation. Yesterday, after hearing Geno's guarantee of victory ("we're not going to lose and there's nothing Colorado State can do about it"), Holtz confided that Geno certainly seemed arrogant.

But 24 hours later, Randy Holtz is coming away with a different impression. "I've been here all weekend," Holtz tells Geno, "and I haven't heard you once mention your two injured All-Americans. Aren't you tempted to provide yourself with that excuse if your team doesn't win or even play as well?"

Geno peers at Holtz thoughtfully. "There's an old saying that I have," Geno replies. "'If you're not careful, there's a danger of leaving the back door open.'

"You know, you can be trapped in a bar," he explains, "and if you know there's another way out, you may not fight as hard. If the only way out is through the front door, then you're going to give it everything you got. We gotta remember that the back door is closed."

There are always three postgame press conferences at Gampel: There's the one in the classroom, where the official quotes are gleaned. There's the one just outside the classroom, where Geno gives the TV people their soundbites and then speaks a little more informally with the same writers he has just spoken to inside the classroom. And then there's the one at the bottom of the stairs, after he has left the main concourse level where the classroom is and returned to court level, where the locker room and basketball offices are located.

Tonight, at the bottom of the stairs, Geno looks as if he could talk another hour or two. Like he doesn't want to say goodbye to Gampel, to this season here, just yet. He expounds on everything from Schuey's improved play ("She's like a lot of females: She likes when you like her. Right now, the way she's playing, I love her"), to yesterday's "A-game" comment ("I know, I sound like a cocky smartass"), to Tamika Williams being underappreciated ("She scored her thousandth point the other night and nobody said 'Boo'; I doubt she even knew"), to Swin's self-absorption ("You can bet Swin knows how many points she has; she's the Wade Boggs of women's basketball") to—

"That's it!" barks Ann Marie Person. It is one minute after midnight. UConn's sports information director just wants everyone to go home. She wants to go home. "C'mon, Coach, time to go."

Ann Marie has been through this before and this much she knows: No one's going to get much sleep in the next week and a half.

Wednesday, March 21 . . . Svetlana Abrosimova is now off crutches. She wears a plastic boot, and the added mobility allows her to participate in practices somewhat. This morning Chris Dailey has her stationed out on a wing, throwing entry passes to post players for a low-post shooting drill.

"Sveta," says CD, "I want you to throw poor passes so they have to work harder to get them."

Sveta turns to a few courtside reporters. "She wants me to make bad passes," Sveta says. "I don't know how to do that."

"You don't know how to do it?" says CD. "I consider you an expert at that."

The levity is short-lived. Practice, which began at 10:00 a.m., will end shortly after noon. Then the Huskies will board a bus that will take them to Bradley International Airport, from where they will fly to Pittsburgh for the East Regional. UConn, now 30-2, plays North Carolina State on Saturday. The players' bags are packed but Geno intends to determine in these two hours if they are ready to go.

"Line up, blue!" he says, after the first team of Sue Bird, Diana Taurasi, Swin Cash, Asjha Jones, and Kelly Schumacher are beaten on defense three straight times. The entire squad, not just those five, line up on the baseline to run a suicide.

Two plays later, Diana allows herself to be screened, giving the white team an easy shot, which they make. "Get off, D," Geno scolds. "You haven't done anything in a week."

"Don't worry about it, we beat Colorado State by a hundred," Geno says as they line up for another suicide. "We beat LIU. They're going to give you a national championship for beating LIU."

Without Shea Ralph or Sveta, the Huskies practice listlessly. Geno whips them verbally, especially Diana, but they do not respond. They look as if they feel sorry for themselves. Eight times he has taken UConn to the Sweet Sixteen (i.e., the third round of the tournament). This attitude, he knows, won't cut it where they're going.

Before they line up for Five Spots, Geno tells them as much. "I can't remember the last time that the team who pouts the most wins," he says. "Except back in third grade, you'd get rewarded for pouting."

Afterward, Geno gathers them together at one free-throw circle. "We can either count on you guys or not," he tells them. He is specifically addressing Kennitra Johnson and the three frosh, Diana, Maria Conlon and Morgan Valley. "See, I'm not like other coaches. I don't want to find out if I can count on you or not in Pittsburgh. I want to find out right now. That's why I'm putting you through this shit. I don't want to find out with ten minutes to play on Saturday if we are going to get back to the Final Four."

Thursday, March 22 . . . The Huskies are well-rested and well-fed. Last night they ate at Morton's Steakhouse; Pittsburgh

Penguin legend Mario Lemieux also happened to be there. A few of the players—Asjha Jones, Kelly Schumacher, Sue Bird, and Tamika Williams—sauntered past Lemieux's table to get a glimpse.

"He's even better-looking in person," Schuey commented after they passed Lemieux's table.

"Schuey," said Sue, who had noticed, "you were looking at the wrong table."

"Oh."

Pittsburgh.The auxiliary gym at Duquesne University is a featureless, windowless space with no seating. It's blah-ness mirrors the Huskies' effort this morning, and the usual suspects—Diana Taurasi and Kennitra Johnson—draw Geno's wrath. On successive plays, D fails to catch a pass, allowing one to ricochet off her nose. Then she throws a no-look pass that squirms through Tamika's hands and out of bounds.

A few plays later Tom Tedesco, who is playing with the white team, makes a sharp backdoor cut. KJ, who is supposed to be guarding him, falls asleep on defense and is easily beaten.

"Tom," Geno asks, "did KJ guard you?"

"No," he replies.

"That's okay," Geno tells the squad, "I should've expected you to be sluggish."

He stands near the door, the only way in or out of this prison cell of a gym. The entire team stands in the free throw lane, anxious. Angry is bad; sardonic is worse. They wonder if he is about to abort practice.

"That's okay. We only spent twenty-six hundred on dinner last night," Geno says. "Twenty-six hundred, but we shouldn't expect you to be ready to practice this morning."

The players get the message. In the next ten minutes the blue squad look as sharp as they have in weeks. Diana hits two straight jumpers. Then she finds Swin Cash on a pick-and-roll play. Next she finds Asjha open, who feeds Swin for an uncontested layup. Diana makes two more baskets. KJ makes three straight buckets. They are groovin', scoring nine straight times against the white defense.

"Get some water," says Geno, looking relieved. "Good job."

After dinner this evening, a small group convenes in the stately Harvest Bar at the Westin Hotel. Geno's disciples grow in number come March. A retinue of UConn administrators, boosters, and fans linger around him. The circus draws more followers these days, but the ringmaster behaves the same.

At about 10:00 p.m. Barb Jacobs, the Big East supervisor of officials, walks into the bar. She joins the gathering. "So," Geno asks her, "who's working Saturday's game?"

She looks flustered. He smiles. "Relax, Barb," he says. "I'm only kidding."

Friday, March 23 . . . Chris Dailey has organized a scavenger hunt to keep the Huskies occupied this morning. She divides the players and managers into four teams, providing each with a Polaroid camera and a list of items that must either be collected or photographed. The four teams will have between 10:00 a.m. and 11:45 a.m. to pillage Pittsburgh.

"The important thing here is creativity," CD says as they begin their sorties. "There's one rule: Nothing illegal. Be back here on time."

One of the items on this morning's list is a photograph taken with a hotel maid. "You get extra points if it's with a maid in a different hotel," says Marci Czel, "or if you help her make a bed."

Marci Czel's squad decides to help a maid make a bed, but loses valuable time when the maid insists it help with the rest of the room. Asjha Jones and Jessica Moore have a bigger problem. They are saddled with two crippled teammates, Shea Ralph and Svetlana Abrosimova. The foursome embark upon a hike to the Mellon Arena, where Louisiana Tech is practicing.

"Getting a photo taken with a La. Tech person," says Shea, "gets you serious extra-credit points."

Arriving at the end of practice, the foursome charm Lady Techster coach Leon Barmore into taking a photo with them. He gladly poses with Shea and Sveta, the latter of whom dons a La. Tech practice jersey for the photo.

"We are going to win," says Shea, as seemingly determined to win this scavenger hunt as a national championship. "Nothing can stop us."

Alas, as fans take notice that Shea and Sveta are here, they approach in hopes of obtaining an autograph. Shea and Sveta cannot say no. Asjha and Jessica wait anxiously, aware that time is wasting and the two cripples cannot run back to the hotel.

"We gotta go!" says Asjha, looking like a bodyguard as she hustles Shea and Sveta away from their fans. Watching them depart, Coach Barmore grins and shakes his head. Two All-Americans on a scavenger hunt. Do they do this in men's basketball?

Saturday, March 24 . . . At 7:00 a.m. you can find Shea inside the Westin's workout room. Her left knee wrapped, she runs on the treadmill for 45 minutes before embarking on a four-station weightlifting circuit.

Shea can still lift weights, of course, and straight-ahead running is also manageable. She has even taken to donning her game sweats and, underneath them, her uniform, during the games. Just in case. Geno has already said that Shea's college career is *finito* but expressed gratitude at her fashion choice. "It's better," he says, "than seeing Shea in one of her Erin Brockovich get-ups."

Shea's mom has been combing the ground for change like a squirrel after acorns. "I've been finding money all week," Lake reports.

Geno has fun with superstition, too. When the Huskies enter the Pittsburgh Penguins' locker room today, he assigns his players lockers according to Penguins they most resemble. Sue Bird, for example, is given the locker of Jaromir Jagr, the NHL's most dynamic skater. Swin Cash is assigned the locker of Wayne Primeau, a hard-hitting forward. "Nobody gets Lemieux's locker," he tells them. "Nobody deserves it."

Inside the plush locker room, someone turns on the big screen TV to watch the final moments of the Mideast regional semifinal between Tennessee and Xavier from Birmingham, Ala. ESPN's Nancy Lieberman-Cline was one of many observers who thought that the Mideast was stacked in the Lady Vols' favor, calling it "the path of least resistance" to the Final Four. Today, though, the Musketeers are shocking the nation, knocking off the Lady Vols, 80-65.

As the Huskies and the Wolfpack of North Carolina State take the court at Mellon Arena, a livid Summitt takes the podium in Birmingham in the wake of Tennessee's earliest exit from the tourney in seven years. "I can teach a lot of things, but I can't teach effort," she says. "I'm disappointed. I'm sick. I guess I'm as mad as I've ever been in my life."

Tennessee's letdown is a lesson to the Huskies, who score the game's first 12 points. UConn's backcourt of Diana Taurasi and Sue combine to score 31 first-half points in staking the Huskies to a 45-26 halftime lead, though the Huskies' familiar demons—Diana's dumbass passing, Sue's reticence on offense, foul trouble—reemerge. Midway through the first half Diana's bounce pass to nobody is, fortuitously for her, deflected out of bounds by an NC State defender.

"Who was that pass to?" Geno pleads with his freshman. "That was the worst pass I've ever seen."

On the ensuing inbounds play, Diana knocks down a jumper, two of her 19 first-half points.

Later in the half Sue dribbles the ball ambivalently at the top of the three-point circle. The offense looks stalled. In exasperation Geno, from the far end of the court, takes a few steps up the sideline toward midcourt. "Just look at the basket, Sue!"

She dribbles behind a screen and promptly drains a jumper. Geno marches back toward the bench, his arms outstretched as if to ask, What's so difficult to comprehend?

The second half is a quagmire. The Wolfpack, whose coach, Kay Yow, ranks fifth all-time in career wins (611), quickly trim the Huskies' lead nearly in half, 49-38. When UConn goes for the knockout punch, Coach Yow's resilient NC State unit puts them in a clinch. They don't die easy.

"Kay Yow, she's a legend," Missouri coach Cindy Stein said yesterday. Earlier today Missouri lost to Louisiana Tech in the other game in this regional.

And Geno Auriemma, someone asked? "He's good to look at," Stein replied.

Geno may be handsome, but there are no aesthetics to this second half. Aggressive play, by both teams, is rewarded with multiple foul calls.

If there is any solace for Geno, it is that the complaint department is seated directly to his left. Carol Sprague, a member of the tournament-selection committee, sits at the scorer's table with a few other NCAA officials adjacent to the UConn bench. Because Sprague cannot eject Geno from a game, she bears the brunt of his invective. For those within earshot, it is far superior commentary to anything that TV or radio has to offer.

"This is an embarrassment!" Geno yells, after Diana is whistled for a foul on what appeared to be a cleanly swatted shot. "Year after year it's the same shit. Get in the tournament, everything's a foul. It's an embarrassment."

The Huskies escape with a 72-58 win. After UConn's 12-0 head start, the teams played to a virtual draw. Diana again dazzled a national television audience, going 6-6 from three-point range.

After the game, in the locker room, before the press is allowed to enter, Geno dissects the victory. He admonishes Sue for playing the second half as poorly (four points, three turnovers) as she had played the first flawlessly (12 points, 0 turnovers). Swin, despite scoring 11 points and grabbing 11 rebounds, is deservedly chewed out for shooting 1-8 from the free-throw line. "I'm happy we won," Geno tells them, "but the best thing we can do is just burn the tape of this game and move on."

Geno looks around the locker room. Staring back at him are 16 mopey faces. Didn't they just win a Sweet Sixteen game? "Okay," he says. "Okay. Who in here thinks I'm being an ass?"

One by one 16 hands go up.

He turned 47 yesterday, Geno did, but the party is more apropos tonight, in the wake of a win. At the Westin's oyster bar tales are swapped. Geno is having a laugh about Cindy Stein's quote, about his being "good to look at".

"That's me," he says. "Don't worry about my record. I'm just another pretty face."

Randy Smith, one of a gaggle of friends orbiting around Geno, cannot resist a comeback. "Your looks," says R. Smith, "are so overrated."

Geno appraises R. Smith's mileage-laden face. "I wish," the coach replies, "I had a mirror for you to look into right now."

Sunday, March 25 . . . Lew Perkins, UConn's athletic director, is so big, so tall, so utterly mountainous that he ought to have a tree line. Today Perkins, 55, stands at the back of the press area watching UConn's media session, which is playing out like vaudeville. Seated from end to end, in order, are Geno, Sue Bird,

Swin Cash, Asjha Jones, Kelly Schumacher and Diana Taurasi. Two comics flanking four straight men.

Geno is asked to account for the veritable pipeline of High School All-Americans and Players of the Year who find their way to secluded Storrs each autumn.

"I think one of the coaches said it earlier," he replies. "I'm really great to look at. I could say all the other things, but I think it's that I'm just another pretty face."

"Diana," someone else follows, "Is that what he told you?"

"No," D replies, her eyes sailing to the back of the room, "I came here because of the AD."

For dinner the Huskies board the team bus and head ten miles southeast to the McKeesport YMCA. Swin's mother, Cynthia Cash, and friends have cooked a soul-food dinner that includes fried chicken, ribs, macaroni and cheese, collared greens, yams, and even pigs' feet. With Swin, whose extended family includes 11 aunts and uncles (not including their spouses) and 78 cousins, a YMCA is a more practical setting for a reunion than a home.

"We had to cancel a Swin family reunion," Geno said this afternoon, "because the new [Pittsburgh Steelers] football stadium isn't finished yet."

After dinner, on the way back to the hotel, the frosh, restless, start acting up. The din is too much for Svetlana Abrosimova, who hobbles to the front of the bus, where the coaches sit.

"I need to sit up here," says Sveta, a slightly annoyed look on her face. "They're too loud."

"Congratulations, Svet" says Jamelle Elliott. "You're growing up."

This is no banner evening for maturity, though. The confluence of young women and an extended stay at a hotel, be it the Huskies here at the Westin or Eloise at The Plaza, is mischief.

Kathryn Fieseler is the instigator. She has chosen this evening to exact revenge upon Stacy Hansmeyer, who short-sheeted her bed on the eve of the Villanova game in Philadelphia last month. After a little duplicity with the front desk clerk, Kathryn obtains the key to Stacy's room and ransacks it while the team is watching tape in Geno's suite.

Kathryn returns to her room, feeling pretty pleased. Ten minutes later, her phone rings.

"Um, Kathryn, that was pretty funny," says Stacy soberly. "I'm guessing it was you. Not that I didn't deserve it but, well, I'd left my national championship ring on my bed. Now I can't find it."

Kathryn's smile disappears. She runs to Stacy's room. "I don't know where to look first," Stacy says. "Maybe I'll try the bathroom."

"Oh, Stace, I'm really sorry," says Kathryn. "I didn't mean—"

"That's okay," says Stacy. "Maybe if we organize the room a little we'll find it."

Kathryn tidies up Stacy's closet and makes her bed. She folds Stacy's clothes and puts them away. All the while Stacy is searching for her ring.

"I found it!" says Stacy, who'd been looking beneath the bed. "Hey, thanks for helping me out."

"No problem, Stace," says Kathryn. "I'm just sorry. . ."

"Don't worry about it," says Stacy. "Everything turned out okay."

Tomorrow morning at breakfast Stacy is still laughing. "Can you believe Kathryn fell for that?" she says. "'I lost my ring'."

Monday, March 26 . . . Sally Bell is a legend among women's basketball officials. She is experienced and knowledgeable and generally well-liked. Next Sunday evening she will officiate the national championship game, her tenth appearance at the women's Final Four in its 20 seasons of existence under NCAA jurisdiction. In terms of on-court deployment, only Pat Summitt has worked more Final Fours (11) than Bell has.

Sally Bell lives less than 100 miles from Knoxville as the crow flies and works primarily Southeastern Conference games (Tennessee's league). Because of that, fervent UConn fans consider her a sixth man for the opposition.

In last season's national championship game, Kelly Schumacher blocked an NCAA record-tying nine shots. She blocked what would have been a record-setting tenth Tennessee shot, but Sally Bell whistled her for a foul on the play. At UConn's victory parade in Hartford the following weekend, someone displayed a sign that read: "SCHUMACHER: 10 + SALLY BELL = 9 BLOCKS".

Geno would never go so far as to impugn Sally Bell's integrity. His beef with her is that she represents the disease that afflicts women's basketball officiating and, hence, the sport: whistle fever. A surfeit of calls disrupts the pace of the game, a disadvantage to teams that like to run (read: UConn). A foul-plagued game can also be drudgery to watch: No one pays to see players shoot free throws.

Geno wants a leaner game. A more fluid game. One that resembles the first six minutes of February's game in Knoxville, when the clock stopped not once, and even the fans were beginning to pant from exhaustion. A game with fewer restrictions, fewer interruptions. One without all the Bell and whistles.

So tonight, as UConn walks on the court for the opening tipoff, there is Sally Bell waiting for them. Geno is anxious. "Today is the longest day of the season," he said earlier, referring to regional finals in general. "You've got to wait to see if your season was a success or not."

Geno is anxious. Diana Taurasi is not. As she walks past Sally Bell and toward the midcourt circle for the opening tip, she gives the referee a playful pat on the butt.

UConn grabs a quick 6-0 lead but the Lady Techsters, who have a pair of go-to players in center Takeisha Lewis and Ayana Walker, battle back. They crawl to within one point at 11-10, but then the Huskies, as they have done dozens of times this season, go on a double-digit scoring run. Twelve straight points later, there is some breathing room, 23-10.

Midway through the first half, Geno's two concerns are Sue Bird and the officials. "Hey, Sue Bird," he asks, "you afraid to shoot the ball? What's the matter with you?"

After Bell whistles Asjha Jones for an offensive foul away from the ball, her second, Geno pleads to referee John Morningstar. "This is a national championship game," Geno says, his eyes embers, his face contorted. "Come on, John. Let the players decide the game."

As Morningstar jogs downcourt, Geno turns to Carol Sprague, who again is seated adjacent to the Husky bench. "Jesus Christ," he says, smoldering. "I'm sick of this."

La. Tech pulls to within six, 25-19, when Kelly Schumacher reaches over the back of forward Cheryl Ford in attempting to grab an offensive rebound. Bell rings her up for her second foul—all three UConn frontcourt starters have two fouls.

"Let the players decide the game, Sally!" Geno implores her. "Let the players decide the game. This isn't girls' basketball any more. It's *women's* basketball."

Bell, in Geno's opinion, is insinuating herself too deeply into the proceedings. And Sue, not enough. "Why is Sue Bird so tentative with the ball?" he asks his assistant coaches. "Why doesn't Sue Bird just shoot the ball?"

Fortunately for UConn and what appears to be the majority of the 9,397 fans here, Diana is treating the Mellon Arena court as if it is her driveway in Chino. With 0:16 remaining in the first half she grabs a defensive rebound in the corner, in front of the UConn bench.

"Clear out!" Geno orders. The Huskies have never practiced such a play, but all are schooled enough in the game to know what to do: Get out of Diana's way.

D dribbles past halfcourt guarded by La. Tech's Brooke Lassiter, a scrappy defender. A few steps above the top of the key D pauses, the basketball a yo-yo in her right hand. She takes one dribble to her right, feints in that direction, and then swiftly crosses the ball over to her left hand, gliding past Lassiter.

It is impressive enough that Diana has executed the crossover dribble so keenly, but then she does something that is seldom seen in women's—or men's—basketball. She shoots the layup with her weak hand, her left hand. The ball caroms off the backboard and in the basket just before the halftime buzzer.

For all intents and purposes, the game is finished. UConn wins, 67-48. Diana owns the arena. At one point late in the game, she crouches in front of the scorer's table, waiting to check into the game. Soon she is joking with two of the official scorers, all of them immune to the gravity of the moment.

Geno's biggest concern when he wakes up tomorrow will be Sue, who attempts only a pair of three-pointers. Yesterday she learned that she had won the Nancy Lieberman-Cline Award, given to the nation's top point guard, for the second consecutive season. Tonight she has Geno wondering about her reliability. "What the hell's gotten into Sue Bird?" he asked the bench after she took an errant shot. "When did she forget how to shoot the ball?"

Otherwise, Geno is relieved. The longest day of the year is over. Later, in the press area, Geno gushes about Diana, who has become the first freshman ever to be named Most Outstanding Player of the East Regional. It is as if, now that she has delivered on her promise, he can at last exhale and share his sentiments about her.

"I put a lot of pressure on her, calling her the best freshman I'd ever recruited," he says. "But she has a chance to be . . . well, her future's right in front of her, as the old baseball guys used to say.

"Diana Taurasi wasn't named Rookie of the Year in our league," Geno says, "but she may be one of the five best players in the country. To be honest, I think the league blew it."

It is nearly 11:00 p.m. In less than 48 hours the Huskies will be in St. Louis for the Final Four. On Friday they will play, one more time, Notre Dame. The turnaround is so quick, the magnitude of the game before them so hard to fathom at this late hour, that it is difficult to even conjure. Someone asks Sue what it will take to win in St. Louis.

"Pass the ball to Diana," Sue says. "All the time."

Thursday, March 29 . . . The road to the women's Final Four, "The March to the Arch" as some are calling it, has at last come to St. Louis. The gateway to the west, St. Louis is a gateway to the future of the women's game as well. Much has changed since 1982, when Louisiana Tech won the first NCAA championship, beating Cheyney State, which was coached by C. Vivian Stringer.

For the inaugural title game in Norfolk, Va., 37 media credentials were issued. This year the NCAA issued a record 785 credentials. Nineteen years ago 9,531 fans, a respectable number, watched the Lady Techsters win. This weekend the 19,404-seat Savvis Center is sold out. Buoyed by attendance figures, the NCAA is taking the sport to the next level: The women's Final Four will be held in domed arenas in 2002 and 2003.

It has been a gateway season for the sport, from Michelle Snow's dunk to Jackie Stiles record-breaking bucket. Stiles not only broke the NCAA career scoring record; she and her Southwest Missouri State teammates have advanced to the Final Four.

In the last month the Claflin Comet has traveled further and dazzled more admirers than any Kansan since Dorothy. Stiles has averaged 29.5 points per game in Southwest Missouri State's four NCAA tourney victories. She and the rest of the Bears have also taken the most indirect of "roads" to the Final Four, going from Springfield, Missouri, to New Brunswick, New Jersey, to Spokane, Washington, to St. Louis: approximately 5,400 miles to reach a destination that is a three-and-a-half hour drive from their campus in Springfield.

All the while Stiles's legend grows so that, in the "Show Me State", it now rivals the Arch in stature. "What's it like," one writer asks Southwest Missouri State coach Cheryl Burnett, "to be living the last two and a half weeks with Michael Jordan and Julia Roberts?"

Later Geno takes the podium in front of more than 100 credentialed media in the cavernous press area. I arrive late, my tape recorder in one hand and notes in another. I scurry to find a seat amongst the sea of inhabited folding chairs as Geno is speaking at the dais. Bumbling into a row, I trip over the foot of Jeff Goldberg of *The Hartford Courant*.

The chair will save me, I think, but the back of it gives with my weight. I fall through the chair with Chevy Chase aplomb, looking like an absolute doofus and making quite a noise. Beautiful ESPN reporter Ann Werner, seated directly behind the carnage, pretends she hasn't noticed. But Geno has.

"You all right, John?" he says, laughing. Sue Bird, also on the dais, just shakes her head.

"That's one of Notre Dame's finest," Geno says, clueing in everyone to my alma mater. "If they play like that tomorrow, we'll be fine."

Friday, March 30 . . . The Adams Mark hotel, located just a Diana Taurasi three-pointer from the St. Louis Arch, is ground zero for women's basketball today. The Women's Basketball Coaches Association (WBCA) is holding its annual convention here and many of the sport's most luminous figures abound.

Illinois' Theresa Grentz is having lunch in the lobby restaurant. So is Georgia's Andy Landers. Tennessee's Pat Summitt, accompanied by Sally Jenkins of *The Washington Post*, strolls through the lobby doors after a midday run along the Mississippi.

Upstairs Katie Post is maintaining the plush Nike coaches suite, the second-toughest ticket and latest closing bar in St. Louis this weekend. The toughest tickets, for tonight's doubleheader, are being brokered for anywhere from $250 to $1,250 a seat.

The opener features two first-team WBCA Kodak All-American guards, Katie Douglas of Purdue and Jackie Stiles of Southwest Missouri State (SMS). The latter is the rubber match between UConn and Notre Dame. "I wonder," says ESPN's Doris Burke, "if more people will watch tonight's game than Sunday's."

Purdue beats SMS, 81-64. The Boilermakers come out in a box-and-one against Jackie Stiles, forcing her to expend energy to find open shots. "Purdue just made me work so hard in the first half," says Stiles, who scored 22 points and leaving the game with a minute remaining to a standing ovation. "In the second half, I just ran out of gas."

Shortly after 8:30 p.m Central time, the final chapter of the UConn-Notre Dame trilogy is minutes away from beginning. A capacity crowd of 20,551 fill the Savvis Center, including Lily and Mario Taurasi, watching their daughter play in person for the first time since November.

Back in Connecticut, where the hour is nearing ten o'clock, more people in the Hartford-New Haven TV market are tuned in to the game than to any primetime show this year except the Super Bowl and the Oscars.

The difference in starting lineups is familiarity. If you were to add each member of the Irish's starting five by their respective number of starts this season, you'd find that of 175 possible starts (35 games x 5 starters), this quintet started 163 of them. That's 96%. Contrast that with UConn, whose starting five tonight started 69% of the Huskies' 35 games.

That disparity is caused in large part by the season-ending injuries of Shea Ralph and Svetlana Abrosimova. "It's got two days to catch up to us," Geno said yesterday of their absence. "What we'll miss the most is the steadying influence they might bring."

At 8:43 the Irish, each of them tattooed with green-leprechaun decals on their triceps, take the court. Then UConn. The

Huskies win the tip and patiently pass the ball four times before Diana attempts an open three-pointer at the top of the key.

Someone—many people, actually— had asked Geno about Diana yesterday, positing that "she doesn't play like a freshman".

"That's because you don't see her every day like I do," Geno replied cheekily. "You're like grandparents. They only see the kids once in a while. Send them home thinking that they're angels."

Diana's three-pointer hits the front of the rim and misses. Both teams miss a few more shots before Sue Bird begins the scoring with a baseline three.

After another ND miss, Sue aggressively drives the distance of the court. "Sue's passive," Geno said yesterday. "She likes to get others involved until the end of the game. Then she takes the shot."

Geno spoke to Sue about this earlier today, and she listened. Though she misses the layup, Kelly Schumacher grabs the rebound, scores and is fouled by Niele Ivey. UConn leads 6-0.

The Savvis Center is at fever pitch. During a television timeout, ESPN courtside reporter Pam Ward tries in vain to listen to her producer's voice in her earpiece, as the Notre Dame band plays the school's fight song behind her.

"They're killin' me," Ward says. "The band's killin' me."

"C'mon, Pam, suck it up," play-by-play announcer Mike Patrick, listening in on his earpiece, chides. "You're not deaf yet."

On the Husky bench, Sveta, in a chartreuse top, and Shea, in her uniform sweats, sit next to the coaches and one another. Whenever there is a reason to cheer, Shea leaps off the bench, impervious to her torn ACL. At timeouts, she sprints out to be the first to slap hands with her teammates.

For the next eight minutes the teams neutralize one another as the lead remains at six, 28-22. Nearly as important as the score is the foul situation. With 10:21 remaining Diana picks up her second foul while helping Schuey on a double-team versus Ruth Riley in the low post.

"Hey!" Geno says disbelievingly to the NCAA official seated closest to him, pantomiming Diana's defensive stance. "Since when is a kid not allowed to do this?"

The calls, as they usually do, even out. With 6:35 remaining and UConn up, 28-22, Riley again parks in her favorite spot, midway along the right lane. However, as Schuey is taking a well-deserved breather (she will score ten points and grab nine rebounds in the first half alone), Riley is guarded by the much lighter Swin Cash. Using her butt to create space for herself, Riley moves Swin about three feet. She is called for the foul, her second.

Riley, incredulous, walks to the sideline as a timeout is called. The moment ESPN cuts away for a commercial break, color analyst Ann Meyers turns to partner Mike Patrick, "Terribly weak call," she says.

"Yep," he concurs.

Half a minute of game action later, Diana is whistled for a foul. Riley and Diana are both done for the half, one which they'd both as soon forget. Each has as many points as the other's jersey number: Riley has three, Diana zero. As she sits on the Notre Dame bench, Riley scratches off her leprechaun decal as if it's a voodoo curse. On the opposite bench Diana sits in frustration. Ann Meyers, noting that Diana is 0-7 from the field, tells the TV audience, "She looks a little tight this game."

With 4:17 left Kennitra Johnson, who has eight first-half points, commits her third foul. Geno sends in Maria Conlon, who only five months ago was taking layup lessons from Michael Auriemma. She takes a pass on the right wing from Sue and nonchalantly drains a three. 42-31, UConn, the largest lead of the game.

A few plays later Sue steals the ball from Alicia Ratay and hurls it upcourt to Maria, who is behind everyone. About 15 feet from the basket, Maria is shoved from behind by Ericka Haney, but no foul is called. Maria continues in for the layup and then a foul is called, though it does not look as if anyone touches her as she shoots.

"She got pushed in the middle of the floor and no call!" Geno tells the NCAA rep, chuckling and glaring simultaneously. "Did you see that? Mind-boggling. You're lucky I got a sense of humor. "

The Fighting Irish have bigger concerns than the officiating. Maria's layup and free throw have opened a 16-point Husky lead. No team has ever trailed by so much in the Final Four and

271

come back to win. Just before halftime Alicia Ratay, freed by a screen that Kelley Siemon sets on Sue, drains a three to bring the Irish within 12 at the intermission.

"Who let her get that three?" Geno asks Chris Dailey, Jamelle Elliot and Tonya Cardoza just before they enter the locker room. "Who set the screen to let her get that three?"

Back in Norristown, Pennsylvania, Ferruccio Auriemma grabs the car keys and heads out the door. His nerves already spent, he will spend the entire second half driving around town alone. "I just had a bad feeling about the second half," he will say later. "I didn't want to watch."

Inside the Notre Dame locker room, a minor miracle occurs. Alicia Ratay speaks. "We're only down twelve," the laconic sophomore tells her team.

"It's not so much that Alicia gave a stirring speech," Coach McGraw later says. "That Alicia said anything was the big deal."

Sue starts the second half with a wide-open three from the corner, and the Huskies are up again by 15. Then the dam breaks. The Irish go on a 24-7 run. All five Irish starters score during the spurt. In the UConn fan section, Rebecca Lobo, Jennifer Rizzotti and Nykesha Sales look as if they have seen a ghost. A ghost of themselves.

"It was eerie," Rebecca will say later. "We were cheering for UConn, of course, but we could relate to Notre Dame so much more because they reminded us of ourselves in ninety-five. They're basically a five-man team."

With 12:40 remaining Alicia Ratay completes the stunning about-face as she drains a three with two Huskies in her face. 61-59, Notre Dame.

Meanwhile Diana is still scoreless: 0-9 from beyond the arc, 0-11 overall. When she is benched briefly during the run, Sveta, seated next to her, offers counsel. "You don't have to hit a three," Sveta says. "Just make an easy basket, a layup, to get yourself going."

With 11:12 left Diana takes Sveta's advice. As the 30-second clock winds down she drives to the lane and is fouled as she makes an off-balance 12-footer, her first bucket in 12 attempts. She converts the free throw as well, putting UConn ahead, 63-61.

The Irish tie it at 63, but UConn goes ahead again on its best offensive sequence of the half. Diana, from the top of the key, fires a pass to Schuey at the free throw line. Schuey pivots and passes to Tamika Williams, who is cutting along the baseline and makes an easy layup. It is the only time all half that UConn shreds Notre Dame's 2-3 zone. It is also, at 65-63, their final lead of the season.

The Irish score 14 straight points in the next five minutes. The Huskies, on the other hand, miss nine consecutive three-pointers. They are playing in a panic. "Every fundamental mistake you can make," ESPN's Patrick says after one of UConn's 12 second-half turnovers, "Connecticut is making it right now."

Geno, the top button of his white oxford shirt undone and his burgundy tie loosened, watches helplessly. He calls a time-out with 9:11 left and the Huskies down seven. "We're losing our freakin' mind here," he tells them. "You guys look like the game is already over."

It is. The Irish lead by 12 with four minutes left, when Diana's three-point attempt from the top of the key hits only backboard. It is her final shot of a miserable, 1-15 evening. With 1:24 remaining, she fouls out. She takes a seat on the bench, looking dejected, distraught. Geno crouches in front of her, rests his hands on her shoulders, and tries to provide solace.

The final score is 90-75. The Irish have outscored the Huskies, 53-26, in the second half, going from 15 down to 15 up. It is a simple matter of the Irish playing a near-perfect half while the Huskies play their worst half in two seasons.

In the postgame locker room pockets of players weep, the most emotional among them the freshmen. Diana cries unabashedly until Schuey wraps her up in a hug, cooing, "Come here, baby."

Only Shea and Tamika appear composed enough for the media to approach. "Right now," says Tamika, pointing toward Shea and Sveta, "all you want to say is, 'I'm sorry', to those two."

But there is nothing to be sorry about. The shots did not fall. The Huskies attempted 19 more than the Irish. The shots, the threes especially, simply did not fall.

Fifteen minutes later Geno is ready to leave the Savvis Center with Kathy, Meghan Pattyson, and his kids. They head down a corridor toward the exit. A young man with a media credential, which identifies him as being affiliated with a Notre Dame fan publication, stops him for one final question. He asks Geno if he had been worried about Notre Dame, with its veteran team, as far back as last summer.

This has been a painful loss. All Geno wants is to find a bar and have a drink with his family and friends. He stops, though, and answers. "When we were healthy and had everybody," Geno tells him, "I wasn't scared of anybody. And I know you write for Notre Dame and want to write that I was worried. But, to be honest with you, I wasn't. The only thing I was worried about last summer was my tan."

Saturday, March 31 . . . At noon Geno stands outside a small conference room in a deserted area of the Huskies' hotel. He agreed to be a guest on Hartford sports radio WTIC (1080 AM), which is broadcasting from a hotel conference room. As he waits he chats with Kathy, Jamelle Elliott, Tonya Cardoza, Marci Czel, and Svetlana Abrosimova, all of whom will sit here for at least the next hour. Where else do they have to be today?

"I'd love to get this shirt I saw at a T-shirt store last night," Geno tells Marci Czel. "It read, 'Do I look like an f___ing people person?'. That's the perfect shirt for today."

Three block away eight former Huskies —Carla Berube, Courtney Gaine, Colleen Healy, Kris Lamb, Rebecca Lobo, Jen Rizzotti, Nykesha Sales, and Paige Sauer—are playing basketball. They have found a YMCA with a small, top-floor gym.

For 90 minutes they play fullcourt, all out, games up to 15 by ones. Nykesha, to no one's surprise, rules the court. Paige and Rebecca battle inside, the sight of two 6'5" women drawing stares from the male weekend warriors who wander past.

A steady rain begins to fall outside, and soon someone notices moisture on the court. There is a tiny leak in the roof.

"That's it," says Nykesha, "I ain't blowing my career at some YMCA."

Time to go. Everyone has had a satisfying run, and there is a discernible joy on all eight glistening faces. As Rebecca dons her street shoes, she exudes a childlike happiness.

"I wish," she says, "we could do this every day."

Notre Dame's Kelley Siemon stops a reporter on the street to say hello. "You going to Geno's party?" she asks. "He invited us, too. The coaches and seniors. Maybe if we'd lost we'd be there."

Much like last year's season-ending party, Geno has commandeered the entire third floor of a sizeable eating & drinking emporium in a revitalized area of town known as the Landing. The seniors—Marci Czel, Christine Rigby, Kelly Schumacher, Shea Ralph, and Svetlana Abrosimova—are allowed to attend. Shea and Sveta bounce up and down on the dance floor to the song "Shout", impervious to their injuries.

A sober undercurrent runs through the evening, though. Friends are here for support. Dianne Nolan, the Fairfield University coach who has known Geno since both were summer camp counselors in their early twenties, tells him, "I'm only here tonight because you lost last night."

The loss aches, but there is something else weighing on Geno's mind. Earlier he was given troubling news. Kris Lamb, who played at UConn from 1987-90, informed him that Kerry Poliquin may have multiple sclerosis, the same disease that claimed her mother's life. Preliminary tests, though not conclusive, lead to the diagnosis of the incurable disease. Kerry, who is at the party, is unaware that he knows.

"How are you doing?" Geno asks Kerry, greeting her with a hug.

"Fine."

"No. Really?" he says, looking into her eyes.

"Scared."

There are no guarantees in life. Experience teaches you as much. There is no guarantee that your best player, or both of them, won't get injured. That the best player you've ever seen won't have the worst game of her life when it counts the most. That you won't go from greatest team ever to sentimental underdog in the course of one season. There are no guarantees in life except a lifetime guarantee. And none of us know the expiration date.

"Is there anything I can do for you?" Geno asks.

"Make it go away," she says.

"If I could," he tells her, "I would."

Geno suffers, too. How quickly this epic season unraveled. "In the second half last night," he says, "I felt like that new U2 song."

Which one?

"'Peace on Earth,'" Geno responds. "You know, where [Bono] sings, 'Jesus could you take the time/To throw a drowning man a line.'"

He listens to U2's most recent compact disc, *All That You Can't Leave Behind*, a lot lately. The album parallels the Huskies' season. The first track, "Beautiful Day", is full of joy and promise, as this team was last October 14. But then Shea and Sveta, were lost, and the Huskies, who began the year as, if not the greatest team ever, certainly Geno's, entered St. Louis as underdogs.

So much had changed since October 14, which was in fact a beautiful day. Two All-Americans were lost for the season to injury. A prohibitive preseason favorite, a team whose chief problem seemed to be a surfeit of returning talent, came to rely on a freshman in its final game. Geno guaranteed a championship-repeat last April. A month later, in a conversation with Matt Eagan, an eerie prescience had overcome him. Sure, his team was returning virtually intact, but you still had to play the games. Every season is different. No matter how much one might appear to resemble the next. "You can't dip your foot," he told Eagan, "in the same river twice."

As painful and humbling as this season will always be for Geno and the Huskies, I will always remember it fondly. I saw Cameron Crowe's film *Almost Famous* shortly before I moved from Manhattan to West Hartford and hoped that, like the film's protagonist, the band would come to accept me, a reporter ("the enemy", as one of the band in the film initially terms him), as one of the family. At the advent of the season I had no idea how realistic or unrealistic that hope was.

Then came the first Notre Dame game. By virtue of this project I happened to be in the UConn pregame locker room. As the game was ending, the Irish's upset in hand, I called my editor at *Sports Illustrated*. The magazine, which had professed no interest in the game beforehand, now wanted a short account of the contest. Under a tight deadline, I did so, breaching the trust of the Huskies by providing details from the locker room, details that made UConn appear overconfident.

"You would never have even been in that locker room," Chris Dailey rebuked me a few days later, "if you were there for *Sports Illustrated*."

CD was right. I apologized to the coaches but, for no good reason, not to the players. A week or so later Svetlana, who the day earlier had learned that she would have to sit out the rest of the season, hobbled up to me on crutches during practice. "I am worried about you," she said.

"Me? Why?"

"You seem distant from us. What's wrong? I feel like you are not our friend anymore."

I was stunned. Stunned that Sveta, who had her own problems now, would notice this. I confided in her about the Notre Dame incident.

"You made a mistake," Sveta said. "Just tell everyone you're sorry."

The next day I asked Geno if I could address the team before practice. Standing near midcourt at Gampel, I spoke to all of them. I apologized. "I'm really sorry," I told them.

A moment or two of silence followed. I don't think any of them had ever seen a sportswriter admit he was wrong. Then Shea, her biceps never more robust and imposing, spoke. A slight, almost imperceptible smile crossed her lips. But not enough of a smile to disabuse me of the notion that she was dead serious. "Just don't," she warned, "let it happen again."

I didn't.

This season will always be bittersweet for Geno and the Huskies. They sold out every game, went 32-3 and advanced to the Final Four minus their two leaders, Shea and Sveta. Unfortunately, they will probably remember it for having fallen short of their goal.

I hope that they don't. I hope, as the years slide past, that they recall all the bends in the river, the moments that rendered the journey, if not one of ultimate triumph, unforgettable all the same. I hope that they see the joy on their own faces when Sue hit that game-winning shot, hear the anguish in Shea's voice after her final drive to the basket, taste the tears that ran down Sveta's face as she hobbled to midcourt on Senior Night, and feel the crisp slap of Marci Czel's palms as she celebrated yet another three-pointer by Diana or Sue.

I hope that they remember being so happy. And so sad. That they were, indeed, together. And I hope they will realize how lucky they were to care about anything this much. I know I will.

EPILOGUE

Notre Dame won the national championship. Barely. The Irish defeated Purdue, 68-66.

The finish provided an eerie *deja vu* for the Irish. Ruth Riley was fouled while lunging for an entry pass into the low post with 5.8 seconds remaining and the score tied. The All-American center buried both free throws, and this time Notre Dame was prepared for its opponent's furious, final dash down-court.

"After the Big East final," said Muffet McGraw, "we devoted at least twenty minutes every practice to defending last-shot scenarios."

Purdue's Katie Douglas did launch an off-balance three-pointer as time expired, but it glanced harmlessly off the rim. Notre Dame had its first national championship in women's basketball, culminating a dreamy 34-2 season in which its two losses came by a total of three points.

After the game Jeff Goldberg of *The Hartford Courant*, the JFK conspiracy theorist, happened to run into Alicia Ratay by pure coincidence. Ratay, you will recall, is the player who'd noted in her bio that her first act as president would be to solve that mystery.

"So," asked Goldberg by way of introduction, "who *do* you think killed JFK?"

Ratay wagged her finger reprovingly at him. "I'm not president yet," she replied.

The Huskies never saw the national championship game. Their charter flight, which was scheduled to land at 3:30 p.m., was delayed due to inclement weather in Hartford. UConn spent several hours on the tarmac in St. Louis before arriving at Bradley International Airport at 11:00 p.m.

Governor John G. Rowland and at least 500 fans, some of whom had waited 12 hours in the biting wind and rain, were at the terminal to greet them. Meanwhile, in West Lafayette, Indiana, an angry mob of Purdue students were turning over cars and setting fires in the wake of their team's narrow defeat to Notre Dame. Yes, students rioting over a women's basketball game.

Notre Dame-bound Teresa Borton led Yakima West Valley High School to the Washington 3A state championship. She was named Most Valuable Player of the tournament.

Stacy Hansmeyer went home to Norman, Oklahoma. She was hired as an assistant coach at the University of Oklahoma where she will work under head coach Sherri Coale, her former coach at Norman High School.

In late April Geno and Svetlana Abrosimova went to Secaucus, New Jersey, to attend the WNBA rookie draft. The Minnesota Lynx selected Sveta seventh overall, three slots behind Jackie Stiles and two behind Ruth Riley. When Sveta approached the interview podium, a WNBA official directed her to make an opening statement and then open the floor to questions.

"Hello!" said Sveta, wearing a smile that stretched from the Baltic Sea to the Bering Strait. "That is my opening statement. You can ask me questions now."

Shea Ralph was drafted in the third round, the 40th pick overall, by the Utah Starzz. She stayed in Storrs on draft day, anxiously avoiding televisions. When her name was announced, she was running on a treadmill in the trainer's room inside Gampel.

Diana Taurasi really did hit the books in the spring semester. She earned a 3.4 GPA and was recognized by the school as a scholar-athlete.

In July Geno coached the US Junior National team, which included Jessica Moore and Diana, at the Junior World Championships in Brno, the Czech Republic. Before the tournament it was announced that via an NCAA-sanctioned stipend from USA Basketball, each member of the team would earn a cash reward for her participation. Each player would receive $5000 if the team won the gold medal, $4,000 for the silver and $3,500 for the bronze. "I'm buying a Lexus," crowed Diana upon hearing the news. "I don't care what color it is."

The US Juniors lost to the host Czechs in the semifinal round, 92-88. Diana scored 25 points in the loss but fouled out. Not that Geno said anything, but the host Czechs attempted 42 free throws to the Americans' 17.

On July 19 Shea, who was spending the summer in Storrs undergoing rehab, was walking her new dog, a bull mastiff puppy she had named Gracie. Suddenly she felt a strange but unfortunately familiar sensation in her left knee. No one was with her and the campus was fairly deserted, so she called Paige Sauer on her cellphone.

"Paige," she said, "I think I tore my ACL again."

"Are you sure?" asked her friend.

"I know that feeling."

Later that week she underwent surgery in Birmingham, Ala., for her fourth ACL tear in a little more than four years. "I'm expecting to be back in December," she said.

Earlier in the summer I ran into Geno at a WNBA exhibition game in Hartford. "Here's something else for your book," he told me. "Boris [Lelchitski, the Russian-born agent who had first clued in Geno to Sveta] told me about this high school girl. She's six-seven and supposedly can really play."

Where's she from? I asked him.

"That's the interesting part," he replied. "Italy."

John Walters was born in Red Bank, New Jersey, and attended the University of Notre Dame. He worked at *Sports Illustrated* from 1989-2001 and lives in New York City.